Survival

GLOBAL POLITICS AND STRATEGY

Volume 62 Number 5 | October–November 2020

'While viruses do not respect borders, their spread and their chances of survival have long depended greatly on the laws, policies and acts of states. However, not all states are up to the job.'

Adam Roberts, Pandemics and Politics, p. 31.

'If ASEAN is seen as unresponsive to regional crises, international actors will fill the void. The ICJ's genocide case against Myanmar was brought by Gambia, a West African country, and buoyed by unprecedented support from the Organization of Islamic Cooperation.'

Rebecca Barber and Sarah Teitt, The Rohingya Crisis: Can ASEAN Salvage Its Credibility?, p. 44.

'The moral complexity is unavoidable. If you think that the noble end of protecting your state and your fellow citizens justifies whatever means deliver the goods, then the opportunities and temptations to push the limits of acceptable behaviour will multiply.'

Rodric Braithwaite, Proper Spying, p. 195.

T0333850

Survival
GLOBAL POLITICS AND STRATEGY
Volume 62 Number 5 | October–November 2020

Contents

On the cover
'The Devotion of Monsignor de Belsunce During the Plague of Marseille, 1720' by Nicolas André Monsiaux (1754–1837).

On the web
Visit www.iiss.org/ publications/survival for brief notices on new books on the Middle East, Economy and South Asia.

Survival **editors' blog**
For ideas and commentary from *Survival* editors and contributors, visit www.iiss.org/blogs/ survival-blog.

Survival
GLOBAL POLITICS AND STRATEGY

The International Institute for Strategic Studies

2121 K Street, NW | Suite 801 | Washington DC 20037 | USA
Tel +1 202 659 1490   Fax +1 202 659 1499   E-mail survival@iiss.org   Web www.iiss.org

Arundel House | 6 Temple Place | London | WC2R 2PG | UK
Tel +44 (0)20 7379 7676   Fax +44 (0)20 7836 3108   E-mail iiss@iiss.org

14th Floor, GBCorp Tower | Bahrain Financial Harbour | Manama | Kingdom of Bahrain
Tel +973 1718 1155   Fax +973 1710 0155   E-mail iiss-middleeast@iiss.org

9 Raffles Place | #51-01 Republic Plaza | Singapore 048619
Tel +65 6499 0055   Fax +65 6499 0059   E-mail iiss-asia@iiss.org

Survival Online www.tandfonline.com/survival and www.iiss.org/publications/survival

Aims and Scope *Survival* is one of the world's leading forums for analysis and debate of international and strategic affairs. Shaped by its editors to be both timely and forward thinking, the journal encourages writers to challenge conventional wisdom and bring fresh, often controversial, perspectives to bear on the strategic issues of the moment. With a diverse range of authors, *Survival* aims to be scholarly in depth while vivid, well written and policy-relevant in approach. Through commentary, analytical articles, case studies, forums, review essays, reviews and letters to the editor, the journal promotes lively, critical debate on issues of international politics and strategy.

Editor **Dana Allin**
Managing Editor **Jonathan Stevenson**
Associate Editor **Carolyn West**
Assistant Editor **Jessica Watson**
Editorial Intern **Niklas Hintermayer**
Production and Cartography **John Buck, Kelly Verity**

Contributing Editors

Ian Bremmer	Bill Emmott	Erik Jones	'Funmi Olonisakin	Angela Stent
Rosa Brooks	Mark Fitzpatrick	Jeffrey Lewis	Thomas Rid	Ray Takeyh
David P. Calleo	John A. Gans, Jr	Hanns W. Maull	Teresita C. Schaffer	David C. Unger
Russell Crandall	John L. Harper	Jeffrey Mazo	Steven Simon	Lanxin Xiang
Toby Dodge	Matthew Harries			

Published for the IISS by
Routledge Journals, an imprint of Taylor & Francis, an Informa business.

About the IISS The IISS, a registered charity with offices in Washington, London, Manama and Singapore, is the world's leading authority on political–military conflict. It is the primary independent source of accurate, objective information on international strategic issues. Publications include *The Military Balance*, an annual reference work on each nation's defence capabilities; *Strategic Survey*, an annual review of world affairs; *Survival*, a bimonthly journal on international affairs; *Strategic Comments*, an online analysis of topical issues in international affairs; and the *Adelphi* series of books on issues of international security.

SUBMISSIONS

To submit an article, authors are advised to follow these guidelines:

- *Survival* articles are around 4,000–10,000 words long including endnotes. A word count should be included with a draft.
- All text, including endnotes, should be double-spaced with wide margins.
- Any tables or artwork should be supplied in separate files, ideally not embedded in the document or linked to text around it.
- All *Survival* articles are expected to include endnote references. These should be complete and include first and last names of authors, titles of articles (even from newspapers), place of publication, publisher, exact publication dates, volume and issue number (if from a journal) and page numbers. Web sources should include complete URLs and DOIs if available.
- A summary of up to 150 words should be included with the article. The summary should state the main argument clearly and concisely, not simply say what the article is about.

- A short author's biography of one or two lines should also be included. This information will appear at the foot of the first page of the article.

Please note that *Survival* has a strict policy of listing multiple authors in alphabetical order.

Submissions should be made by email, in Microsoft Word format, to survival@iiss.org. Alternatively, hard copies may be sent to *Survival*, IISS–US, 2121 K Street NW, Suite 801, Washington, DC 20037, USA.

The editorial review process can take up to three months. *Survival*'s acceptance rate for unsolicited manuscripts is less than 20%. *Survival* does not normally provide referees' comments in the event of rejection. Authors are permitted to submit simultaneously elsewhere so long as this is consistent with the policy of the other publication and the Editors of *Survival* are informed of the dual submission.

Readers are encouraged to comment on articles from the previous issue. Letters should be concise, no longer than 750 words and relate directly to the argument or points made in the original article.

ADVERTISING AND PERMISSIONS

For advertising rates and schedules

USA/Canada: The Advertising Manager, Taylor & Francis Inc., 530 Walnut Street, Suite 850, Philadelphia, PA 19106, USA Tel +1 (800) 354 1420 Fax +1 (215) 207 0050.

UK/Europe/Rest of World: The Advertising Manager, Routledge Journals, Taylor & Francis, 4 Park Square, Milton Park, Abingdon, Oxfordshire OX14 4RN, UK Tel +44 (0) 207 017 6000 Fax +44 (0) 207 017 6336.

SUBSCRIPTIONS

Survival is published bimonthly in February, April, June, August, October and December by Routledge Journals, an imprint of Taylor & Francis, an Informa Business.

Annual Subscription 2020

	UK, RoI	US, Canada Mexico	Europe	Rest of world
Individual	£162	$273	€ 220	$273
Institution (print and online)	£585	$1,023	€ 858	$1,076
Institution (online only)	£497	$869	€ 729	$915

Taylor & Francis has a flexible approach to subscriptions, enabling us to match individual libraries' requirements. This journal is available via a traditional institutional subscription (either print with online access, or online only at a discount) or as part of our libraries, subject collections or archives. For more information on our sales packages please visit http://www.tandfonline.com/page/librarians.

All current institutional subscriptions include online access for any number of concurrent users across a local area network to the currently available backfile and articles posted online ahead of publication.

Subscriptions purchased at the personal rate are strictly for personal, non-commercial use only. The reselling of personal subscriptions is prohibited. Personal subscriptions must be purchased with a personal cheque or credit card. Proof of personal status may be requested.

Dollar rates apply to all subscribers outside Europe. Euro rates apply to all subscribers in Europe, except the UK and the Republic of Ireland where the pound sterling rate applies. If you are unsure which rate applies to you please contact Customer Services in the UK. All subscriptions are payable in advance and all rates include postage. Journals are sent by air to the USA, Canada, Mexico, India, Japan and Australasia. Subscriptions are entered on an annual basis, i.e. January to December. Payment may be made by sterling cheque, dollar cheque, euro cheque, international money order, National Giro or credit cards (Amex, Visa and Mastercard).

Survival (USPS 013095) is published bimonthly (in Feb, Apr, Jun, Aug, Oct and Dec) by Routledge Journals, Taylor & Francis, 4 Park Square, Milton Park, Abingdon, OX14 4RN, United Kingdom.

The US annual subscription price is $1,023. Airfreight and mailing in the USA by agent named WN Shipping USA, 156-15, 146th Avenue, 2nd Floor, Jamaica, NY 11434, USA. Periodicals postage paid at Jamaica NY 11431.

US Postmaster: Send address changes to Survival, C/O Air Business Ltd / 156-15 146th Avenue, Jamaica, New York, NY11434.

Subscription records are maintained at Taylor & Francis Group, 4 Park Square, Milton Park, Abingdon, OX14 4RN, United Kingdom.

ORDERING INFORMATION

Please contact your local Customer Service Department to take out a subscription to the Journal: **USA, Canada:** Taylor & Francis, Inc., 530 Walnut Street, Suite 850, Philadelphia, PA 19106, USA. Tel: +1 800 354 1420; Fax: +1 215 207 0050. **UK/ Europe/Rest of World:** T&F Customer Services, Informa UK Ltd, Sheepen Place, Colchester, Essex, CO3 3LP, United Kingdom. Tel: +44 (0) 20 7017 5544; Fax: +44 (0) 20 7017 5198; Email: subscriptions@tandf.co.uk.

Back issues: Taylor & Francis retains a two-year back issue stock of journals. Older volumes are held by our official stockists: Periodicals Service Company, 351 Fairview Ave., Suite 300, Hudson, New York 12534, USA to whom all orders and enquiries should be addressed. *Tel* +1 518 537 4700 *Fax* +1 518 537 5899 *e-mail* psc@periodicals.com *web* http://www.periodicals.com/tandf.html.

Pandemics and Politics

Adam Roberts

A.J.P. Taylor often observed that great events can have very small causes. The 2020 COVID-19 pandemic is fresh evidence for this proposition. The cause is in all likelihood tiny and accidental: a genetic mutation in a virus, which then spreads into the human population. Like earlier epidemics throughout history, it could have happened with no human intentionality. Its consequences are already momentous and will be even more so before it is over.

The novel coronavirus can easily be seen as a profoundly anti-democratic force. In its first eight months, from early January to mid-August, it produced over 20 million cases of the COVID-19 disease. That disease has killed over 800,000 people and counting; put millions out of work; drastically curtailed travel; precipitated states of emergency; and caused citizens to be placed under detailed and intrusive administrative control, demonstrations to be banned, and elections to be rescheduled or postponed. Bitter disagreements have arisen about when and how to ease restrictions on movement. COVID-19 has generated a revival of conspiracy theories and unjustified recriminations, and prompted absurd denials of medical reality by certain political leaders. Among states, the pandemic has actually heightened some long-existing disputes, most notably those on trade and other matters between China and the United States. The capacity of the United Nations

Adam Roberts is Senior Research Fellow in International Relations, Balliol College, University of Oxford. He is a former President of the British Academy.

Survival | vol. 62 no. 5 | October–November 2020 | pp. 7–40   DOI 10.1080/00396338.2020.1819641

system to address epidemics has been called into question, not least in harsh American criticisms of the World Health Organization (WHO).

It is too simple to cast the pandemic crisis merely as a narrative of rampant authoritarianism versus embattled democracy. The long history of pandemics, earthquakes and other disasters reminds us of the enduring complexity of disaster management, and of the many controversies surrounding it, including the causes of and responses to plagues. States respond in different ways, raising questions regarding the relative effectiveness of democratic versus authoritarian states. International health organisations, especially the WHO, have important roles in dealing with epidemics, whether regional or global. Yet their formal powers are limited and their effectiveness depends on state cooperation. Epidemics, and action to control them, do sometimes play a part in increased authoritarianism, but they can also give rise to more positive initiatives of various kinds.

Pandemic history

The well-documented history of pandemics suggests that we do not live in uniquely dangerous times. We tend to underestimate past threats and disasters because we know that humankind survived them. Yet many past crises appeared at the time to be every bit as menacing and disruptive as the present crisis. The human cost and major consequences of past epidemics of different diseases have long been known. The historian William McNeill, tracing the numerous effects of epidemics on the rise and fall of empires, concluded his masterly and prescient study of *Plagues and Peoples* thus: 'Infectious disease which antedated the emergence of humankind will last as long as humanity itself, and will surely remain, as it has been hitherto, one of the fundamental parameters and determinants of human history.'[1]

In many parts of the world, bubonic plague (recognisable by the swelling of lymphatic glands) has been the type of epidemic most deeply etched into public consciousness. The Hebrew Bible contains reference to such plagues. Most notable was one afflicting the Philistines, as described in the Book of Samuel, which probably happened in about 1350 BCE. While the plague was implicitly understood as the result of the wrath of God, mice were also indicated as a possible causative factor.[2] The first of three outbreaks of bubonic plague that are widely viewed as having amounted to pandemics occurred in 541–49 CE. Known as Justinian's Plague, it affected the Mediterranean countries, Europe and the Near East. It recurred in 588, spreading to what is now France. In 1347–49 came the Black Death pandemic. This killed 30% of Europe's population. For centuries it struck about every ten years, one of the last major outbreaks being the Great Plague of London in 1665–66. Even after that, plagues repeatedly struck cities of North Africa, and also the Ottoman Empire, which endured them up to the first few decades of the nineteenth century. The third plague pandemic occurred in 1855–1900. Believed to have started in Yunnan province in China, it spread to Canton, India and Hong Kong, whence it was reportedly carried by a 'plague ship' (one whose crew and passengers are infected) to Hawaii and San Francisco, causing outbreaks there in 1900.

Epidemics have been linked to a range of phenomena, including grain-storage systems in which rats and fleas can thrive, collapsed or defective health systems, population displacement, revolutions, wars and environmental degradation. Globalisation has been widely seen as another significant factor: epidemic outbreaks have been associated with international trade routes since at least the fourteenth century and still are today.

China, in particular, has been tagged as a possible source of all three plague pandemics, as well as the current coronavirus one. A team of 24 palaeobiologists reported in 2010 that all three historical pandemics had been caused by the same bacterium, *Yersinia pestis*. Regarding its means of transmission, they stated: '*Y. pestis* evolved in or near China, and has been transmitted via multiple epidemics that followed various routes, probably including transmissions to West Asia via the Silk Road and to Africa by Chinese marine voyages.'[3]

In 2013, Ole Benedictow, a Norwegian historian of plagues, agreed that *Y. pestis* was the causative agent, but disagreed about its transmission and with the implication that China was the epicentre of all plagues. In particular, he criticised as 'untenable' the 'highly disparate attempts at explaining the historical spread of *Y. pestis* either by caravans across the Eurasian continent or by sea from China to East Africa whence it could have spread to western Arabia, North Africa and the Middle East'. He proposed a more historically based explanation of how, during the Black Death, *Y. pestis* could have moved from 'the area of the plague focus that stretches from the northern and north-western shores of the Caspian Sea into southern Russia'. He suggests that several plague foci developed over centuries, and that wild rodents played a large part in its transmission.[4] References to plague-like diseases in various classical works and in the Bible reinforce these conclusions.

The historical record is also valuable for what it says about the responses of rulers to pandemics. Even today, most of our methods of combatting COVID-19 are positively ancient. As François Heisbourg has put it: 'The best we currently have are medieval measures such as quarantining, travel bans, wearing masks, confinement and social distancing more broadly.'[5] Different societies do have strikingly divergent approaches to the problem of managing epidemics, based in part on the differing threats they have experienced, distinct cultural traditions on such matters as face masks and handshaking, and disparate forms of governmental and social organisation.

Disasters can transform governments

Disasters of all kinds can of course result in societal breakdown and extreme religious reactions, but they can also give rise to significant transformations of government. The capacity to adapt to disaster appears to have been strong in many European city states. For example, in 1348, during the Black Death, health commissions were set up in Florence and Venice, later developing into 'permanent magistracies monitoring and regulating civic health'.[6] In Milan and Mantua, temporary prohibitions of persons from disease-stricken areas were introduced in 1374.

On the eastern side of the Adriatic Sea, in Dubrovnik (also known as Ragusa), a sophisticated anti-epidemic, and more specifically anti-plague, system was built up from the fourteenth century onwards. Nearby were territories under Ottoman control. It was widely assumed that the plague would continue there, hitting rural communities that formed Dubrovnik's hinterland. The city of Dubrovnik's first regulation on quarantine was passed in 1377, and its first permanent health office was established in 1390. Over centuries, the city developed tough rules on contact tracing, disinfection and quarantining of goods, and prohibitions against physical contact with Ottoman subjects. Though premised on controlling the threat rather than eliminating it entirely, these policies appear to have been more successful than those in various neighbouring Dalmatian cities, purportedly due in part to high standards of public hygiene and good hospital organisation. A Croatian historian, while recognising some failures during the so-called 'plague of the maidservants' in 1691, reaches a favourable verdict on plague control 'thanks to good organisation, broad-based public engagement on this task, as well as substantial government support'.[7]

Over the four centuries following the Black Death, a large body of medical work on epidemics emerged in Europe. Works of this genre came to be known as 'plague tracts' – or, in German scholars' delicious term, *Pestschriften*. These studies are sometimes considered conservative, and excessively preoccupied with ancient astrological, religious or merely speculative theories of plague causation. But they increasingly offered detailed and astute observations, drawing attention to methods of treatment that had been observed to work and addressing the role of government. They noted that the poor were particularly vulnerable, and needed to be fed and sheltered to protect them and others from contagion.[8]

The plague crisis of 1575–78, which posed a threat to the entire Italian Peninsula, led to two important medical developments: the tracking of diseases through detailed health-board statistics, and the instruction of princes on public health and its politics. A good example of both is the work of Sebastiano Tranzi, public doctor of the central Italian town of Lanciano. He was asked by the town's archbishop to publish a plague tract in Italian, 'accessible and beneficial' to the town's citizens. In the resulting book, published in 1587, Tranzi expressed confidence in the present and future preservation of Lanciano from plague based on its 'good rule and governance … that resembled an ancient republic', its magistrates and its laws. He also emphasised the wide range of measures that had kept the city free from the plague's invasion in 1575–78: formation of a public-health board, deployment of eight honoured citizens from the town's best families to guard the gates, and rigorous measures to prevent goods and persons from entering from suspected places.[9] This was an instance of seemingly successful preventive work to save a town from plague.

Samuel Cohn draws two conclusions from his study of plague tracts: firstly, that 'epidemics do not necessarily lead to transcendental religiosity and weakening of states', and, secondly, that effective management of the threat or actuality of plague tended to result in the glorification of leaders and the value of obedience to them, 'thereby boosting absolutist authority at the end of the sixteenth century and into the next'.[10] This invites obvious questions. Were the authorities that had been successful against the plague all 'absolutist'? And were all absolutists successful? Many of the Italian and Dalmatian city states had traditions of relative freedom, regularly changing their consuls to ensure that these officials' lust for power was controlled. These civic traditions had weakened from the thirteenth century onwards, but they were not completely dead.[11]

Pandemics and the utility of history

Historical studies illuminate seven aspects of epidemics. Firstly, they help trace their origin and spread, and the survival and transmission of pathogens between outbreaks. This knowledge helps in forecasting and addressing future outbreaks. They also expose the weakness of conspiracy theories as explanations of epidemics by showing how complex and varied the routes of transmission can be, and how rare it is that complete elimination of a pathogen can be achieved.

Secondly, history is a guide to preventive measures. Historical studies confirm that epidemics are extremely serious, are best tackled as a public-health problem and require, in addition to treatment of the sick, a huge range of preventive measures that have evolved over centuries. As knowledge of pathogens slowly grew from the late nineteenth century onwards, some of these measures were subtly refined but none was considered irrelevant. Past and recent cases confirm the importance of preparedness, including sound organisation of the social response to an epidemic. They also show how a well-oiled and properly financed system of disaster response can itself be a vital ingredient of a city's or state's identity.

Thirdly, historical studies have a place in answering some key clinical questions, including the value of old remedies against new threats – though that place may be distinctly limited. There was not a lot of history involved in the discovery by an Oxford University team in June 2020 that dexamethasone, a cheap steroid first made in 1957 and widely used, reduced deaths among COVID-19 patients on ventilators by a third.[12] However, historical research accompanied by modern epidemiological approaches could clarify what has and has not worked against previous epidemics, and assist in investigating claims for traditional medicine.[13]

Fourthly, a reminder of precedents is salutary. One obvious example concerns the fear of disorder arising in the wake of disaster. After the earthquake in Dubrovnik of

6 April 1667, which killed several thousand citizens, looters and criminals of every description appeared. This led to vulnerability to outside intervention – in that case, from Venice.[14]

Fifthly, past cases can focus attention on key policy issues. A particularly critical issue is whether the aim of public measures is the complete eradication of a pathogen or merely the prevention of its further spread. Over centuries, this was a vexing concern for many territories and municipalities that were located just outside the Ottoman Empire. They knew that they had to live side by side with highly infected societies, and did what they could through quarantine arrangements and limits on movement of travellers.

Sixthly, history reveals protection from epidemics as an evolved attribute of statehood. For centuries, they were viewed as a terrible scourge but not necessarily one that governments could effectively address. Thucydides in around 430 BCE and Thomas Hobbes in the seventeenth century lived in plague-ridden periods – Thucydides caught it himself – but it was especially Italian officials in the sixteenth century who began to see plague management as a key part of statecraft. This view became stronger in the nineteenth century as medical knowledge advanced.

Finally, historical cases raise the question of whether certain national or regional variations in the handling of an epidemic (for instance, on wearing face masks) are constructive or not. Such variations may conform to and draw strength from the cultural traditions of particular societies; and they may also provide a wealth of experience, akin to a series of scientific experiments, on what works and what does not work against epidemics.

Types of states and political systems

Many Asian countries reacted promptly to the first reports of what came to be known as COVID-19. Examples include Singapore, South Korea, Thailand and Vietnam. Even China, after initial denials of the seriousness of the situation, took quick and decisive action in ordering a lockdown in Wuhan and other cities in Hubei province on 23 January 2020. These fast responses in East Asia may have a very simple explanation, which has little to do with the type of political system, and everything to do with lived experience. These countries had been affected by the severe acute respiratory syndrome (SARS) outbreak of 2002–04. They were aware that it was different from influenza – in fact, it is caused by a form of coronavirus – and had a higher fatality rate. Elsewhere, at least up to March 2020, many governments still had a flu model of a likely pandemic, and therefore felt less urgency.

The Wuhan lockdown provided the world with an impressive demonstration of one known way to tamp down an epidemic. But the congratulation and self-congratulation accompanying lockdown's end on 8 April, after almost three months, ignored the fact that in the first weeks of the epidemic there had been a partial cover-up at some state, party and administrative levels.[15]

Assessing the relative performance of democracies and authoritarian states is, in any event, difficult. In this century, the seductive proposition that countries can be divided neatly into two basic categories – constitutional democracies and authoritarian regimes – has run into trouble. As Martin Loughlin of the London School of Economics has observed:

> At the end of the Second World War, there were only 12 established constitutional democracies in the world. By 1987 this number had grown to 66 … and by 2003 the 1987 figure had almost doubled to 121. By the new millennium, almost every state seeking to legitimate its rule in the eyes of its citizens and the world felt obliged to adopt a written constitution incorporating a separation of powers, a commitment to the rule of law, the protection of individual rights, and the holding of free and fair elections. At the end of the 20th century, it appeared that there was only one game in town, and that game was constitutional democracy.[16]

Loughlin goes on to suggest that constitutional democracy had reached its global high point in the period 2006–11 and then went into decline. Democratic states were not overthrown by *coup d'état* or other types of fundamental collapse. Rather, some of them became 'defective democracies' – regimes that retained the formal institutional trappings of constitutional democracies while flouting the norms and values on which they are based.

Consider Brazil. In the 2020 edition of its annual report 'Freedom in the World', Freedom House classifies Brazil as 'free', and describes it as a democracy, but at the same time registers many criticisms: violent attacks on independent journalists and civil-society activists, high rates of violent crime, top-level corruption and disproportionate violence against minorities. Freedom House makes even more criticisms of Peru, but also lists it as 'free'.[17] Both might be candidates for the category of 'defective democracies', but Freedom House does not employ such a category. An additional problem with its methodology is that it is largely silent on issues of health and medical treatment.[18]

One might expect defective democracies, especially those in which press freedom is curtailed, to perform particularly badly in facing major disasters, including pandemics. This would chime with the received view that countries with a free press, independent institutions and the rule of law – in other words, real democracies – are less liable to allow disasters to happen than are authoritarian states. As Amartya Sen and others have pointed out, droughts and other natural disasters may become far more severe if they occur in the absence of political freedoms and independent media. Such institutions tend to act as whistle-blowers, compelling governments and other bodies to mobilise to mitigate material and social damage.[19] In an April 2020 newspaper article on the COVID-19 crisis, Sen mounted a defence of democracy that turned on that kind of contingency:

> Tackling a social calamity is not like fighting a war which works best when a leader can use top-down power to order everyone to do what the leader wants – with no need for consultation. In contrast, what is needed for dealing with a social calamity is participatory governance and alert public discussion.
>
> […]
>
> This applies also to the calamity caused by a pandemic, in which some – the more affluent – may be concerned only about not getting the disease, while others have to worry also about earning an income (which may be threatened by the disease or by an anti-disease policy, such as a lockdown), and – for those away from home as migrant workers – about finding the means of getting back home. The different types of hazards from which different groups suffer have to be addressed, and this is much aided by a participatory democracy.[20]

Is it feasible to measure the comparative performance of different types of state in the early months of the COVID-19 crisis? The answer depends on the existence of some objective metric. One flawed but still useful measure of comparative performance is the number of deaths of COVID-19 patients in different countries. Table 1 illustrates, in a rough-and-ready way, the huge variations in these numbers, both absolutely (column 2) and per million of population at different dates (columns 3 and 4).[21] These statistics need to be viewed with considerable caution. Their obvious limitations include the need to allow for the different threats and circumstances faced by each country; the fact that, in some countries in this list, cases of COVID-19 started much later than in others, so the time frame covered may be shorter; the fact that the death of any individual may have a multiplicity of causes, especially as it is well established that COVID-19's lethality increases in the presence of pre-existing medical conditions; the role of class, ethnicity and other factors; the different practices of states in the attribution of the cause of death; different policies on whether or not those patients who do not go to hospital are tested for COVID-19; and, in many countries, especially those under authoritarian rule, the possibility of widespread and even deliberate undercounting of victims. The 28 countries or territories shown here are merely a sample.

In Table 1, no attempt has been made to formally classify individual countries as democratic or authoritarian, or somewhere in between. This is not only because such classifications would be highly contestable, but also because there is no simple connection between the type of state and its performance. Democracies are all over the place. Take the ten states with the fewest deaths per million of population as of 25 August. Eight of them – Australia, Greece, Iceland, India, Japan, New Zealand, South Korea and Taiwan – are widely accepted as constitutional democracies. Among more authoritarian states, only China and Vietnam are included in the top ten. However, the worst-performing ten states in terms of fatalities per million are all democracies of one kind or another: Belgium, Brazil, France, Italy, Mexico, Peru, Spain, Sweden, the United Kingdom and the United States. Only Mexico fails the Freedom House test, being designated as 'partly free'.

The UK and the US, which have historically seen themselves as the world's leading democratic powers, appear to have set a bad example in the first eight months of the COVID-19 crisis. Particularly in its early weeks, they were slow and indecisive, and American failures have

Table 1: **Reported deaths from COVID-19 in selected countries: totals and per million of population**

Country or territory	Total COVID-19 deaths to 25 August 2020	Deaths to 1 June 2020 per million of population	Deaths to 25 August 2020 per million of population
Australia	517	4.00	20.27
Belgium	9,878	819.35	852.32
Brazil	115,309	137.91	542.48
Canada	9,083	193.28	240.66
China	4,711	3.22	3.27
Denmark	623	99.10	107.56
Finland	335	57.75	60.46
France	30,528	441.25	467.69
Germany	9,277	101.58	110.72
Greece	242	16.79	23.22
Hungary	613	54.45	63.45
Iceland	10	29.30	29.30
India	58,390	3.91	42.31
Italy	35,441	552.66	586.17
Japan	1,196	7.05	9.46
Mexico	60,800	77.02	471.56
New Zealand	22	4.56	4.56
Peru	27,813	136.66	843.54
Poland	1,960	28.11	51.79
Russia	16,448	32.16	112.71
South Africa	13,159	11.52	221.87
South Korea	310	5.29	6.05
Spain	28,924	580.20	618.63
Sweden	5,813	435.18	575.59
Taiwan	7	0.29	0.29
United Kingdom	41,433	551.59	610.33
United States	177,279	315.35	535.58
Vietnam	27	0.00	0.28

Source: Data on cumulative confirmed COVID-19 fatalities and rates per million people is from Our World in Data, 'Coronavirus Pandemic (COVID-19)', https://ourworldindata.org/coronavirus, accessed 25 and 26 August 2020.

remained dramatic as such questions as wearing masks and how to relax lockdowns have been bitterly politicised. The weakness of the UK and US performances is particularly embarrassing in light of the notable disconnect between how these two countries performed in practice in 2020, and how they had been graded only months earlier in the 2019 Global Health Security Index (GHSI). Overall, and also in the specific category of 'Rapid

Response to and Mitigation of the Spread of an Epidemic', the UK and US had been ranked as first and second out of 195 countries. Other states with high death rates in 2020 were also highly rated in the GHSI. France, Spain and Sweden were in the top 15, and Belgium was in 53rd place.[22] In light of their performance in 2020, London and Washington need to acknowledge that they made some poor decisions – in particular, wasting time at the beginning of the pandemic – and that numerous other countries have been more successful in limiting COVID-19 fatalities.

Table 1, of course, is merely illustrative. It is compatible with the possibility that an effective state response during a pandemic crisis depends less on the type of political system than on other factors that might include relevant experience in handling epidemics; clear-minded leadership; and an efficient bureaucracy, drawing on a wide range of social organisations.[23] This is not to suggest that there is no moral or practical distinction to be made between authoritarian and democratic states, whether in general or in their performance over COVID-19. On the contrary, some of the most difficult issues in the crisis have arisen because of the instinct of certain authoritarian states and leaders to clamp down on publicity and debate about an epidemic within their realm.

Nevertheless, it would be counterproductive to approach the current COVID-19 crisis as a platform for championing democracy over authoritarianism. Even if democratic states were all performing strongly, global cooperation is needed among all kinds of states on numerous aspects of this crisis, including the manufacture of medicines and equipment, scientific research, immunisation programmes, transport and quarantining.

International organisations

Any attempt to control a pandemic requires both action within states and international cooperation. Ideally, the two would be complementary. International bodies of many types, from Médecins sans Frontières to the UN Security Council, have been involved in the COVID-19 crisis.[24] By far the most important, and controversial, has been the WHO. It has 194 member states, necessarily includes governments of all sorts and has a notably broad range of responsibilities. One of its key guiding documents is the International Health Regulations (IHR), covering 196 countries and revised substantially in 2005, the purpose and scope of which are 'to prevent, protect against, control and provide a public health response to the international spread of disease in ways that are commensurate with and restricted to public health risks, and which avoid unnecessary interference with international traffic and trade'.[25] Under these regulations, the WHO is responsible for deciding when a particular situation should be declared a public-health emergency of international concern (PHEIC). They do not mention the word 'pandemic'.[26]

In this century, before the advent of COVID-19, the WHO played a significant but sometimes controversial role in addressing several major outbreaks of viral diseases. In 2002–04, SARS caused an epidemic of great regional concern in Asia. The WHO did not deem it a PHEIC (the concept was still in development) or identify it as a pandemic. The perception that China had initially covered up this outbreak, and that the WHO's performance had been weak, led to the WHO's adoption of the IHR in 2005.

In contrast, the WHO proclaimed the H1N1 influenza (or 'swine flu') outbreak a PHEIC on 26 April 2009 and a pandemic on 11 June 2009. The mortality rate was low. But the WHO was accused both of exaggerating the danger and of being slow to determine that this was a pandemic.

In 2012, the WHO issued a global alert about Middle East respiratory syndrome (MERS), a coronavirus disease that had broken out mainly in Saudi Arabia and some neighbouring countries, and which later revived in South Korea. The WHO did not designate MERS as a PHEIC.

In 2013–14, the WHO's slowness in declaring the Ebola-virus outbreak in West Africa a PHEIC increased the scale and severity of this health crisis. The WHO eventually designated it as a PHEIC on 8 August 2014.[27] (Subsequently, on 17 July 2019, it designated an Ebola outbreak in the Democratic Republic of the Congo as a PHEIC.)

As its erratic performance suggests, the WHO is a problematic organisation. Its IHR, which prioritise multilateral cooperation, have proved difficult to implement in many countries. Some of the WHO's wounds have been self-inflicted: in October 2017, it appointed Robert Mugabe, then president of Zimbabwe, as a goodwill ambassador, a decision quickly withdrawn after an uproar over Mugabe's atrocious record on governance, corruption and human rights. But all international organisations, even those concerned with matters of health, have been riven by differences among member states at some point. A harbinger of the United States' current hostility arose in the 1920s and 1930s, when it refused to join the Geneva-based Health Organisation of the League of Nations.[28] The US did remain a member of the Office International d'Hygiène Publique, based in Paris, but its rejection of the League of Nations doomed efforts to merge the Geneva- and Paris-based bodies. Thus, Europe hosted two rival global-health organisations until the WHO was established in 1948. The WHO too has had its inter-state difficulties. In 1949, the Soviet Union left the organisation for a variety of stated reasons, including Moscow's purportedly superior understanding of the causes and cures of diseases, and its denial of the worth of collective WHO action against disease.[29] China also had its suspicions of the WHO, which, along with other UN bodies, had until 1971 recognised Taiwan as the official Chinese government.

Now, ironically, the US and others have impugned the WHO for China's supposed sway within the organisation. The WHO recognised the coronavirus outbreak as a PHEIC on 30 January 2020, named the disease COVID-19 on 11 February and characterised its spread as a pandemic on 11 March.[30] But accusations surfaced that the WHO had been unduly tolerant of the dilatoriness and sparseness of China's required reporting on the epidemic, especially on human-to-human transmission. There appears to be some truth to these claims.

From 12 December 2019 onwards, some patients in Wuhan, the most populous city in Central China, were identified as suffering from an unusual infection of the lungs. Teams of Chinese medical professionals concluded that this illness involved a new virus strain closely related to the SARS virus experienced in China from 2002 onwards. They noted the potential for human-to-human transmission, and on 3 February their findings were promptly published on the website of the international journal *Nature*. One article was based on a single patient.[31] A second article was based on five patients.[32]

Alongside such evidence of openness there were also signs of a partial cover-up. On 30 December 2019, several medical professionals in Wuhan had circulated messages expressing concern about a cluster of cases of a flu-like disease, possibly SARS, that had been treated at hospitals in the city. One hospital's supervision department rebuked one of these doctors, Dr Ai Fen, director of the Emergency Department of Wuhan Central Hospital, for 'spreading rumours'. Dr Li Wenliang, an ophthalmologist at the hospital, was detained for several days by the Wuhan police for circulating some messages about the cases, accused of 'making false comments on the Internet about unconfirmed SARS outbreak' and ordered to 'stop spreading rumours'. Dr Li soon died from COVID-19.[33]

On 31 December 2019, the authorities in Wuhan reported to the WHO China Country Office an outbreak of cases of 'pneumonia of unknown etiology' in the city. In information provided on that day or a few days later, the Chinese authorities said 44 cases were involved, that some patients worked in the Huanan Seafood Market and that there was 'no evidence of significant human-to-human transmission'.[34] Also on 31 December,

There were signs of a partial cover-up

Taiwan reportedly sent an email to the WHO, warning of cases of atypical pneumonia in Wuhan.[35] On 11 January 2020, Dr Yong-Zhen Zhang of the Shanghai Public Health Clinical Center and School of Public Health shared on open websites the full sequence of the coronavirus genome, as detected in samples taken from the first patients. This was an important step towards developing diagnostic tests for the virus.[36] The move was widely praised internationally, but the next day the Chinese government closed the clinic 'for rectification'.[37] Also on 11 January, Chinese media reported the first death from the novel coronavirus – that of a 61-year-old man who had frequently visited the live-animal market in Wuhan.

Early official Chinese statements about the coronavirus outbreak in Wuhan minimised the significance of these events, conveyed the impression that there was no human-to-human transmission and indicated that the outbreak was exclusively connected with the animal market in Wuhan. Then, after the extreme threat posed by the virus had become apparent, criticisms of China for its handling of the issue mounted. Many reports indicated that the number of those who had contracted the new illness from November

2019 onwards was significantly higher than had been admitted in official statements.[38] The WHO's reaction throughout January was to seek more information from China about the outbreak. It experienced difficulties, of which some details emerged in early June, especially following a detailed investigation by the Associated Press (AP) that uncovered transcripts of tape recordings of meetings in January between Chinese health officials and representatives of the WHO. The AP article describes

> significant delays by China and considerable frustration among WHO officials over not getting the information they needed to fight the spread of the deadly virus … Despite the plaudits, China in fact sat on releasing the genetic map, or genome, of the virus for more than a week after three different government labs had fully decoded the information. Tight controls on information and competition within the Chinese public health system were to blame, according to dozens of interviews and internal documents.

> The recordings suggest that rather than colluding with China, as Trump declared, WHO was itself kept in the dark as China gave it the minimal information required by law. However, the agency did try to portray China in the best light, likely as a means to secure more information. And WHO experts genuinely thought Chinese scientists had done 'a very good job' in detecting and decoding the virus, despite the lack of transparency from Chinese officials.[39]

US President Donald Trump initially lavished extraordinary praise on the Chinese government for its handling of the coronavirus crisis. On 24 January he said in a tweet: 'China has been working very hard to contain the Coronavirus. The United States greatly appreciates their efforts and transparency. It will all work out well. In particular, on behalf of the American People, I want to thank President Xi!'[40] Consistent in inconsistency, Trump rapidly became more critical of both China and the WHO. He showed no awareness of the contribution of Chinese medical professionals to the world's knowledge of COVID-19. On 14 April he announced that he planned to halt

US funding of the WHO, which he described as 'severely mismanaging and covering up the spread of the coronavirus'. He also repeatedly expressed his fury at the WHO's opposition to US-supported travel bans stopping flights from China.[41] On 30 April he reiterated his claim (with no substantiation) that the Wuhan Institute of Virology was the origin of this virus.[42] When the CIA was asked to support this theory, it reported promptly that it could find no evidence for it.[43] Later in the summer a detailed response by Shi Zhengli of the Wuhan institute also rejected the claim.[44]

In a four-page letter dated 18 May 2020, Trump said that if the WHO failed to commit to major improvements in the next 30 days, he would make the temporary freeze on US funding for the organisation permanent.[45] On 29 May, not waiting for the expiry of the deadline he himself had set, he announced the United States' severance of all relations with the WHO, stating that the US would redirect its funds to other global public-health needs.[46] However, instant gratification was not available in this case. Subject to congressional requirements, the US withdrawal from the WHO would be effective on 6 July 2021, long after the US presidential election.[47] The American Medical Association and other professional medical institutions strongly opposed the move.[48]

Many of the US criticisms of the WHO were illogical or poorly supported. The complaint about uncritical statements on China made by Tedros Adhanom Ghebreyesus, director-general of the WHO, may have been reasonable in a vacuum, but was undermined by Trump's comparable effusiveness about China. The widespread suspicion was that Trump was blaming China in order to deflect attention from his own failure to effectively address the COVID-19 crisis in the US.[49] Sadly, the whole episode confirms how easily, even over an issue on which there are powerful reasons for international cooperation, national-level suspicion and rancour can gain traction.[50]

Political consequences of pandemics

Major disasters, especially if they can be blamed on particular governments, may spur significant political developments. But the connections can be hard to trace. For example, as Richard Evans has suggested, although many outbreaks of cholera in Central Europe in the nineteenth century roughly coincided with revolutions, 'epidemics were less causes than consequences of revolutionary upheavals and the government reactions associated with them'.[51]

The 'Spanish flu' pandemic of 1918–19, however, could possibly have given momentum to the incipient Indian independence movement. That pandemic has been well described by Laura Spinney in her book *Pale Rider*.[52] In an interview, Spinney reflected on the connection:

> People were dying in droves and in the absence of any British doctors.
>
> […]
>
> The people who stepped into that [medical] breach tended to be the militants, the grassroots militant activists for independence who had already worked out how to cross caste barriers and work together for a different goal, i.e. independence.
>
> Once the pandemic passed, emotion against the British was even higher than it had been before … Those people were far more united than they had been. And now they came together behind Gandhi. He found that suddenly, he had the grass roots support that he had been lacking until then.[53]

It is a heady thought that a pandemic may have ultimately yielded the independence of India in 1947, and thus triggered decolonisation. However, the proposition that there was a close connection between the pandemic and the rise of activism in India has been challenged. David Arnold, emeritus professor of Asian and global history at Warwick University, and a pioneer in the field of colonial medicine, confirmed the terrible scale of the pandemic's carnage in India.[54] But Arnold assessed that the pandemic coincided with a diminution of resistance:

> If some of India's leading dissidents, such as Bal Gangadhar Tilak and Annie Besant, were less vocal than they had been in 1917, a new whirlwind force was emerging in Mohandas Gandhi, who in a matter of months switched from recruiting soldiers for the Raj to riding the wave

of anti-colonial discontent. Recovering from a protracted illness of his own, he called for non-violent resistance against the repressive Rowlatt Act and so sparked a fresh round of protest and defiance. It might be excessive to argue that agitational politics drove endemic hunger from the newspapers' front pages, or that, imperial violence supplanting epidemic violence, the Amritsar massacre of April 1919, with its nearly 400 deaths, put the twelve million influenza deaths in the shade; but something of that order helps explain why influenza did not command more intense and lasting attention. The Indian middle classes, so vocal over plague, were far more muted over influenza.[55]

Sometimes it is measures taken to tackle epidemics that can lead to public objections – whether on religious, health, prudential or other grounds. This is not a new phenomenon. In 1691, during Dubrovnik's last major urban plague, people who were suspected of infection and had been forcibly relocated to the island of Lokrum rebelled, apparently due to over-crowded conditions.[56] In the UK this year, one reason for the delay in the governmental decision on lockdown (eventually imposed on 23 March) was nervousness about the potential risk of popular discontent.[57] Meanwhile, in the US, some of the resistance to lockdowns was anti-science, anti-federal government and violent.

In the first months of 2020, there was a tendency in many countries to accept implicitly a simple set of assumptions about the political conse-quences of pandemics: that COVID-19 is such a deadly threat to societies that only governments can deal with it, thus fulfilling their most basic responsibility, namely the protection of the people. The corollary was that the time for strikes and opposition movements was over. This was war and required unity.

The war analogy is of course imperfect. I am reminded of a British officer whom I met years ago, who at the end of the Second World War had been military governor of Perugia. A visiting general asked him why he had failed to wage war against the mosquitoes in the area. He replied: 'But we did.' And what happened, asked the general. 'The mosquitoes won.' The struggles against mosquitoes, and against viruses, are by nature very different from war. A better analogue of the struggle against the virus may be civil resistance to tyranny. Both courses of action are based on an understanding that the adversary – be it an autocrat needing obedient citizens, or a virus needing a warm host to enable it to replicate and spread – is dependent on people for daily cooperation. Both methods aim to undermine the adversary's sources of power, not so much by fighting as by depriving it of essential resources. And both tend to take a long time to achieve results, leading to frustration among those who have made sacrifices for the cause.

Of course, there are sharp differences. Lockdown tends to be a state activity, while civil resistance is more often initiated by civil-society groups. Even so, lockdown is not in every case a product of government inter-vention, but can also result from citizen initiative.

Viruses depend on people

Lawrence Freedman has observed that in the UK in March 2020, even before a government-imposed lock-down became mandatory, the public 'was already taking their own action. By 18 March there was a 40% reduction in transport use in London. Some 45% of Londoners had stopped visiting leisure venues.'[58] The fact that scientists were heavily and publicly involved in official processes that led to government-mandated lockdown conveyed the message that this was not a government-imposed grab for power, but rather a socially and scientifically necessary step.

Any similarities between lockdowns and civil-resistance movements do not make them natural allies. On the contrary, many governments that have presided over COVID-19 lockdowns have taken a tough line on demonstrations, not least through lockdown rules illegalising all meetings beyond family units. Yet in periods of lockdown, many move-ments, whether on grounds of health or political prudence, have eased up on demonstrations. Other movements have tried to adapt their policies and modi operandi. On 28 May 2020, Extinction Rebellion announced a series of demonstrations in the UK in which people were to be physically distanced at three metres apart and were asked to wear protective face masks. It was not in opposition to the lockdown as such, but it did reflect a criticism of government failure to 'listen to the science' on environmental matters as much as on COVID-19.[59]

Of the many social movements active during the COVID-19 crisis, the most visible and influential has been 'Black Lives Matter'. George Floyd, an African-American man, was killed in Minneapolis on 25 May 2020 when a policeman knelt on his neck for over eight minutes; he repeatedly said 'I can't breathe'. This established a symbolic link with COVID-19, many survivors of which had given graphic descriptions of their difficulties in breathing. Especially in the US, a further connection arose from the discrepancy between the rough and arbitrary police treatment of African Americans, and the much gentler treatment of right-wing, anti-lockdown demonstrators. Added to this was growing evidence that COVID-19 was much more likely to kill poor people, and those from Black, Asian and minority ethnic (BAME) groups, as recognised in a report published in the UK on 2 June – just eight days after Floyd's death.[60] This confluence of facts fed a sense of injustice. Suddenly, in many parts of the world, Black Lives Matter demonstrations burgeoned – many of them playing havoc with lockdown and social-distancing rules. The police could do little about it.

Yet the COVID-19 crisis continued to have illiberal consequences. In over 60 countries and territories, it was the basis for postponing national and local elections.[61] In some places, it has also been a basis for introducing emergency legislation suspending a range of constitutional procedures and citizen rights. Two examples are Hungary and Hong Kong.

In Hungary, the long-standing goal of Prime Minister Viktor Orbán is to create what he has called 'illiberal democracy'. On 30 March 2020, the Hungarian parliament passed a law styled the 'Act on Protection Against the Coronavirus' enabling the government to rule by decree to the extent necessary to address the pandemic's consequences. This special legal order was widely criticised.[62] On 17 April, the European Parliament condemned it as 'totally incompatible with European values'.[63] In an interview on Hungarian radio on 22 May, Orbán presented this rationale for his use of exceptional powers under the law of 30 March. In his view, the end justified the means:

> The special legal order was one of our best decisions, primarily because we were able to make every subsequent decision in good time. So, if you look at countries which are usually considered to be better than us – say

Austria, the Italians or the French – you'll see that in every case here we enacted the first protection measures a week or two earlier than the other countries … the defence operation in Hungary was so effective that in the end there was no mass infection, the epidemic did not cross over into mass infection … The special rule of law was a great help to me, because if something happened in a care home, in the economy or at a border crossing, I didn't have to go to Parliament with a decree to quarrel and engage in a tug-of-war with this left-wing opposition; instead I could react as the situation required – within an hour, if necessary.[64]

Four days later, on 26 May, Orbán submitted a 250-page bill to parliament to end the country's state of emergency by mid-June. This bill's complex provisions would allow the government to rule again by decree for an indefinite period of time. A separate bill gave the government the power to declare a state of medical crisis, to last for at least six months. The Hungarian parliament passed these bills on 16 June, by a vote of 190 to nil, and the state of emergency formally ended on 20 June. Unsurprisingly, this transparent ploy was criticised as offering only an illusion of the end of the state of emergency.

In Hong Kong, the problems that provoked a major crisis in 2020 were of long standing. The 1984 Sino-British Joint Declaration, the key international treaty guaranteeing Hong Kong's autonomy except in foreign affairs and defence, was supposed to chart the status of the Hong Kong Special Administrative Region for 50 years from the restoration of the territory to China on 1 July 1997.[65] Among the inhabitants, fears of erosion of the existing degree of autonomy were strong. From 2005 onwards there were many large and mainly non-violent demonstrations, generally demanding more democracy. The 2014 student-led 'Umbrella Movement', demanding reforms of Hong Kong's election laws, was strikingly well organised. Then, from June 2019, huge demonstrations, mainly student-led, were triggered by fears about a proposed new Hong Kong law that would have provided for extradition to mainland China of fugitive offenders. Carrie Lam, chief executive of Hong Kong, withdrew the bill on 4 September, but would not concede the demonstrators' other demands, which included, for example, her own resignation, retraction of the designation of certain demonstrations as 'riots' and an independent investigation of police brutality. Protests continued, being countered, as before, by extensive police use of tear gas and protesters' use of face masks. There was also increasing violence from a small but significant minority of the demonstrators. Parties supporting the demonstrators' aims won a landslide victory in the Hong Kong District Council elections on 24 November 2019.

In early 2020, the pandemic brought a change of focus. It appeared to increase the determination of the authorities in Hong Kong and Beijing to end the embarrassing displays of public hostility. In late March, with encouragement from Beijing, the Hong Kong authorities passed a regulation prohibiting gatherings of more than four people on the pretext of disease control.[66] It failed to stop the demonstrations. Bypassing the Hong Kong authorities completely, the Standing Committee of the National People's Congress in Beijing passed a sweeping new 'National Security Law' for Hong Kong on 30 June, effective immediately.[67] The UK government declared that the new law was a 'clear and serious' violation of the 1984 Joint Declaration on Hong Kong.[68]

The new law pays lip service to 'ensuring the resolute, full and faithful implementation of the policy of One Country, Two Systems under which the people of Hong Kong administer Hong Kong with a high degree of autonomy'. It includes an article on human rights, stipulating that the provisions of both the International Covenant on Civil and Political Rights, and the one on Economic, Social and Cultural Rights, are to be protected. But its main thrust is its enunciation of new rights and powers for the Chinese authorities in Hong Kong, and its listing of a range of loosely defined offences. In a long list of 'terrorist activities', Article 24 includes 'dangerous activities which seriously jeopardise public health, safety or security'. Article 20, on secession, prohibits many acts 'whether or not by force or threat of force', effectively criminalising even non-violent forms of political action.[69]

Following the law's passage, the Hong Kong government became harsher. On 30 July, 12 pro-democracy politicians were disqualified from standing in elections to the Legislative Council scheduled for 6 September

2020. A day later, these elections were postponed for a year under the Emergency Regulations Ordinance – according to Lam, 'purely on the basis of protecting the health and safety of the Hong Kong people'.[70] In addition to seeing COVID-19 per se as an excuse for tighter civil control, China may have regarded the weakened international positions of the US and the UK in light of their poor performance in the pandemic crisis as increasing its freedom of action to impose authoritarian measures without provoking a strong international response.

In several countries with a history of internal conflict, such as Sri Lanka, the armed forces were given increased law-enforcement responsibility.[71] At the same time, Steven Simon has looked at other countries, including Hungary, the Philippines and the US, in which the virus threat might be used in order to 'inure the public to the erosion of civil liberties and the expansion of executive power'. He has judiciously observed that such moves have other causes as well, and that 'the current crisis does not really seem to rise to the status of game changer in the long-standing tussle between liberal and illiberal democracies – or competitive democracies – and authoritarian regimes'.[72] Francis Fukuyama has offered a range of scenarios that COVID-19 could encourage, some pessimistic (rising fascism) and some optimistic (resilient democracy). He entertains the hope that the crisis will have a beneficial selection effect in leading to the exposure of recklessly authoritarian figures such as President Jair Bolsonaro of Brazil. Professionalism and competence may again come to be valued. More broadly, Fukuyama has noted that:

> Major crises have major consequences, usually unforeseen. The Great Depression spurred isolationism, nationalism, fascism, and World War II – but also led to the New Deal, the rise of the United States as a global superpower, and eventually decolonization. The 9/11 attacks produced two failed American interventions, the rise of Iran, and new forms of Islamic radicalism. The 2008 financial crisis generated a surge in anti-establishment populism that replaced leaders across the globe. Future historians will trace comparably large effects to the current coronavirus pandemic; the challenge is figuring them out ahead of time.[73]

Past epidemics suggest a wide range of effects. One obvious one stands out. The United States' reputation as a serious international actor has undergone a major decline. The trend began long ago with the Vietnam War, and gained momentum with fraught conflicts in Afghanistan and Iraq. But Trump's wilful alienation of allies and international institutions has accelerated and intensified the problem. In his serially gormless involvements in the COVID-19 crisis, he has failed to look after his own country. His repeated verbal attacks on China, and on the WHO, have shown an inability to temper disagreement with basic civility and attention to facts. In a long line of major missteps, Trump's crowning failure has arguably been his complete abdication of responsibility for mobilising international cooperation in the pandemic.

*   *   *

The long-term effects of epidemics have been huge. Dealing with them has always been difficult and remains so today. The history of epidemics suggests that the present crisis is likely to have a long tail, and that other epidemics are to be expected. The scope of the threat is undoubtedly international – COVID-19 spread fast around the globe largely because of modern means of travel – and vigorous international collaboration among medical professionals has been one redeeming feature of this crisis.[74] The specialised roles of international bodies such as the WHO remain essential. Yet the very scale and expense of the tasks faced, the continuing suspicion among states and the tendency of great-power disagreements to be dragged into such organisations make them unable to assume overall responsibility for managing pandemics.

Tackling epidemics is first and foremost a task for national governments. This responsibility dates back to the fourteenth century, when city states in the Italian Peninsula and the Adriatic began to develop systems for taking administrative measures against plagues. While viruses do not respect borders, their spread and their chances of survival have long depended greatly on the laws, policies and acts of states. However, not all states are up to the job. Their effectiveness in addressing pandemics does not appear to turn on what position they occupy on the democratic–authoritarian divide. The key factors are rather the competence of leaders, their capacity to make quick decisions, their willingness to listen to scientists, the effectiveness of their bureaucratic machinery and the degree of trust they engender in citizens.

In this crisis there has been much discussion of the performance of women heads of government. Most of the 12-plus governments under female leadership made prompt decisions about lockdowns and other measures, and were effective at communicating with the public. In most cases, their countries suffered relatively low death rates. In the literature analysing this, there are various preliminary explanations as to why women performed relatively well in this crisis, and the phenomenon calls for further investigation.[75]

Struggles against epidemics necessarily involve the hazard-strewn task of goal-setting. In the case of COVID-19, the capacity of the virus to stage a second rise in cases after it had been beaten in a particular area is one of many reasons for caution in promising and claiming successes. Complete worldwide elimination of the virus should of course be an ultimate goal, but is almost certainly unrealistic in the short or medium term. In the meantime, the main aims must be to use a wide range of measures to reduce the circulation of the virus among the population and minimise the susceptibility of the population to it. These include old-fashioned quarantines as well as the sophisticated development of vaccines.

Trust in leadership is essential because struggles against infectious diseases necessitate a degree of individual sacrifice for the social good. If people are required to stay indoors for months, to socially distance, to deploy their skills on the front line or to accept a vaccine despite a barrage of hostile internet propaganda, they need a sense that the advice they are getting comes from an honest source, is given for good reasons and contemplates a plausible goal. While the war analogy is tempting, it does not sit well with struggles against epidemics because the process of coping with virus-laden threats is necessarily slow, decentralised and unspectacularly administrative and social.

The process of ending pandemic lockdowns and other measures may yet prove more socially divisive than their initial implementation had been. It requires some very difficult and controversial judgements about whether and how to relax certain measures and the risks involved. Within communities, care-home staff or schoolteachers may feel it is unsafe to resume their normal pattern of work without access to certain evidence, protective equipment, test procedures and other support. Within states, there may be fundamental disagreements about how policies and institutions need to change in light of varying experiences with this pandemic. In the international context, disagreements may arise when one country's action, or refusal to act, poses risks for other states and their citizens. Notwithstanding the obstinacy of some leaders, there is no denying the pressing need to coordinate and harmonise policies between all levels of government and across borders.

Notes

1   William H. McNeill, *Plagues and Peoples* (New York: Doubleday, 1998), p. 295. This book is about epidemic infections generally, and is not therefore confined to those specifically known as plagues. Compared to the first edition, published in 1976, McNeill did not alter his conclusions at all, but he did add a preface, largely about the AIDS epidemic, in which he reiterated the book's central theme of 'our extraordinary capability for altering natural balances, and the limitations of those capabilities'. McNeill, *Plagues and Peoples*, p. 16.

2   See the First Book of Samuel, chapters 5 and 6, in the Old Testament; and Frank R. Freeman, 'Bubonic Plague in the Book of Samuel', *Journal of the Royal Society of Medicine*, vol. 98, no. 9, September 2005, p. 436.

3   Giovanna Morelli et al., 'Phylogenetic Diversity and Historical Patterns of Pandemic Spread of *Yersinia pestis*', *Nature Genetics*, vol. 42, no. 12, December 2010, pp. 1,140–3.

4   Ole Benedictow, 'Yersinia Pestis, the Bacterium of Plague, Arose in East Asia. Did It Spread Westwards via the Silk Roads, the Chinese Maritime Expeditions of Zheng He or over the Vast Eurasian Populations of Sylvatic (Wild) Rodents?', *Journal of Asian History*, vol. 47, no. 1, 2013, pp. 12, 19, 29–30.

5   François Heisbourg, 'From Wuhan to the World: How the Pandemic Will Reshape Geopolitics', *Survival*, vol. 62, no. 3, June–July 2020, p. 7.

6   Paul Slack, 'Introduction', in Terence Ranger and Paul Slack (eds), *Epidemics and Ideas: Essays on the Historical Perception of Pestilence* (Cambridge: Cambridge University Press, 1992), pp. 15, 16.

7   Rina Kralj-Brassard, 'A City Facing the Plague: Dubrovnik, 1691', *Dubrovnik Annals*, vol. 20, September 2016, p. 110.

8 See Samuel K. Cohn, *Cultures of Plague: Medical Thinking at the End of the Renaissance* (Oxford: Oxford University Press, 2009), pp. 8, 211–16, 299.

9 Sebastiano Tranzi, *Trattato di Peste* (Rome: Heredi di Giovanni Gigliotto, 1587), dedication to the Archbishop of Lanciano, on six unnumbered pages, final page.

10 Cohn, *Cultures of Plague*, pp. 294, 297–9.

11 See Quentin Skinner, *The Foundations of Modern Political Thought*, Volume 1: *The Renaissance* (Cambridge: Cambridge University Press, 1978), pp. 3–7, 15–17, 23–8, 41–6, 53.

12 'Dexamethasone Reduces Death in Hospitalised Patients with Severe Respiratory Complications of COVID-19', University of Oxford, 16 June 2020, http://www.ox.ac.uk/news/2020-06-16-dexamethasone-reduces-death-hospitalised-patients-severe-respiratory-complications.

13 Reports in the UK media of use of indigenous medicines in areas of Brazil affected by COVID-19 have included Peter Stubley, 'Brazil's Remote Tribes in Amazon Turn to Tree Bark and Honey to Treat Coronavirus', *Independent*, 20 May 2020, https://www.independent.co.uk/news/world/americas/brazil-coronavirus-amazon-tribe-tree-bark-plants-honey-cure-bolsonaro-a9524551.html; and Lindsey Hilsum, 'How an Amazon Rainforest Village Survived Covid-19 with Modern and Traditional Medicine', Channel 4 News, 8 June 2020, https://www.channel4.com/news/how-an-amazon-rainforest-village-survived-covid-19-with-modern-and-traditional-medicine.

14 See Robin Harris, *Dubrovnik: A History* (London: Saqi, 2003), pp. 333, 347.

15 See Lily Kuo, 'Birth of a Pandemic: Inside the First Weeks of the Coronavirus Outbreak in Wuhan', *Guardian*, 10 April 2020, https://www.theguardian.com/world/2020/apr/10/birth-of-a-pandemic-inside-the-first-weeks-of-the-coronavirus-outbreak-in-wuhan.

16 Martin Loughlin, 'The Contemporary Crisis of Constitutional Democracy', *Oxford Journal of Legal Studies*, vol. 39, no. 2, Summer 2019, pp. 436–7.

17 For the detailed Freedom House assessment of all countries in 2019–20, see https://freedomhouse.org/countries/freedom-world/scores.

18 See Freedom House, 'Freedom in the World 2020 Methodology', https://freedomhouse.org/reports/freedom-world/freedom-world-research-methodology; and Freedom House, 'Principles for Protecting Civil and Political Rights in the Fight Against Covid-19', 24 March 2020, https://freedomhouse.org/article/principles-protecting-civil-and-political-rights-fight-against-covid-19.

19 See, for example, the detailed studies pointing to this conclusion in Jean Drèze, Amartya Sen and Athar Hussein (eds), *The Political Economy of Hunger* (Oxford: Clarendon Press, 1990), vol. I, *Entitlement and Well-Being*, pp. 6–7, 23–4, 146–89; and vol. II, *Famine Prevention*, pp. 145, 153, 159–60, 190–1.

20 Amartya Sen, 'Overcoming a Pandemic May Look Like Fighting a War, But the Real Need Is Far From That', *Indian Express*, 8 April 2020, https://indianexpress.

com/article/opinion/columns/
coronavirus-india-lockdown-amartya-
sen-economy-migrants-6352132/.

21 Table 1 is based on data from
the European Centre for Disease
Prevention and Control. These figures
take account of changes in certain
countries' methods of calculating the
number of deaths due to COVID-19.
For example, Public Health England
announced on 12 August 2020 that
it was ceasing to count as COVID-19
deaths all those who had tested positive for the disease more than 28 days
before they died, unless COVID-19
was also mentioned on the death cer-
tificate. This change was intended to
reduce the risk of over-counting – for
example, of those who had recovered
from COVID-19 but subsequently
died of unrelated causes.

22 Global Health Security Index, October
2019, pp. 20–2, https://www.ghsindex.
org/wp-content/uploads/2019/10/2019-
Global-Health-Security-Index.pdf.
The GHSI is the result of cooperation between the Nuclear Threat
Initiative, the Johns Hopkins Center
for Health Security and the Economist
Intelligence Unit. The GHSI did note
that 'national health security is fundamentally weak around the world. No
country is fully prepared for epidemics or pandemics, and every country
has important gaps to address.'

23 See Francis Fukuyama, 'The Pandemic
and Political Order', *Foreign Affairs*, vol.
99, no. 4, July/August 2020, pp. 26–8.

24 UN Security Council Resolution
2532, passed unanimously on 1 July
2020 after protracted negotiations,
expressed 'grave concern about the
devastating impact of the COVID-

19 pandemic across the world,
especially in countries ravaged by
armed conflicts' and demanded 'a
general and immediate cessation
of hostilities in all situations on its
agenda', but added, unusually, that
this call 'does not apply to military
operations against the Islamic State'
and other named terrorist groups.
Owing to US objections, this resolution (unlike earlier Security Council
resolutions on HIV/AIDS and Ebola)
contains no mention of the WHO. For
background, see Julian Borger, 'US
Blocks Vote on UN's Bid for Global
Ceasefire over Reference to WHO',
Guardian, 8 May 2020, https://www.
theguardian.com/world/2020/may/08/
un-ceasefire-resolution-us-blocks-who.

25 Foreword, *International Health
Regulations*, 3rd edition (Geneva:
WHO, 2016), p. 1. The full text of the
IHR is on pp. 6–39.

26 WHO sources have defined 'pandemic' as referring to the worldwide
spread of a new disease. However, the
emphasis on the newness of a disease
has not been consistent, and on the
day the WHO declared a pandemic
regarding the H1N1 virus, the director of the Centers for Disease Control,
a US federal agency, indicated that
the use of the term 'pandemic' does
not suggest that there has been any
change in the behaviour of a virus,
but only 'that it is spreading in more
parts of the world'. Centers for Disease
Control and Prevention, 'CDC Press
Conference on Investigation of Human
Cases of Novel Influenza A H1N1',
11 June 2009, https://www.cdc.gov/
media/transcripts/2009/t090611.htm.

27 For a succinct summary of its poor

performance in many crises including the 2014 Ebola epidemic, see Francesco Checchi et al., 'World Health Organization and Emergency Health: If Not Now, When?', *British Medical Journal*, 2016, https://www.bmj.com/content/352/bmj.i469.long.

28 See 'Message of 25 April 1921 from the President of the Permanent Committee of the Office International d'Hygiène Publique to the Secretary-General of the League of Nations', in Norman Howard-Jones, *The Scientific Background of the International Sanitary Conferences 1851–1938* (Geneva: WHO, 1975), pp. 93–4.

29 See Charles E. Allen, 'World Health and World Politics', *International Organization*, vol. 4, no. 1, February 1950, pp. 40–2.

30 See 'Statement on the Second Meeting of the International Health Regulations (2005) Emergency Committee Regarding the Outbreak of Novel Coronavirus (2019-nCoV)', WHO, 30 January 2020, https://www.who.int/news-room/detail/30-01-2020-statement-on-the-second-meeting-of-the-international-health-regulations-(2005)-emergency-committee-regarding-the-outbreak-of-novel-coronavirus-(2019-ncov).

31 Fan Wu et al., 'A New Corona Virus Associated with Human Respiratory Disease in China', *Nature*, vol. 579, 12 March 2020, pp. 265–9. It was also published online on 3 February 2020 at https://www.natureindex.com/article/10.1038/s41586-020-2008-3. This article was the work of 19 researchers, six in Wuhan, and almost all affiliated with Chinese public-health institutions. The study was conceived and designed by Yong-Zhen Zhang of Fudan University, Shanghai.

32 Peng Zhou et al., 'A Pneumonia Outbreak Associated with a New Coronavirus of Probable Bat Origin', *Nature*, vol. 579, 12 March 2020, pp. 270–3. It was also published online on 3 February 2020 at https://www.nature.com/articles/s41586-020-2012-7. This article was the work of 29 researchers, all affiliated with public-health institutions in Wuhan.

33 He passed away on 7 February 2020, having caught the disease from an eye patient who was not known to have been infected. In March, the Chinese Communist Party issued an apology to him and revoked the admonishment. Helen Davidson, 'Chinese Inquiry Exonerates Coronavirus Whistleblower Doctor', *Guardian*, 21 March 2020, https://www.theguardian.com/world/2020/mar/20/chinese-inquiry-exonerates-coronavirus-whistleblower-doctor-li-wenliang.

34 On 31 December 2019, the WHO China Country Office was informed (evidently by the Wuhan Municipal Health Commission) of the outbreak in Wuhan. Details, including those about the WHO response in early January 2020, are summarised in WHO, 'Pneumonia of Unknown Cause – China', 5 January 2020, https://www.who.int/csr/don/05-january-2020-pneumonia-of-unkown-cause-china/en/.

35 On the action by Taiwan on 31 December 2019, see 'The Facts Regarding Taiwan's Email to Alert WHO to Possible Danger of COVID-19', Taiwan Centers for Disease Control, 11 April 2020, https://www.

cdc.gov.tw/En/Bulletin/Detail/PAD-lbwDHeN_bLa-viBOuw?typeid=158. The 31 December warning from Taiwan is also mentioned in Lawrence Freedman, 'Strategy for a Pandemic: The UK and COVID-19', *Survival*, vol. 62, no. 3, June–July 2020, p. 30. It is not indicated in the timeline on COVID-19 published on the WHO website. Whether the Taiwan statement, or some advance notice of it, preceded (and therefore potentially triggered) the official statement by Wuhan authorities is unclear.

36 Two open websites on which the genome was shared were virological. org and the US government-run National Library of Medicine, https://www.ncbi.nlm.nih.gov/sars-cov-2/. See also Jon Cohen, 'Chinese Researchers Reveal Draft Genome of Virus Implicated in Wuhan Pneumonia Outbreak', *Science*, 11 January 2020, https://www.sciencemag.org/news/2020/01/chinese-researchers-reveal-draft-genome-virus-implicated-wuhan-pneumonia-outbreak.

37 Zhuang Pinghui, 'Chinese Laboratory that First Shared Coronavirus Genome with World Ordered to Close for "Rectification", Hindering Its Covid-19 Research', *South China Morning Post*, 28 February 2020, https://www.scmp.com/news/china/society/article/3052966/chinese-laboratory-first-shared-coronavirus-genome-world-ordered.

38 For a newspaper summary of evidence about early Chinese cases of COVID-19, see Josephine Ma, 'Coronavirus: China's First Confirmed Covid-19 Case Traced back to November 17', *South China Morning Post*, 13 March 2020, https://www.scmp.com/news/china/society/article/3074991/coronavirus-chinas-first-confirmed-covid-19-case-traced-back.

39 'China Delayed Releasing Coronavirus Info, Frustrating WHO', Associated Press, 3 June 2020, https://apnews.com/3c061794970661042b18d5aeaaed9fae.

40 Donald J. Trump (@realDonaldTrump), tweet, 24 January 2020, https://twitter.com/realdonaldtrump/status/1220818115354923009?lang=en. Even after extensive evidence had emerged of a possible cover-up by the Chinese authorities on certain points, similar praise was heaped on China. See, for instance, Donald J. Trump (@realDonaldTrump), 7 February 2020, https://twitter.com/realdonaldtrump/status/1225728756456808448?lang=en.

41 White House, 'Remarks by President Trump in Press Briefing', 14 April 2020, https://www.whitehouse.gov/briefings-statements/remarks-president-trump-press-briefing/.

42 White House, 'Remarks by President Trump on Protecting America's Seniors', 30 April 2020, https://www.whitehouse.gov/briefings-statements/remarks-president-trump-protecting-americas-seniors/.

43 See Jonathan Stevenson, 'CIA Agonistes', *Survival*, vol. 62, no. 3, June–July 2020, p. 258.

44 See Shi Zhengli of the Wuhan Institute of Virology, email of 15 July 2020, published in Jon Cohen, 'Wuhan Coronavirus Hunter Shi Zhengli Speaks Out', *Science*, 31 July 2020, https://www.sciencemag.org/news/2020/07/trump-owes-us-

apology-chinese-scientist-center-
covid-19-origin-theories-speaks-out.

45 Letter to Dr Tedros Adhanom
Ghebreyesus, director-general of the
WHO, from President Donald Trump,
White House, 18 May 2020, https://
www.whitehouse.gov/wp-content/
uploads/2020/05/Tedros-Letter.pdf.

46 'Coronavirus: Trump Terminates US
Relationship with WHO', BBC, 30 May
2020, https://www.bbc.co.uk/news/
world-us-canada-52857413?intlink_
from_url=https://www.bbc.co.uk/
news/topics/c207p54m4pnt/
world-health-organization-who&link_
location=live-reporting-story.

47 See 'Trump Moves to Pull US Out of
World Health Organization', BBC,
7 July 2020, https://www.bbc.co.uk/
news/world-us-canada-53327906.

48 American Medical Association,
'Statement on Withdrawal of U.S.
from the World Health Organization',
7 July 2020, https://www.ama-assn.
org/press-center/ama-statements/
statement-withdrawal-us-world-
health-organization.

49 For a critique of President Trump's
verbal attacks on China and the WHO
over COVID-19, see Jessica McDonald
et al., 'FactChecking Trump's Attack
on the WHO', FactCheck.org, 15
April 2020, https://www.factcheck.
org/2020/04/factchecking-trumps-
attack-on-the-who/.

50 Something was achieved as a result
of pressure on the WHO. On 19
May, a virtual meeting of the World
Health Assembly agreed to a long
resolution establishing an 'impartial,
independent and comprehensive
evaluation' of lessons learned from
the international health response to
COVID-19. Resolution on 'COVID-19
Response', WHO, 73rd World Health
Assembly, adopted by consensus on
19 May 2020, https://apps.who.int/
gb/ebwha/pdf_files/WHA73/A73_
CONF1Rev1-en.pdf.

51 Richard J. Evans, 'Epidemics and
Revolutions', in Ranger and Slack
(eds), *Epidemics and Ideas*, p. 162.

52 Laura Spinney, *Pale Rider: The Spanish
Flu of 1918 and How it Changed the
World* (London: Jonathan Cape, 2017),
pp. 8, 254–60.

53 Patt Morrison, 'What the Deadly
1918 Flu Epidemic Can Teach Us
About Our Coronavirus Reaction',
Los Angeles Times, 11 March 2020,
https://www.latimes.com/opinion/
story/2020-03-11/1918-flu-epidemic-
coronavirus. This article states that
Mahatma Gandhi was among those
who had caught the Spanish flu
and survived.

54 See David Arnold, 'Death and the
Modern Empire: The 1918–19 Influenza
Epidemic in India', *Transactions of
the Royal Historical Society*, vol. 29,
December 2019, pp. 181–200. (Lecture
delivered at Strathclyde University, 5
October 2018.)

55 *Ibid.*, p. 198.

56 See Kralj-Brassard, 'A City Facing the
Plague', pp. 134, 139.

57 See Freedman, 'Strategy for a
Pandemic', p. 26.

58 *Ibid.*, p. 53.

59 See Extinction Rebellion, 'Extinction
Rebellion to Hold Socially Distanced
Protests Across the UK Demanding
People Have a Voice over Their
Future', 28 May 2020, https://rebellion.
earth/2020/05/28/30th-may-12pm-
extinction-rebellion-to-hold-socially-

distanced-protests-across-the-uk-calling-for-a-citizens-assembly-on-covid-19-recovery/.

60 Public Health England, 'Disparities in the Risk and Outcomes of COVID-19', 2 June 2020, pp. 4–8, https://www.gov.uk/government/publications/covid-19-review-of-disparities-in-risks-and-outcomes. This report was heavily criticised for failing to include a plan of action to protect vulnerable groups, and for not reflecting the input of many advocacy groups. See Gareth Iacobucci, 'Covid-19: PHE Review Has Failed Ethnic Minorities, Leaders Tell BMJ', *British Medical Journal*, 8 June 2020, https://www.bmj.com/content/369/bmj.m2264.

61 See International IDEA Institute for Democracy and Electoral Assistance, 'Global Overview of COVID-19: Impact on Elections', 18 March 2020, https://www.idea.int/news-media/multimedia-reports/global-overview-covid-19-impact-elections.

62 For a critique of the special legal order passed by the Hungarian parliament on 30 March 2020, see Domokos Lazar, 'A State in Danger – Special Legal Order Introduced in Hungary', Heinrich Böll Stiftung, 1 April 2020, https://eu.boell.org/en/2020/04/01/state-danger-special-legal-order-introduced-hungary.

63 Quoted in Vlagyiszlav Makszimov, 'EP Condemns Hungary and Poland's Controversial Coronavirus Moves', Euractiv, 17 April 2020, https://www.euractiv.com/section/justice-home-affairs/news/ep-condemns-hungarys-and-polands-controversial-coronavirus-moves/.

64 Viktor Orbán, interview with Kossuth Radio on 22 May 2020, available at Government of Hungary, 'Danger Has Not Passed, Preparedness Must Be Maintained', https://www.kormany.hu/en/the-prime-minister/news/danger-has-not-passed-preparedness-must-be-maintained. In this interview, his brief look at the numbers of deaths in other countries omitted mention of Poland. In Poland, the cumulative fatality rate per million was 25.68 as of 22 May 2020 – substantially better than Hungary's 49.27 – and Poland has remained ahead. See Our World in Data, 'Coronavirus Pandemic (COVID-19)', as of 22 May 2020, https://ourworldindata.org/coronavirus#coronavirus-country-profiles.

65 'Joint Declaration of the Government of the United Kingdom of Great Britain and Northern Ireland and the Government of the People's Republic of China on the Question of Hong Kong', *United Nations Treaty Series*, vol. 1,399, 19 December 1994, pp. 61–73, https://treaties.un.org/doc/Publication/UNTS/Volume%201399/v1399.pdf.

66 Chief Executive Council, 'Prevention and Control of Disease (Prohibition on Group Gathering) Regulation', Hong Kong e-Legislation, 29 March 2020, https://www.elegislation.gov.hk/hk/cap599G. This regulation was scheduled to expire at midnight on 28 June 2020.

67 The roles of the National People's Congress of the People's Republic of China regarding Hong Kong are mentioned in Article 3 (12) and Annex I of the 1984 Joint Declaration.

68 William James, 'UK Says China's Security Law Is Serious Violation

of Hong Kong Treaty', Reuters, 1 July 2020, https://www.reuters.com/article/us-hongkong-protests-britain/uk-says-chinas-security-law-is-serious-violation-of-hong-kong-treaty-idUSKBN2425LL.

69 'Law of the People's Republic of China on Safeguarding National Security in the Hong Kong Special Administrative Region', Articles 1, 4 and 12–30. For a complete English text, see 'English Translation of the Law of the People's Republic of China on Safeguarding National Security in the Hong Kong Special Administrative Region', Xinhuanet.com, 1 July 2020, http://www.xinhuanet.com/english/2020-07/01/c_139178753.htm. For an assessment, see 'Hong Kong's Security Law', IISS Strategic Comment, July 2020, https://www.iiss.org/publications/strategic-comments/2020/hong-kongs-security-law.

70 For the Hong Kong chief executive's statements in defence of these actions, see Government Responses to Recent Events, 'Press Releases', https://www.isd.gov.hk/response2019/eng/press.html. British colonial authorities originally promulgated the Emergency Regulations Ordinance in 1922.

71 Since March 2020, for example, the chief of Sri Lanka's National Operation Centre for Prevention of COVID-19 Outbreak has been Lieutenant-General Shavendra Silva, chief of the Defence Staff. For critical views on the lack of civilian oversight and claimed unsuitability of some of the personnel, see 'Sri Lanka's Militarisation of Covid-19 Response: Infographic by ITJP', Colombo Telegraph, 9 April 2020, https://www.colombotelegraph.com/index.php/sri-lankas-militarisation-of-covid-19-response-infographic-by-itjp/.

72 Steven Simon, 'Subtle Connections: Pandemic and the Authoritarian Impulse', Survival, vol. 62, no. 3, June–July 2020, pp. 105–6.

73 Fukuyama, 'The Pandemic and Political Order', p. 26.

74 See, for example, Gigi Kwik Gronvall, 'The Scientific Response to COVID-19 and Lessons for Security', Survival, vol. 62, no. 3, June–July 2020, pp. 77–92.

75 See Supriya Garikipati and Uma Kambhampati, 'Leading the Fight Against the Pandemic: Does Gender "Really" Matter?', Discussion Paper No. 2020-13, University of Reading, Department of Economics, http://www.reading.ac.uk/web/files/economics/emdp202013.pdf.

The Rohingya Crisis: Can ASEAN Salvage Its Credibility?

Rebecca Barber and Sarah Teitt

For many years, the government of Myanmar, a majority-Buddhist country, has systematically repressed the country's Rohingya Muslims, an ethnic, religious and linguistic minority residing primarily in Rakhine State on Myanmar's western coast. The government does not consider them one of the country's official ethnic groups, and since 1982 has denied them citizenship, effectively rendering them stateless. The Rohingya, for their part, have resisted official mistreatment, and several hundred have joined the Arakan Rohingya Salvation Army, which the government claims, but the group denies, is Islamist. In August 2017, its militants attacked around 30 police posts, reportedly killing a dozen officers. In response, the government dispatched the army. Within a month, troops supported by local Buddhist mobs burned Rohingya villages and attacked civilians, reportedly raping and abusing women and killing almost 7,000 people, including more than 700 young children. Subsequently, the government bore down on Rakhine State, where most Rohingya settled, apparently torching more than 300 villages, building government facilities on some of the sites and leaving others scorched. The government denies these allegations, while admitting that some members of the security forces have committed war crimes and

Rebecca Barber is a PhD candidate at the TC Beirne School of Law and the Asia-Pacific Centre for the Responsibility to Protect (APR2P) of the School of Political Science and International Studies, University of Queensland. **Sarah Teitt** is an Australian Research Council DECRA Senior Research Fellow and Deputy Director of the APR2P.

Survival | vol. 62 no. 5 | October–November 2020 | pp. 41–54   DOI 10.1080/00396338.2020.1819642

violations of human rights and domestic law. Since 2017, over 700,000 Rohingya have fled from Myanmar to Bangladesh, which as of March 2019 was no longer accepting refugees. With over half a million Rohingya still living in Rakhine State, subject to continuing abuses by security forces and at risk of deprivation, violence and ethnic cleansing, an independent fact-finding mission established by the United Nations Human Rights Council has warned that there is an ongoing risk of genocide.[1]

In January 2020, the International Court of Justice (ICJ) ordered the Myanmar government to take 'provisional measures' to prevent the commission of genocide against the Rohingya ethnic minority.[2] The order came just two months after the International Criminal Court announced that it had authorised an investigation into alleged crimes against the Rohingya, indicating that there was a 'reasonable basis to believe widespread and/or systematic acts of violence may have been committed' that could qualify as crimes against humanity (persecution and deportation).[3] In contrast to this international response, the Association of Southeast Asian Nations (ASEAN) has not issued a single statement even acknowledging the allegations against the Myanmar government and its senior officials. Instead, its high-level consensus statements have consistently reiterated the association's support for the government of Myanmar.[4]

It is in ASEAN's interest to take a more interventionist approach to the Rohingya crisis. In the past, ASEAN's principles of non-interference and consensus have occasionally been relaxed, and they could be so now. If ASEAN wishes to preserve its centrality and legitimacy, it must reassess the reputational and political costs of action versus inaction.

Risks to ASEAN

ASEAN's traditional principles of sovereignty, non-interference and consensus decision-making, enshrined in the ASEAN Charter and numerous other agreements and declarations, explain, if they do not justify, the organisation's handling of the Rohingya crisis.[5] Some scholars view these principles as insurmountable. One, for example, has assessed that ASEAN 'does not possess ... the ability to realise' its human-rights commitments.[6] Others appear resigned to ASEAN members' intolerance of interference, arguing that 'ASEAN states have proven time and again that they are not prepared' to allow the organisation to intrude in their domestic affairs.[7]

In practice, however, ASEAN has not interpreted the principle of non-interference as absolute.[8] Dating back to at least 2003, when ASEAN foreign ministers expressed concern about the pace of democratisation in Myanmar itself, the organisation has issued challenging statements with respect to the country's domestic issues. In 2005, for example, it pressured Myanmar to forfeit its role as ASEAN chair for 2006–07 amid external criticisms of its governance. Also in 2005, Malaysia, as ASEAN chair, informed Myanmar that the organisation would 'no longer be able to defend [Myanmar] internationally' unless it made progress towards democracy.[9] In 2007, Singapore's foreign minister issued a statement on behalf of ASEAN foreign ministers criticising Myanmar's crackdown on peaceful protests.[10] In 2008, ASEAN leaders pressured the country to accept international aid in the wake of Cyclone Nargis.[11]

ASEAN's tentatively interventionist stance on Myanmar during this period was underpinned by its calculations regarding the cost of inaction. The United States as well as European Union member states were threatening to withdraw development funding. Concerns arose that issues in Myanmar might prevent the US from acceding to ASEAN's Treaty of Amity and Cooperation in Southeast Asia. And ASEAN had a keen institutional interest in preventing Myanmar's fraught governance from derailing ASEAN's integration agenda.[12] Despite the risk of antagonising Naypyidaw, ASEAN asserted itself because its interests required it to do so.

The current Rohingya crisis calls for a similar but more decisive balancing of the costs of action versus inaction. In opting for a comparatively conservative position, ASEAN has underestimated the reputational and political costs of being perceived as unresponsive to a major regional crisis, and risks undermining its own organisational aspirations.

Since 2010, ASEAN statements and policies have consistently reaffirmed the importance of the organisation's geopolitical centrality. In 2018, its leaders agreed on 'centrality and unity' as the first of ten key principles underscoring their vision of a 'resilient and innovative ASEAN'.[13] Many of ASEAN's recent high-level statements have similarly affirmed the need to 'maintain ASEAN centrality and ASEAN's role as the primary driving force in the regional architecture'.[14]

Over the past decade, however, its salience has been threatened by shifting regional dynamics as major powers have sought to establish alternative regional frameworks. The Comprehensive and Progressive Agreement for Trans-Pacific Partnership, for example, involves some ASEAN member states but not the organisation itself. As ASEAN members interact more frequently and independently with external partners and trading regimes, the importance of a Southeast Asian regional association may be diminished. Great-power focus on the region – in particular, the confrontation between the US and China in the South China Sea – arguably marginalises ASEAN even further. In addition, Indonesia, traditionally ASEAN's dominant member, is a rising middle power and may be increasingly disinclined to operate within the framework of an ineffectual ASEAN.[15]

> ASEAN must be publicly engaged on the crisis

A status quo policy of inaction will not offset these threats. To maintain influence, relevance and legitimacy, ASEAN must be publicly and visibly engaged on the Rohingya crisis in a manner commensurate with the gravity of the situation. It must also demonstrate that it is capable of forging unity on the issue among its members. And it must adhere to its own human-rights commitments.

If ASEAN is seen as unresponsive to regional crises, international actors will fill the void. The ICJ's genocide case against Myanmar was brought by Gambia, a West African country, and buoyed by unprecedented support from the Organization of Islamic Cooperation (OIC). A key reason was that when ASEAN failed to push Myanmar to protect the Rohingya, Malaysia turned to the OIC.[16] Malaysia's representative to the ASEAN Intergovernmental Commission on Human Rights (AICHR) warned recently that if ASEAN now fails to respond to the ICJ's provisional-measures order, it risks 'becoming a bystander while the resolution to the Rohingya crisis is sought elsewhere'.[17]

In spite of ASEAN's perceived inaction, there appears to be domestic pressure – in some cases, mainstream support – in its key member states for a more activist approach. Protests have occurred in Indonesia and Malaysia outside Myanmar's embassies, demanding a stronger stance.[18] In Indonesia, Islamist extremists have exploited public anger over the persecution of fellow Muslims to attack the Joko Widodo (Jokowi) administration.[19] In 2018, 132 Southeast Asian parliamentarians issued a statement calling on ASEAN to exert greater pressure on Myanmar and, in 2020, a major survey found that the majority of respondents in seven of ten ASEAN member states disapproved of the organisation's handling of the Rohingya issue.[20]

Even among senior officials in some member states, the prevailing perception is of an organisation that is both unable to manage a regional security crisis and out of touch with the demands of its constituencies for a more principled and energetic response. In 2017, Malaysian foreign minister Anifah Aman publicly disassociated Malaysia from the ASEAN chairman's anodyne statement on the situation in Rakhine State.[21] The following year, Malaysian prime minister Mahathir Mohamad said that 'if ASEAN just allows these people to be massacred, it doesn't seem we are acting responsibly', while Vivian Balakrishnan, Singapore's minister of foreign affairs, told his parliament that ASEAN leaders had 'expressed their grave concern to Myanmar' at the sidelines of the UN General Assembly.[22] Indonesian President Joko Widodo has also expressed his concern to Naypyidaw bilaterally, and even Philippine President Rodrigo Duterte – not known as a staunch humanitarian – has described the situation in Myanmar as genocide.[23] The public frustration of such officials seems to confirm their own concern about the reputational cost to ASEAN of its failure to respond to such a high-profile human-rights crisis.

ASEAN leaders have had cause in the past to recognise the cost of division. In 2012, they found themselves unable to reach a common position on the South China Sea and, for the first time in the organisation's history, failed to issue an annual joint communiqué. As one commentator noted: 'ASEAN officials acknowledged that the incident had a negative impact on ASEAN's credibility' and 'soon after the meeting … went into damage-control mode', subsequently announcing the Six-Point Principles on the South China Sea, which temporarily 'allayed concerns that ASEAN cannot reach a common position on the issue'.[24]

Granted, ASEAN's human-rights commitments – in particular those enshrined in its 2012 Human Rights Declaration – were driven more by an interest in establishing ASEAN's legitimacy as a regional organisation than by ideology.[25] Nevertheless, those commitments have created standards to which ASEAN must now hold itself to preserve that legitimacy. As Mathew Davies has recognised, because ASEAN 'has committed to human rights rhetorically', it 'is now embedded in a wider range of processes and engagements ... which expose it and its members to a wider set of pressures to engage meaningfully with human rights'.[26] Helen Nesadurai has observed that the association cannot indefinitely 'sustain the gap between its rhetorical commitment to human rights and its actions before it loses legitimacy as a rightful regional organisation'.[27]

Options for a strengthened ASEAN response

More constructive engagement by ASEAN in the Rohingya crisis could take several forms. At least two of the organisation's many forums could be utilised to greater effect.

As many commentators have observed, the AICHR was never designed to 'push too strongly against ASEAN's fundamental principles of respect for sovereignty and non-intervention'.[28] While its primary purpose is to promote and protect human rights, its guiding principles include respect for sovereignty and non-interference, recognising the primary responsibility of member states for the protection of their citizens' human rights and pursuing a constructive and non-interventionist approach.[29] The AICHR is bound by consensual decision-making procedures, and is not empowered to hear individual complaints, investigate allegations or conduct monitoring visits.[30] It has been robustly criticised by civil-society organisations for hiding 'behind the non-interference principle' and neglecting 'the fulfilment [of] human rights on the ground'.[31]

For all its flaws, however, AICHR representatives acknowledge that the functionality of the commission could be improved without changing its Terms of Reference. For example, as of late 2019, the AICHR had not formally considered the Rohingya situation purportedly because it had been unable to reach consensus regarding the need to do so.[32] But there is nothing in the AICHR's Terms of Reference requiring it to reach consensus before considering a given issue. The AICHR could simply reconsider its modus operandi and free itself up to confront human-rights crises and meet with stakeholders without a consensus decision. In response to the Rohingya crisis in particular, the AICHR could offer assistance to Myanmar in complying with the provisional measures required by the ICJ's order. This would fall within the AICHR's mandate to provide technical assistance. Also worth noting is the provision in the AICHR's Terms of Reference that allows the commission to 'perform any other tasks as may be assigned to it by the ASEAN Foreign Ministers Meeting', which affords the AICHR the flexibility to perform tasks other than those explicitly specified.[33]

If ASEAN really is to solidify its legitimacy, however, it will need to go beyond such incremental shifts and show that its human-rights body is substantially capable of protecting human rights on the ground. To achieve this, the AICHR's Terms of Reference would need to be revised.[34] Possibilities for strengthening them include empowering the commission to request information from, and make recommendations to, member states; authorising it to undertake country visits; and allowing exceptions to consensus decision-making when an ASEAN state is accused of grave violations of human rights.[35]

Another body that could play a more constructive role is the ASEAN Coordinating Centre for Humanitarian Assistance on Disaster Management (AHA Centre), ASEAN's mechanism for promoting 'regional collaboration in disaster management and emergency response'.[36] Thus far, it has responded primarily to natural disasters, though ASEAN agreements leave open the possibility of the AHA Centre playing a greater role in conflict-related crises.[37] In Rakhine State, it has assisted with the coordination of humanitarian assistance, and has deployed its ASEAN–Emergency Response and Assessment Team (ASEAN–ERAT) to monitor the distribution of humanitarian relief and assess conditions for the repatriation of refugees.[38]

Several factors constrain the capacity of the ASEAN–ERAT to respond to conflict-related crises, however. Firstly, it operates under the 'supervision and control' of the affected state, and thus cannot function as an independent humanitarian actor.[39] Secondly, there are no guidelines on how its response should be tailored in conflict contexts as compared with natural disasters. Thirdly, even when it does respond to conflict-related crises, its mandate tends to be interpreted as excluding engagement in the protection of human rights or in humanitarian operations. Following the ASEAN–ERAT's assessment of conditions for repatriation in Rakhine State in 2019, Human Rights Watch criticised ASEAN for ignoring persistent human-rights violations that were preventing the voluntary return of refugees from Bangladesh.[40] AHA Centre Executive Director Adelina Kamal responded by stating that the ASEAN–ERAT's expertise was 'disaster management', and that it could not go beyond its mandate.[41]

However limited in its effect, the AHA Centre's engagement in Rakhine State does reflect the desire of ASEAN member states to usefully engage on the crisis without damaging fragile relationships. They see light humanitarian support and refugee-repatriation assistance as relatively uncontroversial. But if ASEAN is to realise its vision of becoming a 'global leader on disaster management and emergency response', it will need to assume a more substantial role in responding to humanitarian crises.[42] This will require specific guidance for the ASEAN–ERAT on how to operate in conflict-induced crises, serious consideration of the degree of independence required for it to function in such contexts, and the development of dedicated expertise on humanitarian operations in such crises, including humanitarian protection.

*   *   *

Among member states, there is considerable support for a more robust ASEAN response to the human-rights violations against the Rohingya. At a meeting of the ASEAN Institute for Peace and Reconciliation in 2017, Singapore's representative said that there was consensus within the organisation on at least three core issues: that the violence must stop; that humanitarian assistance should be provided; and that ASEAN should play a role. At the same meeting, the Philippines' representative chimed in that on the sidelines of that year's UN General Assembly session in New York, 'nine Ministers closeted themselves in a room and agonized over how to help'.[43] This is common ground upon which to build.

Over the past several decades, ASEAN has asserted its geopolitical centrality in the Asia-Pacific region, and has increased its credibility by rhetorically committing to human rights. There are valid political constraints that preclude a comprehensively more interventionist ASEAN. But the Rohingya crisis in Myanmar has rendered ASEAN's resolutely non-interventionist approach politically imprudent and damaging to its legitimacy.[44] By reorienting existing mechanisms, ASEAN could feasibly adopt a more forward-leaning and effective approach to upholding human rights, within the bounds of recognised political constraints.

Notes

1   See, for instance, 'Genocide Threat for Myanmar's Rohingya Greater than Ever, Investigators Warn Human Rights Council', UN News, 16 September 2019, https://news.un.org/en/story/2019/09/1046442. For background, see 'Myanmar Rohingya: What You Need to Know About the Crisis', BBC, 23 January 2020, https://www.bbc.co.uk/news/world-asia-41566561; Edith Lederer, 'UN Condemns Human Rights Abuses Against Myanmar's Rohingya', Associated Press, 28 December 2019, https://apnews.com/20020daebe7 5507606546560d5e24d83; Human Rights Watch, 'Burma: Scores of Rohingya Villages Bulldozed', 23 February 2018, https://www.hrw.org/news/2018/02/23/burma-scores-rohingya-villages-bulldozed; and Médecins Sans Frontières, 'Rohingya Refugee Crisis', https://www.msf.org.uk/issues/rohingya-refugee-crisis.

2   International Court of Justice, 'Application of the Convention on the Prevention of the Crime of Genocide (The Gambia v. Myanmar): Request for the Indication of Provisional Measures', 23 January 2020, https://www.icj-cij.org/files/case-related/178/178-20200123-ORD-01-00-EN.pdf.

3   International Criminal Court, 'ICC Judges Authorise Opening of an Investigation into the Situation in Bangladesh/Myanmar', press release, 14 November 2019, https://www.icc-cpi.int/Pages/item.aspx?name=pr1495.

4   See, for example, ASEAN, 'Chairman's Statement of the 34th ASEAN Summit', 23 June 2019, https://asean.org/storage/2019/06/Final_Chairs-Statement-of-the-34th-ASEAN-Summit-rev.pdf.

5   See, in particular, ASEAN, 'Charter of the Association of Southeast Asian Nations', 2007, articles 2 and 20, published in *United Nations Treaty Series*, vol. 2,624, no. 46,745 (New York: United Nations, 2009), pp. 223–98; and 'Treaty of Amity and Cooperation in Southeast Asia', 1976, article two, published in *United Nations Treaty Series*, vol. 1,025, no. 15,063, pp. 316–22 (New York: United Nations, 1976).

6   Mathew Davies, 'Important but De-centred: ASEAN's Role in the Southeast Asian Human Rights Space', *TRaNS: Trans-Regional and -National Studies of Southeast Asia*, vol. 5, no. 1, January 2017, pp. 99, 114.

7   See, for example, Shaun Narine, 'The ASEAN Regional Security Partnership: Strengths and Limits of a Cooperative System', *Contemporary Southeast Asia*, vol. 38, no. 1, 2016, pp. 154, 157.

8   See, for example, Mathew Davies, 'A Community of Practice: Explaining Change and Continuity in ASEAN's Diplomatic Environment', *Pacific Review*, vol. 29, no. 2, 2016, pp. 211, 215; and Helen E.S. Nesadurai, 'ASEAN During the Life of the Pacific Review: A Balance Sheet on Regional Governance and Community Building', *Pacific Review*, vol. 30, no. 6, 2017, pp. 938, 943.

9   Jurgen Haacke, 'The Myanmar Imbroglio and ASEAN: Heading Towards the 2010 Elections', *International Affairs*, vol. 86, no. 1, 2010, pp. 153, 160.

10 See Mathew Davies, 'The Perils of Incoherence: ASEAN, Myanmar and the Avoidable Failures of Human Rights Socialization', *Contemporary Southeast Asia*, vol. 34, no. 1, 2012, p. 9.

11 See Jurgen Haacke, 'Myanmar, the Responsibility to Protect, and the Need for Practical Assistance', *Global Responsibility to Protect*, vol. 1, no. 2, 2009, pp. 156, 173.

12 See Haacke, 'The Myanmar Imbroglio and ASEAN', p. 165.

13 ASEAN, 'ASEAN Leaders' Vision for a Resilient and Innovative ASEAN', 27 April 2018, https://asean. org/wp-content/uploads/2018/04/ ASEAN-Leaders-Vision-for-a-Resilient-and-Innovative-ASEAN.pdf.

14 ASEAN, 'Chairman's Statement of the 35th ASEAN Summit', 3 November 2019, https://asean.org/ storage/2019/11/Chairs-Statement-of-the-35th-ASEAN-Summit-FINAL.pdf. See also ASEAN, 'Joint Communiqué of the 52nd ASEAN Foreign Ministers' Meeting', 31 July 2019, https://asean.org/storage/2019/07/ CIRCULATE-Joint-Communique-of-the-52nd-AMM-FINAL.pdf; and ASEAN, 'ASEAN Community Vision 2025', 2015, https://www.asean.org/ storage/images/2015/November/ aec-page/ASEAN-Community-Vision-2025.pdf.

15 See Mark Beeson, 'The Great ASEAN Rorschach Test', *Pacific Review*, vol. 33, nos 3–4, 2020, pp. 574, 578; and Christopher B. Roberts and Leonard C. Sebastian, 'Ascending Indonesia: Significance and Conceptual Foundations', in Christopher B. Roberts, Ahmad D. Habir and Leonard C. Sebastian (eds), *Indonesia's Ascent: Power, Leadership and Regional Order* (Basingstoke: Palgrave Macmillan, 2015), p. 1.

16 See 'Malaysia Says OIC Will Push Myanmar to Halt Rohingya Crisis', AP News, 18 January 2017, https://apnews.com/ def675bb06fb40fob58a1136d9754c19/ Malaysia-says-OIC-will-push-Myanmar-to-halt-Rohingya-crisis.

17 Eric Paulsen, 'Comment: Why ASEAN Must Act on ICJ Ruling on the Rohingya', *Star*, 23 February 2020, https://www.thestar.com. my/news/focus/2020/02/23/

comment-why-asean-must-act-on-icj-ruling-on-the-rohingya.

18   See 'Thousands of Indonesians Join Anti-Myanmar Rally in Jakarta', Reuters, 6 September 2017, https://www.reuters.com/article/us-myanmar-rohingya-indonesia/thousands-of-indonesians-join-anti-myanmar-rally-in-jakarta-idUSKC-N1BH0T6; and Ram Anand and Azril Annuar, 'Why Thousands of Rohingya Protested in KL on Merdeka Eve', *Malay Mail*, 2 September 2017, https://www.malaymail.com/news/malaysia/2017/09/02/why-thousands-of-rohingya-pro-tested-in-kl-on-merdeka-eve/1456113.

19   See James M. Dorsey, 'Plight of Myanmar's Rohingya: Militant Islam's Next Rallying Call?', *South China Morning Post*, 9 September 2017, https://www.scmp.com/week-asia/politics/article/2110176/plight-myanmars-rohingya-militant-islams-next-rallying-call.

20   ASEAN Parliamentarians for Human Rights (APHR), 'Myanmar Authorities Must Be Brought Before International Criminal Court, Say Southeast Asian Lawmakers', 24 August 2018, https://aseanmp.org/2018/08/24/mp-state-ment-rohingya-crisis/; and S.M. Tang et al., 'The State of Southeast Asia: 2020 Survey Report', ISEAS–Yusof Ishak Institute, 16 January 2020, p. 12, https://www.iseas.edu.sg/images/pdf/TheStateofSEASurveyReport_2020.pdf.

21   'Malaysia Disassociates Itself from ASEAN Statement on Myanmar's Rakhine State', Channel News Asia, 24 September 2017, https://www.channelnewsasia.com/news/asia/malaysia-disassociates-itself-from-asean-statement-on-myan-mar-s-9246494.

22   'Mahathir: ASEAN Must Press Suu Kyi over Rohingya Crisis', *Dhaka Tribune*, 17 December 2018, https://www.dhakatribune.com/world/south-asia/2018/12/17/mahathir-asean-must-press-suu-kyi-over-rohingya-crisis; and Yasmine Yahya, 'Parliament: Vivian Balakrishnan Reiterates Call for Myanmar to Provide for Safe Return of Rohingya Refugees', *Straits Times*, 2 October 2018, https://www.straitstimes.com/politics/parliament-vivian-reiterates-call-for-myanmar-to-provide-for-safe-return-of-rohingya.

23   See Marguerite Alfra Sapiie, 'Indonesia Wants End to Rohingya Crisis, Jokowi Tells Myint', *Jakarta Post*, 28 April 2018, https://www.thejakartapost.com/news/2018/04/28/indonesia-wants-end-to-rohingya-crisis-jokowi-tells-myint.html; and 'Philippines' Duterte Cites "Genocide" in Myanmar, Says Will Take Refugees', *Straits Times*, 5 April 2018, https://www.straitstimes.com/asia/se-asia/philippines-duterte-cites-genocide-in-myanmar-says-will-take-refugees.

24   Mely Caballero-Anthony, 'Understanding ASEAN's Centrality: Bases and Prospects in an Evolving Regional Architecture', *Pacific Review*, vol. 27, no. 4, 2014, pp. 479, 563.

25   See, for example, Shaun Narine, 'Human Rights Norms and the Evolution of ASEAN: Moving Without Moving in a Changing Regional Environment', *Contemporary Southeast Asia*, vol. 34, no. 3, 2012, p. 367; and Mathew Davies, 'ASEAN and Human Rights Norms: Constructivism,

Rational Choice, and the Action–Identity Gap', *International Relations of the Asia-Pacific*, vol. 13, no. 2, 2013, p. 221.

26 Davies, 'Important but De-centred', p. 111.

27 Nesadurai, 'ASEAN During the Life of the Pacific Review', p. 942.

28 Narine, 'Human Rights Norms and the Evolution of ASEAN', p. 375.

29 See ASEAN, 'Terms of Reference of ASEAN Intergovernmental Commission on Human Rights' (hereafter 'AICHR TOR'), 2019, http://hrlibrary.umn.edu/research/Philippines/Terms%20of%20Reference%20for%20the%20ASEAN%20Inter-Governmental%20CHR.pdf.

30 See Hao Duy Phan, 'Promotional Versus Protective Design: The Case of the ASEAN Intergovernmental Commission on Human Rights', *International Journal of Human Rights*, vol. 23, no. 6, 2019, p. 919.

31 APHR, FORUM–ASIA and Centre for Strategic and International Studies (CSIS), 'Joint Statement: ASEAN Needs a Stronger Human Rights Mechanism', 9 May 2019, https://aseanmp.org/2019/05/09/joint-statement-asean-hrmechanism/.

32 Author interviews with a senior official of an ASEAN member state, conducted in June 2019.

33 ASEAN, 'AICHR TOR'.

34 See Phan, 'Promotional Versus Protective Design', p. 14.

35 See Vitit Muntarbhorn, 'Responsibility to Protect Through the Human Rights Lens: Implications for Southeast Asia', speech delivered at the Dr Surin Pitswan Memorial Oration, Asia-Pacific Centre for the Responsibility to Protect, September 2019, https://r2pasiapacific.org/files/3868/speech_surinpitsuwan_2019oration_vititmuntarbhorn.

36 ASEAN, 'Agreement on the Establishment of the ASEAN Co-ordinating Centre for Humanitarian Assistance and Disaster Management', 2011, https://ahacentre.org/wp-content/uploads/2017/02/Agreement-of-AHAC-Establishment-A5-20140703.pdf.

37 See ASEAN, 'ASEAN Vision 2025 on Disaster Management', 2015, https://www.asean.org/storage/2012/05/fa-220416_DM2025_email.pdf.

38 See, for example, AHA Centre, 'AHA Centre Delivers 80 Tons of Relief Materials to Rakhine State, Myanmar', press release, 26 October 2017, https://ahacentre.org/press-release/aha-centre-delivers-80-tons-of-relief-materials-to-rakhine-state-myanmar/; and ASEAN, 'Press Statement by the Chairman of the ASEAN Foreign Minister's Retreat', 17 January 2020, https://asean.org/storage/2020/01/17.1.2020-AMMR-Press-Statement-Final.pdf.

39 AHA Centre, 'Guidelines: ASEAN–ERAT', 2018, pp. 25, 35, https://ahacentre.org/wp-content/uploads/publications/ASEAN-ERAT-guidelines.pdf.

40 See Human Rights Watch, 'For Rohingya Refugees, There's No Return in Sight: Why They Remain Stuck in Bangladesh', *Foreign Affairs*, 5 June 2019, https://www.foreignaffairs.com/articles/burma-myanmar/2019-06-05/rohingya-refugees-theres-no-return-sight.

41 W.K. Leong, 'AHA Centre Defends

Leaked Report on Rohingya Refugees', Channel News Asia, 10 June 2019, https://www.channelnewsasia.com/news/asia/aaha-centre-defends-leaked-report-on-rohingya-refugees-11613142.

42 ASEAN, 'ASEAN Vision 2025 on Disaster Management'.

43 ASEAN Institute for Peace and Reconciliation (AIPR), 'Strengthening Convergences for Humanitarian Action in ASEAN: An ASEAN AIPR Symposium on International Humanitarian Law', October 2017, p. 45, https://asean-aipr.org/wp-content/uploads/2018/08/Strengthening-Convergences-for-Humanitarian-Action-in-ASEAN.pdf.

44 See Marty Natalegawa, *Does ASEAN Matter? A View from Within* (Pasir Panjang: ISEAS–Yusof Ishak Institute, 2018), p. 228.

The New Threat to the Test-Ban Treaty

Edward Ifft

It has been a difficult time for arms control. The past few months have seen the demise of the Intermediate-Range Nuclear Forces (INF) Treaty; the United States' withdrawal from the Open Skies Treaty, the Arms Trade Treaty and the Joint Comprehensive Plan of Action (JCPOA) with Iran; violations of the Chemical Weapons Convention by Syria and Russia; and postponement of the Non-Proliferation Treaty (NPT) Review Conference. The Treaty on Conventional Armed Forces in Europe is almost comatose and the future of the New Strategic Arms Reduction Treaty (New START) is in doubt. There are urgent calls for China to become more involved in constraining both strategic and tactical arms – a logical step, but a complicating one without an obvious solution. There has been much discussion of the dangers to international security posed by cyber weapons, space weapons, drones and artificial intelligence, but even hypothetical solutions are largely absent.

Despite these difficulties, all existing arms-control negotiating forums appear frozen, except perhaps for the US–Russia negotiations on New START. Diplomatic and military channels between the United States/ NATO and Russia have been severed, with few exceptions. The problems surrounding Iran and North Korea are steadily worsening, without any

Edward Ifft, now a Distinguished Visiting Fellow at the Hoover Institution, Stanford University, helped negotiate and implement many of the key nuclear-arms-control agreements of the past 45 years, primarily as a senior US State Department official.

Survival | vol. 62 no. 5 | October–November 2020 | pp. 55–64   DOI 10.1080/00396338.2020.1819643

negotiations under way to deal with them. Somewhat incongruously, communication channels at the presidential level between Donald Trump and Vladimir Putin, Trump and Xi Jinping, and Trump and Kim Jong-un remain open and are used. This could facilitate solutions.

The next casualty?

On top of all this, the Comprehensive Test-Ban Treaty (CTBT), which Bill Clinton called the 'longest sought, hardest fought' arms-control treaty of them all, has come under threat. The CTBT was negotiated at the Geneva Conference on Disarmament in 1994–96. It has been signed by 184 countries and ratified by 168.[1] Demonstrating that the treaty is far more than just a piece of paper, the Comprehensive Test-Ban Treaty Organization (CTBTO) Preparatory Commission in Vienna has nearly finished creating a rather remarkable International Monitoring System comprising 337 facilities in 89 countries, and employing four key technologies: seismic, radionuclide, hydroacoustic and infrasound. Data from the system's monitoring stations flows daily to all the signatory states. The system has functioned well in detecting all of North Korea's nuclear explosions, and has made important contributions to scientific knowledge of earthquakes and geophysics, to tsunami-warning systems, to the monitoring of nuclear accidents and more. In addition, large field exercises in Kazakhstan and Jordan have contributed greatly to preparations for conducting on-site inspections, should they be needed.[2]

In spite of this impressive preparatory work, the CTBT has not yet entered into force. Eight of the 44 countries whose ratification is required are still delinquent: China, Egypt, India, Iran, Israel, North Korea, Pakistan and the US. (India, North Korea and Pakistan have not even signed.) A worldwide moratorium on nuclear explosions, endorsed by the United Nations Security Council, is holding, and other than those conducted by North Korea, there have been no nuclear explosions since India and Pakistan tested in 1998. Still, the US State Department has concluded that 'Russia has conducted nuclear weapons experiments that have created nuclear yield and are not consistent with the US "zero-yield" standard', and may be guilty of a technical violation of the 1974 Threshold Test

Ban Treaty.[3] The department's 2020 arms-control compliance report also expresses 'concern' that China may be engaging in similar activities.[4] Though artfully worded, these are serious charges. The compliance report also contends that both Russia and China appear to be making preparations for a test explosion.[5] At US insistence, the CTBT does not prohibit such preparations.

Suspicions surrounding Russian and Chinese activities are not necessarily new. As early as 2009, members of the Congressional Commission on the Strategic Posture of the United States (the Perry–Schlesinger Commission) who opposed the CTBT claimed that 'apparently Russia and possibly China are conducting low yield [nuclear] tests'.[6] By agreement, other members of the commission who disagreed with this assessment did not attempt to refute it in the commission's report. In subsequent years, similar allegations have arisen, from inside and outside the US government.[7] However, the 2020 compliance report is the first time the charge has risen to the level of a 'finding'.[8] No public evidence has ever been offered for any of these charges.

The US itself has reportedly considered conducting its first nuclear explosion since September 1992.[9] This would be held at the former nuclear test site in Nevada, where almost 1,000 tests, both in the atmosphere and underground, were conducted during the Cold War. (France is the only country to have permanently closed its test site.) The rationale for a new US test was apparently twofold: to counter the alleged Russian activities, and to pressure both Russia and China into a more favourable stance in negotiations over New START and a possible follow-on treaty. Of course, any such test would violate the United States' own interpretation of the CTBT and other relevant treaties, and would also open the door to resumed testing by other countries, particularly North Korea.

Interpreting the CTBT

Because the CTBT has not yet entered into force, concepts such as 'compliance' and 'violation' must be used carefully. Describing certain activities may require a detailed knowledge of physics, and there is always a risk that governments may interpret the same terms differently.

The basic obligation the CTBT imposes on adherents is to not conduct any 'nuclear explosion'.[10] Yet the treaty does not contain a definition of this term. At first glance, this might appear to be a serious oversight, but the omission was deliberate, resulting from careful consideration. After negotiating at length among themselves and deliberating whether the treaty should allow very-low-yield nuclear explosions, the five permanent members (P5) of the UN Security Council, led by the US, decided to ban all such explosions without exception, this being the 'zero-yield option'.

The popular term 'yield', which is often used when discussing nuclear weapons, is quite clear when expressed in kilotons. However, when discussing extremely small events, the term 'zero yield' could be subject to different interpretations. A more precise description would be to say there is nuclear yield if there is a self-sustaining nuclear reaction (the experiment or test becomes super-critical). Experiments with plutonium which do not cross this line are called 'hydrodynamic', while those that do are termed 'hydro-nuclear'. According to the US interpretation, the former are permitted by the CTBT, while the latter are not. (It appears that it is this line which the US believes Russia has crossed at its test site at Novaya Zemlya.) While there may be general agreement on this legal fine point, it is not clear whether political leaders have gotten into this level of detail in their discussions of what is and is not allowed by the treaty. The situation has been further complicated by the introduction of the concept of 'release of nuclear energy' into discussions of compliance.

To deal with possible misunderstandings of the term 'yield', and to avoid unintentionally prohibiting desirable, peaceful nuclear activities, negotiators created a category of 'activities not prohibited', which was described as not exhaustive. Examples cited were computer modelling, inertial confinement fusion, certain scientific research projects involving some release of nuclear energy, nuclear-power and research reactors, hydrodynamic experiments involving fissile material and more.[11]

Additional treaty obligations

The obligation not to conduct nuclear explosions cannot be violated before the CTBT comes into force.[12] However, there are several more treaty obligations that are relevant here.[13] In the no man's land between signature and entry into force, the Vienna Convention on the Law of Treaties requires that signatory states not engage in activities that would 'defeat the object and purpose' of the treaty.[14] This obligation too is open to interpretation. In a statement on 15 September 2016, the P5 declared that any nuclear explosion would violate this standard. Eight days later, the UN Security Council noted this statement in UN Security Council Resolution (UNSCR) 2310. Under the common-sense meaning of 'defeat' – that is, to render impossible the achievement of the treaty's object and purpose – this might have been an overreach. India, Pakistan and North Korea have all conducted large nuclear explosions since 1996, yet this has not put the treaty's object and purpose beyond reach, and all three countries would still be welcomed as parties. Perhaps the intent of the P5 statement and UNSCR 2310 was to make clear that such actions would be 'inconsistent with' or 'contrary to' the treaty's object and purpose, but not actually 'defeat' its goals.

The Vienna Convention also provides that the 'object and purpose' obligation may be set aside if entry into force is unduly delayed. The fact that the CTBT was opened for signature 24 years ago may provide another possible source of misunderstanding. It is worth noting that the US compliance report does not mention the 'object and purpose' obligation at all.

Even though the CTBT has yet to enter into force, all states that have nuclear weapons, even North Korea, are currently observing a moratorium on nuclear explosions. Compliance is unilateral and voluntary, and therefore not legally binding. There is no agreed document laying out each country's understanding of its own moratorium. The US compliance report charges that Russia is not conforming to the US standard in its moratorium.[15] But there is nothing to suggest that Russia has ever explicitly agreed to this standard. It could conceivably have its own standard.

If Russia is in fact conducting nuclear explosions, this would constitute a technical violation of the Threshold Test Ban Treaty. This treaty, which has entered into force, requires advance notice of any nuclear explosion. Russia has never given such notice, but it also denies conducting any such explosions. It also appears to believe that the treaty has been 'overtaken' by the CTBT, in which case such notice would no longer be required.

Russian resistance

Russian responses to the US accusations have been consistent and categorical, but not specific enough to allay suspicions. On 23 April 2020, Russia's Ministry of Foreign Affairs stated: 'We do not conduct non-zero-yield tests. We, like the US and other nuclear states, carry out so-called subcritical tests, which in no way run counter to our obligations.'[16] In a 15 June 2020 interview with *Kommersant*, former deputy foreign minister Grigory Berdennikov, who led the Russian delegation to the CTBT negotiations, took a different approach, stating that the US charges were 'unsubstantiated and cannot be substantiated'.[17] He went on to explain that evidence indicating the precise nature of an explosion could only be obtained through an on-site inspection, which cannot occur until the treaty has entered into force. In a further possible insight into Russian thinking, he claimed that, during the CTBT negotiations,

> we have stated more than once that the treaty must not hinder maintenance of the reliability and safety of our nuclear weapons. We do not intend to expose our nuclear arsenal to danger. It must be maintained in a safe and reliable state. No one has disputed that.

US analysts have also opined that on-site inspections could solve the mystery of whether very small explosions have crossed the line.[18] The problem, as Berdennikov pointed out, is that these are only allowed after entry into force of the CTBT, an outcome that seems highly unlikely if current questions are not resolved. Even if such inspections could be carried out, it is not clear how they would work. Such inspections would require highly intrusive access to underground testing tunnels, something that has not been prepared for in field exercises. Of course, in a highly cooperative environment, even intrusive underground inspections might well be possible, and the CTBT does allow inspectors to enter mines, caverns or other excavations in the 'continuation phase' of an inspection. Still, it should be noted that the explosions in dispute are extremely small, to the point of being undetectable by existing monitoring systems. No suspicious signals from either Russian or Chinese test sites have been reported by the International Data Centre in Vienna, even though the International Monitoring System was designed to have high sensitivity for detecting seismic signals from former nuclear test sites.[19]

A more general approach, and one which need not wait for the CTBT to enter into force, would be to improve the transparency of test sites and relevant activities. There have been repeated calls for this,[20] but the Russian response has generally been to argue that this too must wait for entry into force.[21] For its part, the US has been quite transparent regarding its hydrodynamic experiments in Nevada. A breakthrough might be possible if Russia provided, for example, some information regarding the dates and nature of its experiments with fissile materials, perhaps using confidential channels to do so.

Saving the CTBT

It is clear that any resolution of the CTBT impasse will be very difficult to achieve unless the US provides some explanation for its charges and Russia provides more information regarding its activities at Novaya Zemlya. The most desirable solution would be that detailed technical discussions reveal that the activities in question do not actually violate any current obligations. Another possibility would be that discussions reveal differing understandings in the US and Russia of their current obligations.[22] If the countries were unable to resolve these differences, they might agree not to call the activities in question violations and to be more transparent about them. A better outcome would be for Russia not to admit any fault, but to agree to cease the activities in question. It is possible that Russia or other countries are engaging in activities that they would consider illegal after entry into force, but not before, or that they believe are protected by the 'activities not prohibited' concept. Some may believe that the 'undue delay' clause of the Vienna Convention is relevant.

A more difficult, but perhaps more satisfying, outcome would see the sides harmonise their differing interpretations through compromise prior to the CTBT's entry into force. The distinction between this outcome and the current situation would probably not be verifiable, but would remove the principal point of contention. In any such discussions, the US should be prepared for Russian counter-accusations. These could take the form of questions about possible weapons-related activities at US laboratories, such as the National Ignition Facility at Livermore and the Dual-Axis Radiographic Hydrodynamic Test Facility at Los Alamos.

While all this may appear to be an obscure controversy over relatively minor legal and technical matters, there are disturbing similarities between the questions surrounding the CTBT and last year's INF Treaty disaster. In both cases, problems began with hints and whispers of Russian misbehaviour, with no evidence presented. Arms-control opponents gradually amplified these rumours over several years, with the involvement of think tanks and prominent American lawmakers.[23] Russia at first ignored all this, then issued sweeping denials of any wrongdoing. Some confidential inter-governmental meetings were held, but apparently failed to make progress. The results of these meetings were not made public, meaning that allies, non-governmental organisations and academic experts could not contribute to the process of finding a solution. In the case of the INF Treaty, only when a full-blown crisis was apparent did a few (controversial) facts and creative ideas emerge, but this was too little, too late – the treaty was abandoned and the testing of once-prohibited weapons systems resumed. We can only hope that the CTBT will not follow this same course.[24]

Notes

1   For articles dealing with all aspects of the CTBT, see *Nonproliferation Review*, vol. 23, nos 3–4, June–July 2016.

2   For a discussion of the CTBT verification system, see Andreas Persbo, 'Compliance Science: The CTBT's Global Verification System', *Nonproliferation Review*, June–July 2016, pp. 317–28. See also articles by Raymond Jeanloz, Edward Ifft, Matthias Auer and Mark Prior, and Pierce Corden and David Hafmeister, in Pierce Corden et al. (eds), *Nuclear Weapons and Related Security Issues*,

American Institute of Physics, vol. 1,898, April 2017, available at http://www.proceedings.aip.org.

3   US Department of State, 'Adherence to and Compliance with Arms Control, Nonproliferation, and Disarmament Agreements and Commitments', June 2020, pp. 46, 50, https://www.state.gov/wp-content/uploads/2020/06/2020-Adherence-to-and-Compliance-with-Arms-Control-Nonproliferation-and-Disarmament-Agreements-and-Commitments-Compliance-Report-1.pdf. The

Threshold Test Ban Treaty entered into force in 1990.

4 US Department of State, 'Adherence to and Compliance with Arms Control, Nonproliferation, and Disarmament Agreements and Commitments', pp. 49–50.

5 *Ibid.*, pp. 49–51.

6 US Institute of Peace, 'America's Strategic Posture: The Final Report of the Congressional Commission on the Strategic Posture of the United States', 2009, p. 83.

7 See, for example, 'The Arms Control Landscape', prepared remarks by the director of the Defense Intelligence Agency, Lt-Gen. Robert Ashley, Jr, at the Hudson Institute, Washington DC, 29 May 2019, https://www.hudson. org/research/15063-transcript-the- arms-control-landscape-ft-dia-lt-gen- robert-p-ashley-jr.

8 Previous US compliance reports used statements such as 'U.S. assessments are based on the U.S. position of what constitutes a nuclear explosive testing moratorium', but without saying what this US assessment is. See US Department of State, '2015 Report on Adherence to and Compliance with Arms Control, Nonproliferation, and Disarmament Agreements and Commitments', Part IV, https://2009-2017.state.gov/t/avc/ rls/rpt/2015/243224.htm.

9 See John Hudson and Paul Sonne, 'Officials: Trump Administration Discussed First U.S. Nuclear Test Since 1992', *Washington Post*, 23 May 2020; and 'Viva Las Vegas?', *The Economist*, 27 June 2020, pp. 17–18. The idea of the US conducting a test has created a significant backlash:

see Shannon Bugos, 'US Testing Interest Triggers Backlash', *Arms Control Today*, July–August 2020, pp. 33–4; and Maximilian Hoell, 'The Comprehensive Nuclear-Test-Ban Treaty Is in Danger: Here's How to Save It', European Leadership Network, August 2019.

10 Article I of the CTBT states that 'each State Party undertakes not to carry out any nuclear weapon test explo- sion or any other nuclear explosion, and to prohibit and prevent any such nuclear explosion at any place under its jurisdiction or control'. This for- mulation was carried over from the 1963 Limited [Partial] Nuclear Test Ban Treaty. The text of the CTBT is available at https://www.ctbto.org/ fileadmin/user_upload/legal/CTBT_ English_withCover.pdf.

11 US Department of State, 'Article-by- Article Analysis of the Comprehensive Nuclear Test-Ban Treaty', archived at https://2009-2017.state.gov/t/avc/ trty/16522.htm.

12 The US compliance report acknowl- edges this point by stating: 'This Report does not assess any coun- try's compliance with the CTBT, as it has never entered into force and the United States has no obligations under it.' US Department of State, 'Adherence to and Compliance with Arms Control, Nonproliferation, and Disarmament Agreements and Commitments', p. 48.

13 For further discussion of these obligations, see Edward Ifft, 'An Assessment of Obligations Under the Comprehensive Nuclear-Test- Ban Treaty', European Leadership Network Commentary, 2 June 2020.

14 See Article 18 of the Vienna Convention on the Law of Treaties, 1969, available at https://legal.un.org/ilc/texts/instruments/english/conventions/1_1_1969.pdf.

15 US Department of State, 'Adherence to and Compliance with Arms Control, Nonproliferation, and Disarmament Agreements and Commitments', pp. 50–1.

16 Ministry of Foreign Affairs of the Russian Federation, 'Commentary by the Information and Press Department (MFA of Russia) on Executive Summary of the 2020 Adherence to and Compliance with Arms Control, Nonproliferation, and Disarmament Agreements and Commitments (Compliance Report) – United States Department of State', statement no. 601-23-04-2020, 23 April 2020, https://www.mid.ru/en/foreign_policy/news/-/asset_publisher/cKNonkJE02Bw/content/id/4104977.

17 '"U.S. Accusations Unsupported by Any Evidence"', Kommersant, 15 June 2020, p. 4, https://www.kommersant.ru/doc/4378452.

18 See, for example, Daryl G. Kimball, 'U.S. Claims of Illegal Russian Nuclear Testing: Myths, Realities, and Next Steps', Arms Control Association, 16 August 2019.

19 See Committee on Reviewing and Updating Technical Issues Related to the Comprehensive Nuclear Test Ban Treaty, The Comprehensive Nuclear Test-Ban-Treaty: Technical Issues for the United States (Washington DC: National Academies Press, 2012).

20 See, for example, Frank N. von Hippel, 'Transparency for Nuclear Weapon Test Sites', Physics Today, May 2020, pp. 10–11.

21 The above-cited statements by the Ministry of Foreign Affairs of the Russian Federation and Berdennikov are consistent with this view, as are private conversations the author has had with Russian colleagues.

22 The US compliance report indicates that some such discussions among the P5 have already been attempted. These have evidently not been successful, and no details are provided. See US Department of State, 'Adherence to and Compliance with Arms Control, Nonproliferation, and Disarmament Agreements and Commitments', pp. 50–1.

23 See Paul Sonne, 'U.S. Military Intelligence Steps up Accusation Against Russia over Nuclear Testing', Washington Post, 13 June 2019.

24 Prospects are reasonably hopeful. The proposed 2020 Democratic Party Platform, recommended for approval by the delegates to the Democratic National Convention, includes 'pushing for the ratification of the ... Comprehensive Test Ban Treaty'. See '2020 Democratic Party Platform', Democratic Convention, 31 July 2020, p. 81, https://www.demconvention.com/wp-content/uploads/2020/08/2020-07-31-Democratic-Party-Platform-For-Distribution.pdf.

Is Donald Trump America's First Constructivist President?

Christopher J. Fettweis

Summit meetings between leaders, according to conventional wisdom, are the climax of international diplomacy. They are supposed to occur at the end of long rounds of negotiations, after underlings have worked out the details of complex agreements, and are designed to add final touches and sell deals. Months of meticulous planning should precede the smiles, hand-shakes and photo ops that are the true essence of summitry.

US President Donald Trump disagrees. Early in his term, when the opportunity to meet North Korean leader Kim Jong-un arose, the president consented immediately without consulting advisers or insisting on preconditions. Many in the foreign-policy community reacted quickly and negatively, suggesting this was not how things were done. Normal presidents did not make rash, impulsive, spur-of-the-moment decisions with enormous implications. Trump, however, is not a normal president. He has no interest in precedent or received wisdom, and relies entirely on his instincts, demanding in the process that everyone else adjust. Trump forces analysts and observers to question much of what they thought was true about presidential behaviour and leadership itself.

Christopher J. Fettweis is Professor of Political Science at Tulane University and an adjunct scholar in the Cato Institute's Defense and Foreign Policy Studies Department. His most recent book is *Psychology of a Superpower: Security and Dominance in U.S. Foreign Policy* (Columbia University Press, 2018).

Survival | vol. 62 no. 5 | October–November 2020 | pp. 65–75   DOI 10.1080/00396338.2020.1819645

Accidental theorist

In other words, Trump is effectively America's first constructivist president. He does not know this, of course – he does not read, and even if he did, it seems unlikely that Alexander Wendt's work would find a place on his nightstand – but he is a living experiment in the validity of the constructivist approach to foreign policy.[1] Every day Trump compels long-time watchers of the presidency to rethink what they had previously accepted as true and inevitable, to question the rules and to wonder just what has to be. The American presidency is what Trump makes of it.

One of the great contributions of constructivism in the 1990s was to ask international-relations theorists and practitioners to examine their corpus of knowledge in the hope of separating the eternal from the ephemeral. Many long-accepted rules are socially constructed, dependent not upon law or rule but convention and shared belief. Even the most basic, ubiquitous concepts, such as the balance of power and anarchy, are neither natural nor inevitable, but constructed by international society. If such assumptions were constructed, the obvious implication is that they can they be deconstructed. What is does not have to be. The characteristics of the system, once thought eternal and immutable, are as malleable as the people who devise and maintain them. Fundamental change is not only possible but inevitable, alongside evolutions in society and in the dominant patterns of thought and behaviour. As ideas change, so does behaviour, say constructivists, since they insist that ideas rather than power (according to realists) or institutions and law (per liberals) provide structure to the system.[2]

Trump brought a substantively similar, if intellectually cruder, mindset into the White House. Perhaps vaguely aware of how his predecessors behaved (and perhaps not), Trump was determined to run the government his own way. He was unimpressed with the stodgy, boring, Coolidge-esque dignity that had come to be associated with the office, and uninterested in acting 'presidential'. He was going to entertain and outrage as well as lead, replacing 'no drama Obama' with constant headline-grabbing crises.

Sacrosanct conventional political wisdoms collapsed one after another. Presidential candidates used to release tax returns. They could not openly mock the handicapped or prisoners of war, or discuss their genitals during

debates. They did not contend that the women accusing them of molesta-
tion and assault were liars because they were too ugly to accost.

In office, Trump continued to rewrite the rules. He refused to separate
himself from his business interests or set up a blind trust. He ignored nepo-
tism conventions, putting his grossly unqualified daughter and son-in-law
on the payroll and trusting them with the kinds of major portfolios previously given to seasoned professionals. He carried on public feuds with
members of his own administration, castigating them on Twitter or ridicul-
ing them at campaign-style rallies. He arrived at the office at 11.00 in the
morning and retired to his bedroom at 6.00 in the evening, ending each day
binge-watching cable television. He flouted science in the face of a devastating pandemic. The political class looked on aghast.

By overturning many of the norms and shibboleths previously associated with the presidency, Trump demanded that observers look at the office
with new eyes. What is actually important in a presidency, and what has
been accepted as such merely because of precedent and habit? What does it
mean to be presidential?

Trump remade the policymaking process as well. No longer was the
intelligence community trusted to inform policy, nor were National Security
Council meetings held before major decisions. Notes were irregularly kept
and policy proposals were not written down. There were 'no minutes,
no work product, no materials', according to one observer, and reports
emerged as if they were the 'product of immaculate conception'.[3] Scores
of senior positions have remained unfilled. Messages that might upset the
president never found their way to his desk, lest the messenger be black-
listed and fired by tweet. Large portions of the American political system,
especially within his party, bent to Trump's will. No one has been able to
presidentialise him, as it were, and his supporters have proven content to
watch him deconstruct the office in exchange for Supreme Court justices,
tax cuts and 'maximum pressure' on Iran.

Nowhere is Trump more constructivist than in his rhetoric. Whereas most
observers once believed that demonstrable mendacity could sink a campaign, he proved that functional reality could instead be conjured by force
of presidential personality. Perpetual lying has not significantly affected

Trump's popularity. His supporters know he is a consummate bullshitter and are unbothered.[4] Millions have proven willing to believe Trump over the media and egg-headed experts. They would rather live in the world constructed by Trump, whether it bears any resemblance to reality or not.

The Trump presidency is a multi-year example of what political scientists call a systemic shock: an event that has injected chaos into both domestic and international politics. The coronavirus pandemic will add to the bedlam and shake the system to its foundations. Such shocks can be very instructive. Left standing in their destructive wake are the system's most enduring and viable features, those likely to persist.

Trump is a uniquely perfect storm of psychopathology, political instinct and bunco guile, unforeseeable and still unbelievable to many. His accidental presidency is an ideal test of the strength and robustness of the international-relations canon. When it ends, we will be closer to determining which of our theories, laws, norms, assumptions and beliefs hold up, and which require complete re-examination, separating the venerable and well-nigh immutable aspects of international politics from the vulnerable ones that can change at the whim of an American president. Notwithstanding the wreckage he has visited, it is an unprecedented opportunity, unlikely to be repeated. Early returns are improbably if provisionally reassuring, especially in terms of conflict and overall systemic stability. Events may not bear out widespread expectations of impending doom.

American democracy

Trump has demanded a re-evaluation of the idea of America itself. Most Americans have long assumed that a commitment to democratic practice is deeply ingrained in their political culture, but until now the strength of that commitment has rarely been tested. Can it withstand Trump's authoritarian assault?

The obvious is occasionally worth stating: Trump is no democrat. Much has been made of the various challenges his presidency poses to democracy and domestic institutions.[5] Like all would-be tyrants, Trump has criticised the independent judiciary and called for the prosecution of his political enemies. He has responded to all unfavourable press coverage not with explanations or clarifications but with attacks on reporters. His goal is not to win debates but to undermine the other side, hoping to convince his political base that it too is under attack and that he alone can save his faithful. The president has adopted not only the attitudes and tactics of prior authoritarians but sometimes their phraseology as well, borrowing from Joseph Stalin (the press is the 'enemy of the people') and Adolf Hitler (changing 'lying press' – *Lügenpresse* – only slightly to 'fake news'). Like all good constructivists, Trump knows that rhetoric matters and that word choice shapes debate.

Domestic political institutions have, for the most part, held firm in the face of his relentless assaults. The press remains largely unintimidated, and the judiciary has overruled a number of Trump's initiatives. Questions remain about the independence of the Department of Justice: optimists may point to the appointment of Special Counsel Robert Mueller and continuing investigations into Trump's various misdeeds, but pessimists can respond with the increased influence of William Barr, Trump's second attorney general. If Barr believes in unlimited executive power, however, most of the professionals in his department do not.

By far the greatest check on Trump's authoritarianism has been his incompetence. Any plans he may have had to subvert American democracy have been foiled by his inability to scheme about anything for more than ten consecutive minutes. His wilder suggestions and ideas are immediately leaked to the press, usually by multiple sources. Trump has run into a problem common to all dictators: unwilling to share the limelight with talented advisors, the president has surrounded himself instead with partisan mediocrities, fawning relatives, outright sycophants and unprincipled bureaucratic climbers. He has sacrificed efficiency and expertise for constant adulation and affirmation. Fortunately for champions of the American democratic experiment, Trump is not a calculating evil genius seeking absolute power. He is instead a fantasist showman, immersed in a dystopian world of his own creation, throwing tantrums when reality does not conform to it.

As every nervous flyer can tell you, however, past performance is no guarantee of future success. Revolutionary political behaviour always seems impossible until it happens. While it is true that until now the various constraints built into the US system have inhibited the president's authoritarian tendencies, the Trump test has exposed at least two major weaknesses in the American republic. Firstly, Congress – the primary countervailing power on the executive branch – has been remarkably supine. With very few exceptions, Republican members of Congress who objected to Trump's substance or style have been cowed into silence. The Grand Old Party, especially its leadership in both houses, has enabled Trump from the beginning and proved happy to abandon some of its long-standing concerns, such as support for free trade, alliances and basic decency. Fear of the president's tweets and the reaction of his supporters has removed all semblance of balance from the legislative branch.

The cult that has emerged around Trump's personality is the second reason for long-term concern. Trump's base has not waivered at all through-out his four years. No matter what Trump has done or said, no matter how offensive and transparently insincere he has been, a solid third of the US elec-torate has supported him. They have stalwartly believed Trump's version of events over those provided by the putatively lying media or its Deep State allies. Trump's infamous claim that he could shoot someone in the middle of Fifth Avenue and not lose voters seems true – though he would not gain any, either.

That inability to gain voters might well save the republic. If his first term is any indication, American political institutions look sufficiently robust to survive the Trump test. Should the test extend beyond 2020, however, he may have enough time to weaken them fatally. Furthermore, those who follow Trump in the White House may well play by different rules and might not share his fortuitous incompetence. Future presidents will prob-ably eschew Trump's boorishness and unique rules of grammar. They are unlikely to uproot completely the expanded executive powers that he and Barr have planted. But if he has shown how American democracy could end, he appears incapable of bringing it down himself.

International politics

Trump's campaign to 'Make America Great Again' is part of a worldwide populist movement that swept a number of authoritarian nationalists into office. The elections that brought Trump to power, and others in Hungary, the Philippines, Turkey and elsewhere, should effectively lay to rest one issue that scholars used to debate fiercely: whether democracy produces better leaders than other systems.[6] Apparently it does not. It turns out that pathological narcissists can ride waves of voter anger, fear and resentment right into power, even in the world's most mature democracies. Indeed, it is hard to imagine Trump coming to power in any other system. He lacks the strategic aptitude needed to plot a coup and would never win followers among the various selectorates that control the top positions in durable autocracies. Populists like him need systems in which the voice of the 'poorly educated' masses, to use Trump's words, is as important as any other.[7] Only a democracy fits that bill.

The Trump presidency also demands reconsideration of the 'New Peace' – that is, the widespread and underappreciated decline in violence since the end of the Cold War.[8] Unbeknownst to Trump (and many professional observers of international politics), the world is substantially less violent than it was even a generation ago. The impression he encourages that we live in a complex and chaotic era, one more dangerous than past ones, is empirically false. Large swaths of the globe, including most of Europe, the Pacific Rim and virtually the entire Western Hemisphere, are at peace. Warfare is confined mostly to a broad arc that runs from the Sahel through the Middle East into Pakistan. By almost any measure, the world has become significantly safer.[9] Whether these pacific trends represent a fundamental change in the rules that govern state behaviour or a temporary respite between cataclysms is not yet clear, but there is no doubt that the twenty-first century has thus far been more stable and peaceful than any of its predecessors.

Scholars have pointed to a number of factors that might help account for this phenomenon. Nuclear weapons, democracy, economic interdependence and international institutions have all received credit for the increased peace.[10] Two other proposed explanations – an irenic shift in ideas and norms, and hegemonic stability provided by the United States – could be affected by Trump's presidency.[11] Broad, systemic trends are not dependent upon the actions of any single country, but the strongest ones have a disproportionate influence on the rest. Prior to the onset of the New Peace, the dominant military power being run by an unpredictable nationalist would have set off alarm bells in capitals worldwide. Signs of insecurity, such as intense balancing and sharply increased defence spending, would have arisen. Substantial systemic upset, even chaos, could have ensued. If such tumult does not unfold in the wake of this presidency, the New Peace will have proven durable. Preliminary indications are promising: the world has not experienced a rise in conflict during Trump's term in office, and violence remains at historically low levels. China is spending more on defence, but few others have followed its lead. Not even the Trump administration's targeted killing of Iranian Islamic Revolutionary Guard Corps commander Qasem Soleimani in early January – a singularly reckless provocation – led to military escalation in arguably the world's most unstable region.

The Trump years will also reveal a great deal about the relationship between US commitments and international order. Early on, the Trump White House fashioned itself as an implacable enemy of internationalism, or what senior officials derisively called 'globalism'. The international system, according to Trump and his aides, was rigged against the United States. To correct this imbalance, to adjust bilateral relationships and make them fair, all prior agreements required at least renegotiation and often abrogation. The COVID-19 pandemic only activated Trump's insular nationalism. Rather than seeking cooperation across borders, he sought desperately to deflect blame for his delayed, inadequate response. Trump's nationalist foreign policy may do lasting damage to the image of the United States abroad and the trust that other countries place in its judgement.

The implications of a worldwide loss of confidence in the United States would be enormous. Even allowing for realist scepticism towards liberal internationalists, there is little doubt that after the Second World War, Washington's benevolence and idealism helped construct a system of institutions, laws, norms and rules that gave much of the post-war world its structure.[12] The Trump administration has deprived that system of focused and committed leadership, and perceptions of blinkered US unilateralism have undoubtedly hardened. But if the liberal international order so painstakingly constructed under US leadership survives the Trump years, it is hard to imagine what could bring it to an end.

*   *   *

Trump came into office with a crass nightclub entertainer's instincts, knowing that if he was bored with the presidency then so was the country. He was determined to make politics rude and disruptive, and to govern by his rules, criticism be damned. The Trump administration has been diverting, in the same way a school-bus accident diverts. Yet many of Trump's signature foreign-policy decisions – themselves part of a sustained effort to reverse those of his predecessor – could be undone by the next occupant of the White House.

The Paris agreement on climate change could be re-energised; remnants of the Trans-Pacific Partnership could be rewickered; even the Iran nuclear deal, now on life support, might prove salvageable, since other parties are keen to save it and Iran's breaches remain tentative and reversible. Despite Trump's wilful antagonism towards China, overriding mutual interests suggest that the damage to the bilateral relationship is reparable. Notwithstanding Trump's incessant spitefulness – crowned by his recently announced withdrawal of nearly 12,000 US troops from a supposedly 'delinquent' Germany to punish it for not paying a NATO 'fee' that does not exist as such – the Atlantic Alliance and transatlantic relations, ingrained as they are in the deep structure of the international order, are likely to emerge from at least a truncated Trump era intact, if shaken.[13]

Overall, the erratic nationalist leadership of the world's strongest state appears to have had little net effect on global stability. The New Peace, as well as American democracy and the liberal international order, might thus survive the United States' four-year experiment in presidential recklessness and incompetence. If so, Trump, our first constructivist president, will have unwittingly moved our understanding of the fundamental nature of the international system forward, and possibly even increased our confidence in it.

Notes

1   Then again, were Wendt to put Trump's picture on the cover of the next edition of his groundbreaking book, the president might add it to his unread piles. See Alexander Wendt, *Social Theory of International Politics* (Cambridge: Cambridge University Press, 2011). See also

Alexander Wendt, 'Anarchy Is What States Make of It: The Social Construction of Power Politics', *International Organization*, vol. 46, no. 2, Spring 1992, pp. 391–425.

2   In addition to Wendt's work, good introductions to constructivist international-relations theory include Ted Hopf, 'The Promise of Constructivism in International Relations Theory', *International Security*, vol. 23, no. 1, Summer 1998, pp. 171–200; Peter J. Katzenstein (ed.), *The Culture of National Security: Norms and Identity in World Politics* (New York: Columbia University Press, 1996); and John Gerard Ruggie, 'What Makes the World Hang Together? Neo-utilitarianism and the Social Constructivist Challenge', *International Organization*, vol. 52, no. 4, Autumn 1998, pp. 855–85.

3   Quoted in Evan Osnos, 'Trump vs. the "Deep State"', *New Yorker*, 21 May 2018, https://www.newyorker.com/magazine/2018/05/21/trump-vs-the-deep-state.

4   The term in this case is a philosophical one, meaning rhetoric that creates its own reality, irrespective of its relationship to the truth. See Harry G. Frankfurt, *On Bullshit* (Princeton, NJ: Princeton University Press, 2005).

5   See Madeleine Albright, *Fascism: A Warning* (New York: HarperCollins, 2018); Steven Livitsky and Daniel Ziblatt, *How Democracies Die: What History Reveals About Our Future* (New York: Crown, 2018); and Timothy Snyder, *On Tyranny: Twenty Lessons from the Twentieth Century* (New York: Penguin, 2017).

6   On this issue, see Bruce Bueno de

Mesquita et al., *The Logic of Political Survival* (Cambridge, MA: MIT Press, 2003); and Mancur Olson, 'Dictatorship, Democracy and Development', *American Political Science Review*, vol. 87, no. 3, September 1993, pp. 567–76.

7   See, for example, Josh Hafner, 'Donald Trump Loves the "Poorly Educated" — and They Love Him', *USA Today*, 24 February 2016, https://eu.usatoday.com/story/news/politics/onpolitics/2016/02/24/donald-trump-nevada-poorly-educated/80860078/.

8   Steven Pinker first coined the phrase in his *The Better Angels of Our Nature: Why Violence Has Declined* (New York: Viking, 2011).

9   Conflict numbers tell only part of the story. By almost any measure, the world has become significantly safer, with appreciable declines in coups, repression, the chances of dying in battle, border wars, conquest, genocide and violence against civilians. In addition to Pinker's *The Better Angels of Our Nature*, see Joshua Goldstein, *Winning the War on War: The Decline of Armed Conflict Worldwide* (New York: Dutton, 2011); John Mueller, *The Remnants of War* (Ithaca, NY: Cornell University Press, 2004); and Steven Pinker, *Enlightenment Now: The Case for Reason, Science, Humanism, and Progress* (New York: Viking, 2018), especially pp. 156–66. For a review of this literature, see Christopher J. Fettweis, *Psychology of a Superpower: Security and Dominance in US Foreign Policy* (New York: Columbia University Press, 2018), chapter one.

10   On nuclear weapons, see Lawrence

Freedman, 'Stephen Pinker and the Long Peace: Alliance, Deterrence and Decline', *Journal of Cold War History*, vol. 14, no. 4, September 2014, pp. 657–72. On democracy, see Michael W. Doyle, 'Liberalism and World Politics', *American Political Science Review*, vol. 80, no. 4, December 1985, pp. 1,151–70. On capitalism, see Erik Gartzke, 'The Capitalist Peace', *American Journal of Political Science*, vol. 51, no. 1, January 2007, pp. 166–91. On international institutions, see Goldstein, *Winning the War on War*; and Virginia Page Fortna, 'Is Peacekeeping "Winning the War on War"?', *Perspectives on Politics*, vol. 11, no. 2, June 2013, pp. 566–70.

[11] Regarding norms, see John Mueller, 'War Has Almost Ceased to Exist: An Assessment', *Political Science Quarterly*, vol. 124, no. 2, Summer 2009, pp. 297–321; and Pinker, *The Better Angels of Our Nature*. Concerning hegemonic stability, see Robert Kagan, *The World America Made* (New York: Alfred A. Knopf, 2012).

[12] On that order, consult the work of G. John Ikenberry, including most recently 'The Next Liberal Order', *Foreign Affairs*, vol. 99, no. 4, July/August 2020, pp. 133–42. See also Hanns W. Maull, 'The Once and Future Liberal Order', *Survival*, vol. 61, no. 2, April–May 2019, pp. 7–32; and Stewart M. Patrick, 'Trump and World Order', *Foreign Affairs*, vol. 96, no. 2, March/April 2017, pp. 52–7. For the sceptical view, see Graham Allison, 'The Myth of the World Order', *Foreign Affairs*, vol. 97, no. 4, July/August 2018, pp. 124–33; and Patrick Porter, *The False Promise of Liberal Order: Nostalgia, Delusion and the Rise of Trump* (Cambridge: Polity, 2020).

[13] See, for instance, Thomas Gibbons-Neff, 'U.S. Will Cut 12,000 Forces in Germany', *New York Times*, 29 July 2020, https://www.nytimes.com/2020/07/29/world/europe/us-troops-nato-germany.html.

Noteworthy

Inflection point

'I'm in Philadelphia, where our Constitution was drafted and signed. It wasn't a perfect document. It allowed for the inhumanity of slavery and failed to guarantee women – and even men who didn't own property – the right to participate in the political process. But embedded in this document was a North Star that would guide future generations; a system of representative government – a democracy – through which we could better realise our highest ideals. Through civil war and bitter struggles, we improved this Constitution to include the voices of those who'd once been left out. And gradually, we made this country more just, more equal and more free.

The one Constitutional office elected by all of the people is the presidency. So at minimum, we should expect a president to feel a sense of responsibility for the safety and welfare of all 330 million of us, regardless of what we look like, how we worship, who we love, how much money we have – or who we voted for.

But we should also expect a president to be the custodian of this democracy. We should expect that regardless of ego, ambition or political beliefs, the president will preserve, protect and defend the freedoms and ideals that so many Americans marched for and went to jail for; fought for and died for.

I have sat in the Oval Office with both of the men who are running for president. I never expected that my successor would embrace my vision or continue my policies. I did hope, for the sake of our country, that Donald Trump might show some interest in taking the job seriously; that he might come to feel the weight of the office and discover some reverence for the democracy that had been placed in his care.

But he never did. For close to four years now, he's shown no interest in putting in the work; no interest in finding common ground; no interest in using the awesome power of his office to help anyone but himself and his friends; no interest in treating the presidency as anything but one more reality show that he can use to get the attention he craves.

Former US president Barack Obama speaks at the Democratic National Convention on 19 August 2020.[1]

No generation ever knows what history will ask of it. All we can ever know is whether we'll be ready when that moment arrives. And now history has delivered us to one of the most difficult moments America has ever faced. Four historic crises. All at the same time. A perfect storm. The worst pandemic in over 100 years. The worst economic crisis since the Great Depression. The most compelling call for racial justice since the '60s. And the undeniable realities and accelerating threats of climate change.

[…]

All elections are important. But we know in our bones this one is more consequential. America is at an inflection point. A time of real peril, but of extraordinary possibilities. We can choose the path of becoming angrier, less hopeful and more divided. A path of shadow and suspicion. Or we can choose a different path, and together, take this chance to heal, to be reborn, to unite. A path of hope and light This is a life-changing election

    DOI 10.1080/00396338.2020.1819646

that will determine America's future for a very long time. Character is on the ballot. Compassion is on the ballot. Decency, science, democracy. They are all on the ballot.

Joe Biden accepts the Democratic Party's nomination for president of the United States on 20 August 2020.[2]

This election will decide if we save the American dream or whether we allow a socialist agenda to demolish our cherished destiny. It will decide whether we rapidly create millions of high-paying jobs or whether we crush our industries and send millions of these jobs overseas, as has been foolishly done for many decades. Your vote will decide whether we protect law-abiding Americans or whether we give free rein to violent anarchists and agitators and criminals who threaten our citizens.

[…]

China would own our country if Joe Biden got elected. Unlike Biden, I will hold them fully accountable for the tragedy that they caused all over the world – they caused. In recent months, our nation and the world has been hit by the once-in-a-century pandemic that China allowed to spread around the globe. They could have stopped it, but they allowed it to come out.

[…]

Biden is a Trojan horse for socialism.

President Donald Trump accepts the Republican Party's nomination for president of the United States on 27 August 2020.[3]

Russian immunity

'It works effectively enough, forms a stable immunity and, I repeat, it has gone through all necessary tests.'

Russian President Vladimir Putin announces the approval of what he claims to be a vaccine for the coronavirus that causes COVID-19.[4]

'This is all beyond stupid. Putin doesn't have a vaccine, he's just making a political statement.'

John Moore, a virologist at Weill Cornell medical college in New York City, casts doubt on Putin's announcement.[5]

'This will be the beginning of your end – you will go down on your knees like in Ukraine and other countries and pray, God knows to whom.'

Belarusian President Alexander Lukashenko, whose re-election on 9 August 2020 has been disputed, speaks against his opponents at a pro-government rally on 16 August.[6]

'We of course have certain obligations toward Belarus.'

President Putin reveals during an interview on Russian state television that he has ordered the creation of a reserve of law-enforcement officers at the request of Lukashenko.[7]

'This is really a favourite tool for them. I don't know how plausible it is after so many cases – every time, they say they have nothing to do with this, and it just happens that people who oppose Putin's regime keep having horrible accidents.'

Vladimir Kara-Murza, a Russian democracy activist, comments on the poisoning of fellow activist Alexei Navalny on 20 August 2020.[8]

Sources

1 'Transcript: Barack Obama's DNC Speech', CNN, 20 August 2020, https://edition.cnn.com/2020/08/19/politics/barack-obama-speech-transcript/index.html.

2 Matt Stevens, 'Joe Biden Accepts Presidential Nomination: Full Transcript', *New York Times*, 20 August 2020, https://www.nytimes.com/2020/08/20/us/politics/biden-presidential-nomination-dnc.html.

3 Glenn Thrush, 'Full Transcript: President Trump's Republican National Convention Speech', *New York Times*, 28 August 2020, https://www.nytimes.com/2020/08/28/us/politics/trump-rnc-speech-transcript.html.

4 Andrew E. Kramer, 'Russia Approves Coronavirus Vaccine Before Completing Tests', *New York Times*, 11 August 2020, https://www.nytimes.com/2020/08/11/world/europe/russia-coronavirus-vaccine.html.

5 Carl Zimmer, "This Is All Beyond Stupid." Experts Worry About Russia's Rushed Vaccine', *New York Times*, 11 August 2020, https://www.nytimes.com/2020/08/11/health/russia-covid-19-vaccine-safety.html?action=click&module=Top%20Stories&pgtype=Homepage.

6 'Belarus: Mass Protest Eclipses Defiant Belarus Leader's Rally', BBC News, 16 August 2020, https://www.bbc.com/news/world-europe-53795871.

7 Andrew Higgins, 'Putin Warns Belarus Protesters: Don't Push Too Hard', *New York Times*, 27 August 2020, https://www.nytimes.com/2020/08/27/world/europe/belarus-russia-putin.html.

8 Max Seddon, 'Navalny Poisoning Fits Pattern of Behaviour in Putin's Russia', *Financial Times*, 21 August 2020, https://www.ft.com/content/aac65ce9-1086-4c60-9347-5135916747bc.

Saving Strategic Arms Control

Alexey Arbatov

While national leaders are justifiably preoccupied by the COVID-19 pandemic, arms-control challenges are at a historical low on the world's list of priorities. Without proper attention, the arms-control system – built during the previous half-century but neglected over the last several years – will continue to disintegrate.

Following the collapse of the Intermediate-Range Nuclear Forces (INF) Treaty in 2019, no steps are being considered for preventing a new arms race with medium-range missiles. Discussions between the United States and Russia about extending the 2011 New Strategic Arms Reduction Treaty (New START) beyond its February 2021 expiration date are increasingly controversial. Due to the pandemic, on-site inspections, a key element of the New START verification regime, have been interrupted. For the same reason, the 10th Review Conference of the Nuclear Non-Proliferation Treaty, scheduled for April–May 2020 in New York, has been postponed until next year. Russia suspended the Treaty on Conventional Armed Forces in Europe in 2015, and the United States will leave the treaty in November. In May, the United States announced that it would withdraw from the Treaty on Open Skies, an associated confidence-building measure, due to Russian violations.[1]

Alexey Arbatov is Director of the Center for International Security at the Primakov National Research Institute of World Economy and International Relations, Russian Academy of Science, and is a full member of the Russian Academy of Sciences. He participated in the START I negotiations in 1990, served as deputy chair of the Defense Committee of the State Duma from 1994–2003 and headed the Non-Proliferation Program at the Carnegie Moscow Center from 2004–17.

Survival | vol. 62 no. 5 | October–November 2020 | pp. 79–104   DOI 10.1080/00396338.2020.1819640

The Comprehensive Test-Ban Treaty, which the US, China and some other nuclear powers have not ratified but all observe, could be completely disavowed by Washington in the near future. That could doom the whole nuclear-disarmament architecture. As Sam Nunn and Ernest Moniz, two of the United States' most authoritative strategists and public leaders, have noted, the resumption of nuclear tests by the United States 'would eviscerate any constraints on other nuclear capable states, as well as potential adversaries, like Russia and China. Moreover, a resurgence of nuclear testing may not be reversible for decades, paving the way to new nuclear weapon states and the development of even more destructive nuclear capabilities and elevated risks from others.'[2]

Thus far, COVID-19 has not affected the main weapons programmes of the United States, Russia, China and other leading military powers, although a discussion of possible savings on procurement has started in the US.[3] A new cycle of nuclear and advanced-conventional arms races is gaining momentum. Against the background of the collapse of nuclear arms-control regimes, this arms race will inevitably exacerbate political tensions among the great powers, creating a high probability of armed conflict and the ensuing risk of nuclear escalation, which would make the pandemic look like a minor nuisance. COVID-19 must not serve as a pretext for ignoring or postponing urgently needed efforts to break current arms-control deadlocks.[4] A systemic approach is crucial.

Saving INF constraints

New START is up against a hard deadline, and the top priority should be to get it extended. While saving the INF Treaty is not realistic, it would still be best if the United States and Russia could find a way to avoid deploying intermediate-range missiles in Europe. In 2019, the United States announced that it would withdraw from the INF Treaty due to alleged Russian violations by deploying the 9M729 ground-launched cruise missile (US/NATO designation SSC-8 *Screwdriver*). Although China was not a party to that agreement, the US had also become increasingly concerned by growth in the size and capabilities of Chinese INF-class systems. Any US plans for new missile deployments in the Indo-Pacific would be linked to Chinese programmes; it is up to Washington and Beijing to search for mutual accommodation, however difficult this presently looks.

In Europe, American and Russian medium-range-missile deployments should be avoided at all costs. In 1987, the INF Treaty, which notably eliminated an entire class of weapons rather than merely limiting its numbers, constituted the most dramatic step toward ending the Cold War and the nuclear arms race. Now, as William Perry, the US secretary of defense in 1994–97 and a renowned strategic thinker, wrote in his recent book:

> By withdrawing from the INF Treaty, it is not hyperbole to say that President Trump is ushering in a new Cold War. There have been other elements of US and Russian diplomacy that have moved us in this dangerous direction, but it seems to us that withdrawing from the INF Treaty was the most decisive … This is how an arms race starts.[5]

Others would argue that this particular race did not start in Washington, but rather when Moscow developed and then deployed a 2,500-kilometre-class ground-launched cruise missile. In any case, the US withdrawal accelerated it.

New medium-range missiles in Europe would be highly destabilising in precipitating mutual planning for pre-emptive strikes.[6] This prospect was implicit in a March 2019 statement by Colonel-General Valery Gerasimov, head of the Russian General Staff: 'The policy of Western "partners" makes us respond to a threat with a threat, by planning in advance to deliver strikes against the decision-making centers and launchers for employment of cruise missiles against targets at Russian territory.'[7]

Such developments also would block any possibility of continuing strategic arms-control cooperation even if New START were extended after its expiration in 2021. This is because American intermediate-range missiles in Europe would be perceived by Moscow now, as they were in the early 1980s, as threatening a decapitating and disarming strike on Russia's strategic deterrent. This perceived threat was blocking progress at START I negotiations until a breakthrough was achieved with the INF Treaty in 1987.

Present controversies around the INF Treaty were not alleviated in January 2019 when Russian officials showed missiles it claimed to be

9M729s, perceived by the United States and NATO as a treaty violation, to foreign military representatives in an aircraft hangar in Moscow. NATO states did not attend the demonstration and declared that the systems displayed were different from the missiles in question.[8]

A temporary deal on this issue, to be in force until the US and China can reach some compromise, should be based on Russia's proposal to NATO states in late 2019 to agree on a moratorium on NATO deployment of medium-range missile systems in Europe and Russian deployment of such systems within range of Europe. In order to fortify this deal, the two sides should jointly develop additional means of verification, using confidence-building measures and on-site inspections, to make sure that the missiles deployed in Russian regular units are the same as those demonstrated in Moscow in 2019. If for some technical reason Russia cannot prove that this missile type has the permitted range (less than 500 km), its deployment should be stopped until such methods are elaborated.

In parallel, Russia's concerns should be addressed. Moscow claims that US missile-defence launchers for Standard-2 interceptors deployed in Romania and Poland could be used to launch offensive *Tomahawk* sea-based cruise missiles, which are deployed on US surface ships with the same Mk-41 launchers as the Standard anti-missiles. The US could alleviate this concern by agreeing to transparency and on-site inspections.

The New START extension

Equally urgent is the need to address strategic arms-control issues in the remaining months before the expiration of New START in February 2021. The latest US position is that extension, just like any START follow-on treaty, is conditioned on China's participation. This is yet another example of Moscow and Washington alternating positions on the same issue, recalling a joke well known to arms-control veterans: both sides take the same position on the same issues but at different times.[9]

For more than a decade, Russia insisted that the bilateral US–Russia arms-control format be transformed into a multilateral one, in particular regarding the INF Treaty and the follow-on to New START (while taking no definite position on the extension of the latter). This position was initially advanced by President Vladimir Putin in his famous Munich speech on 10 February 2007.[10] Later, in 2012, Putin said: 'We will not disarm unilaterally … All nuclear powers should participate in this process. We cannot disarm while other nuclear powers are building up their arms.'[11] The US had been generally sympathetic (except about including Britain and France), but not too persistent. In 2007, the US and Russia advanced a joint UN resolution in favour of making the INF Treaty multilateral but received no positive response.[12]

In 2019, the situation diametrically changed. The Trump administration suddenly became a devoted partisan of multilateral nuclear arms control, while Putin's government opposed it. The stated US reason for withdrawing from the INF Treaty was that it believed Russia was in material breach of the treaty and had been for nearly a decade. A political reason was the United States' perceived need to counter China's medium-range-missile deployment and the necessity of China's participation in any possible new treaty. Likewise, Washington's openness to extending New START and supporting a follow-on START was linked to China's engagement on strategic-arms limitations and reductions.[13]

The Russian stance shifted to the long-standing position of the seven smaller nuclear-arms states: that the United States and Russia have to proceed bilaterally since they possess the overwhelming portion of the world's nuclear weapons. On 5 September 2019 at the Eastern Economic Forum, Putin articulated this U-turn:

> Now the USA have put forward a new version, they want to engage the People's Republic of China in this joint work. But the Chinese are arguing quite reasonably that China's nuclear potential is much lower than Russia's or America's, and they do not understand what they should reduce if they already have fewer delivery vehicles and fewer warheads. This position looks sufficiently logical.[14]

Thus, Moscow extended support to China's rejection of US proposals to join any new version of the INF Treaty or a START follow-on treaty.

The US stance has been in a state of continuous flux. China has said it would join negotiations on the next START only when the US is willing to reduce its strategic arsenal to the same size as Beijing's. This is extremely unlikely in the near to medium term, and Beijing knows it. If Washington has other demands, it should clarify them. Perhaps the US requires China to join the agreement on the New START extension, which may imply China's joining the treaty in whatever form. This would mean, first of all, that China would have to accept New START's verification regime, including exchange of information and on-site inspections. This regime is designed to make sure the two nuclear superpowers observe the treaty limitations, primarily on delivery vehicles and warheads. China would stay well below both ceilings, so this verification regime would be largely irrelevant to its compliance with the treaty. The only useful purpose of inspections might be to learn how many multiple warheads are deployed on its DF-31A(G) (CH-SS-10 mod 3) and DF-41 (CH-SS-20) intercontinental ballistic missiles (ICBMs). It may also be possible to discover differences in the maintenance regimes of Chinese nuclear forces.

Inspecting underground facilities, however, would call for special verification provisions that are now absent in New START. This would mean not just extending but renegotiating the most important part of the treaty, which would probably take much longer than the time left until its expiration in 2021 or even the five-year extension period permitted by the treaty. China's joining New START would serve as legalisation and encouragement of China's building up of its strategic nuclear forces to the New START ceilings of 800 strategic missiles and bombers and 1,550 warheads (thus increasing its current forces by five and ten times, respectively).[15] Obviously, neither the US nor Russia would welcome this prospect.

Hence the New START extension should remain a Russia–US bilateral issue, but with two important mutual understandings. Firstly, the new Russian *Avangard* boost-glide system and *Sarmat* heavy ICBMs must be recognised as subjects of all treaty provisions. According to some suggestions, the same should apply to the medium-range Tu-22M3M (*Backfire*) bomber, since the upgraded version reportedly includes an air-to-air refuelling capability, which the aircraft previously lacked.[16] This is implied by the precedent set by the Strategic Arms Limitation Talks (SALT) II Treaty of 1979. The second understanding is that extending New START is intended not merely to retain the transparency of the treaty-verification regime but also, and even more importantly, to gain additional time to work on a follow-on treaty and make up for the years wasted since New START's ratification in 2011.[17] Issues related to a New START follow-on could be settled during this extra time. Before engaging China, it would be logical to agree in principle on the scope and parameters of further US–Russian arms reductions.

START follow-on: a bilateral agenda

In parallel to discussing a multilateral agreement, Moscow and Washington should proceed with negotiating a bilateral deal as a New START follow-on. Since the nuclear forces of China, the United Kingdom and France will hardly be limited in the next several years, further deep cuts in the strategic forces of the two major powers (following manifold reductions since 1991) are not an urgent goal and may be safely postponed. Hence, the follow-on ceilings can be lowered symbolically – say, by just 100 deployed delivery vehicles and warheads, down to 600 and 1,400 respectively. Far more important is the scope of the next agreement, the main goal of which should be enhancing strategic stability.

In recent years, a new belief has been gaining momentum in the United States and Russia. It is that the newest weapons systems and military technologies are cardinally changing the essence of strategic stability and making traditional arms control obsolete and impotent.[18] The technological novelties that have stimulated this belief are well known to the expert community. They include various long-range, high-precision subsonic conventional systems, which are capable of hitting targets previously accessible only to nuclear weapons.[19] The US is developing still-longer-range hypersonic, high-precision weapons.[20] Russia and China are deploying hypersonic boost-glide and aero-ballistic systems, which may be armed with nuclear or conventional warheads.[21] As pointed out by Harvard's Steven E. Miller, 'technological improvements make it possible to use advanced conventional weapons against strategic targets and nuclear command and control facilities, potentially blurring the line between conventional and nuclear war and possibly creating escalatory risks and pressures in the event of conventional conflict'.[22] More powerful uninhabited aerial and underwater nuclear and conventional delivery vehicles are in development and can potentially operate with the use of artificial intelligence.[23]

Also under way is the rapid expansion of cyber-warfare technology, the development of space arms and the modernisation of missile-defence systems, which are gaining offensive (in particular, anti-satellite) capabilities.[24] Many offensive systems are dual-capable, and any ambiguity as to whether the payload is conventional or nuclear is potentially destabilising. Such weapons, and automated command-and-control and information systems, are blurring the nuclear threshold and could trigger an uncontrollable escalation of a local conflict or even a military accident in a time of crisis.[25] At the same time, the nuclear threshold is eroded by new or revived concepts and means of conducting a limited nuclear war, and the introduction of strategic and tactical low-yield nuclear warheads.[26]

These innovative weapons systems and technologies are cited to assert that the concept of strategic stability at the core of the 1991–2010 START treaties is outdated. The concept was first formulated in the 1990 Soviet–American declaration, which defined strategic stability as a strategic relationship that removes the incentives to launch the first nuclear strike.[27] At that time, such an incentive was perceived as the ability to launch a disarming (that is, counterforce) nuclear strike, thus avoiding a retaliatory strike or reducing its consequences to an acceptable level. Such a capability in a crisis might encourage nuclear aggression or pre-emption. To minimise that threat, the two powers agreed to undertake reductions in their strategic forces, taking into account strategic offence–defence interaction, lowering the concentration of warheads on their delivery vehicles and relying on survivable weapons systems (namely, sea-based and ground-mobile missiles).

A particular Russian concern is that a massive counterforce nuclear attack is an outdated threat and that the new threat is a disarming strike using high-precision, non-nuclear offensive and defensive arms, cyber-warfare systems and space weapons. The corollary is that from now on, a commitment to refrain from a nuclear first strike may still allow a disarming strike using non-nuclear weapons and new military technologies. A related notion is that the impossibility of a disarming strike at a strategic level does not rule out, and might even encourage, the selective use of nuclear weapons on a local and regional scale.[28] This concept is often called 'escalate to de-escalate' – the selective intimidating use of nuclear weapons to prevent an opponent from achieving success in a conventional conflict. This imprudent idea has not been mentioned in the most recent formulations of Russian military doctrine, published in 2010, 2014 and 2018. But top Russian political and military officials should still unequivocally repudiate it. Even better would be a joint US–Russian statement abandoning any limited use of nuclear weapons, thus expanding and enhancing the traditional concept of strategic stability.

All novel dangers and uncertainties notwithstanding, the original concept of strategic stability remains relevant and should be maintained. The salience of that concept in past arms-control treaties has rendered a massive, disarming nuclear strike highly improbable, despite high tensions in Russia–NATO relations since 2014. Besides, there are no reasonable alternatives except ambiguous ideas about 'creating an environment for nuclear disarmament' and working out 'stable rules for military competition'.[29] At the same time, the concept of strategic stability should be updated for and adapted to new technical and strategic realities. In particular, the list of incentives for a first nuclear strike should be broadened to include not only a possibility of a massive counterforce attack, but also a threat of conventional counterforce strikes using long-range non-nuclear weapons systems in conjunction with defensive systems, space weapons and cyber assets.

Russia should repudiate 'escalate to de-escalate'

Furthermore, the operative concept of strategic stability should address the threat of limited nuclear use, which might be aimed at preventing an opponent's victory in a conventional war or solidifying one's own initial gains in such a war. Strategic arms control can limit some weapons systems associated with such concepts. But the main emphasis should be on limiting sub-strategic (tactical) nuclear weapons and reducing and geographically separating conventional forces. This would mitigate the fear of defeat for any party in a local or regional conventional war.

This goal is attainable. Such measures were taken pursuant to the 1990 Treaty on Conventional Armed Forces in Europe, the 1992 Treaty on Open

Skies and the 2011 Vienna Document on confidence-building measures. These agreements paved the way for major, parallel, unilateral cuts in US and Russian tactical nuclear weapons during the 1990s. The modernised concept of strategic stability should now be formulated as 'a strategic relationship that removes the incentives for any use of nuclear weapons'. Such incentives include the traditional threat of a massive disarming nuclear strike, and the newer threat of conventional counterforce strikes and limited use of nuclear weapons in local or regional conventional wars.

The potentially revolutionary impact of technological progress is not new. It is enough to recall the creation of long-range ballistic missiles in the late 1950s, followed by the development of nuclear ballistic-missile-defence systems.[30] Then came another revolution – multiple independently targetable re-entry vehicles (MIRVs) – and the development of compact high-precision intermediate-range cruise missiles in the 1970s. The US Strategic Defense Initiative (SDI, also known as 'Star Wars'), formulated in 1983, called for a greater revolution in military technology than all the current technological innovations combined. However, the progress of US–Soviet political relations and strategic talks enabled the US Senate to save the Anti-Ballistic Missile Treaty and eventually led to the curtailment of the SDI programme by the late 1980s. The 1987 INF Treaty, 1991 START I and subsequent START and Strategic Offensive Reductions treaties imposed deep and stabilising reductions in nuclear forces down to pre-MIRV warhead levels.

Dealing with new threats to strategic stability in the follow-on START treaty requires that the long-range (more than 600 km) air-launched nuclear and conventional cruise and hypersonic missiles and nuclear gravity bombs be included under a common warhead ceiling, and that they be counted according to the actual loading of the heavy bombers.[31] In the past, air-launched missiles were counted under warhead ceilings in the 1991 START I and the 1993 START II treaties.[32] Nuclear gravity bombs on heavy bombers counted as one warhead. Bombers with conventional cruise missiles and bombs were labelled as 'converted for non-nuclear missions'. They were exempt from START counting rules, but had to be deployed at airfields farther than 100 km from nuclear-storage facilities. Under the next START, only bombers armed with conventional bombs and cruise missiles with ranges shorter than 600 km should be discounted as converted for non-nuclear missions. All deployed long-range conventional and nuclear air-launched missiles, and nuclear gravity bombs on deployed heavy bombers, should count against the overall warhead ceiling.

Limits on strategic delivery vehicles and warheads should also cap the innovative weapons systems: ground-based intercontinental cruise missiles and long-range autonomous underwater drones, as well as land- and sea-based boost-glide hypersonic systems with ranges similar to those specified in the SALT and START treaties (for instance, land-based missiles with ranges greater than 5,500 km and sea-based missiles with ranges greater than 600 km).[33] Such weapons should be limited regardless of whether their warheads are nuclear or conventional.

As for verification feasibility, ground-launched, long-range cruise missiles such as the Russian *Burevestnik* type would be easy to numerically limit in a future agreement using the former INF Treaty verification measures.[34] Sea-launched cruise missiles present a much more serious challenge. They are deployed in ships' universal missile launchers along with anti-aircraft and anti-ship missiles, and in launchers of attack submarines' torpedo tubes. The initial solution might be to extend confidence-building measures to missiles of these types with nuclear or conventional warheads, including exchanges of numerical data (as was agreed under START I) and notifications of sea-launched cruise-missile-equipped ships and submarines leaving ports.

Boost-glide hypersonic missiles (the Russian *Avangard* system and the systems being developed under the US Conventional Prompt Global Strike Program) would not pose a serious problem. Boost-glide systems are accelerated by ICBMs or submarine-launched ballistic missiles, and may be verified in the same manner. Hypersonic gliding and high-speed air-launched missiles are to be limited on heavy bombers, together with other systems of this class.

In this way, the most destabilising long-range strategic systems blurring the line between conventional and nuclear warfare (including long-range conventional missiles and low-yield nuclear bombs) would become subject to verifiable arms control. Indirectly, their numbers would be limited, since under common ceilings they would 'compete' with the number of proven and reliable nuclear-tipped strategic ballistic missiles. The latter would also have to be reduced to allow for ground- and air-launched cruise missiles, hypersonic boost-glide and ram-jet missiles, and underwater nuclear drones under the overall limit.

The usual argument against such an approach is that a large number of non-nuclear air-launched (as well as sea-launched) cruise missiles are required for local military operations, like those recently conducted by the United States and Russia in Afghanistan, Iraq, Libya and Syria. However, such strikes hardly require missiles with a range of over 600 km, given the small territory of those countries and the unimpeded access the major powers have to the military theatres. Even if they decided to use longer-range cruise missiles, a large number would not be required. Such weapons can be borrowed from strategic stockpiles and later replenished through new production. Large arsenals of non-nuclear air-launched cruise missiles and hypersonic missile types would only be useful to the great powers in launching strikes against each other. It is these forces and plans that arms-control measures should seek to restrict, since they lower the nuclear threshold.

Counting strategic weapons is relatively easy

Forging a formal treaty on tactical nuclear weapons has been a headache for diplomats and scholars for many decades. These systems profoundly differ from strategic arms, which makes the SALT/START experience largely irrelevant. They generally involve the use of dual-purpose aircraft, medium- and short-range missiles, artillery and naval weapons, which number in the thousands. Tangibly limiting them implies severe cuts of conventional forces, undermining their capabilities in regional non-nuclear missions. In addition, unlike strategic weapons, tactical nuclear arms are not deployed on their delivery vehicles in peacetime, and instead are kept in various types of storage facilities. Hence, reducing them means applying limitations and verification procedures on weapons inside storage sites at home and abroad, and possibly on manufacturing and dismantling plants as well.

Counting strategic weapons is relatively easy provided the locations of ballistic-missile-submarine bases, heavy bombers and silo-launched and mobile ICBMs are known. Counting the number of nuclear warheads and bombs in storage is much more difficult due to their much larger numbers, the co-location of strategic and sub-strategic (medium-range and tactical) weapons, and the complication that some warheads would inevitably be in the process of being dismantled or manufactured. On-site inspections may also interrupt the strictly scheduled routine of checking and servicing weapons in storage for safety and reliability purposes.

Still more difficult would be the task of verifiable dismantlement. For strategic weapons, technical procedures have been developed over decades of SALT and START negotiations, and most have worked well. For non-deployed warheads and bombs, customised procedures would have to be devised and negotiated anew. They would probably require on-site monitoring at manufacturing facilities, which would be challenging to establish without compromising the most guarded technical secrets. Then it would be necessary to monitor large amounts of withdrawn fissile material in nuclear pits and ensure that it is not used to produce new weapons in excess of those needed to resupply active forces or stockpiles under the agreed numerical ceilings. The parties could deal with these technical and economic problems only after agreeing on immensely controversial political and strategic issues, including security commitments to allies and basing on foreign territories. Intrusive regimes of this kind are imaginable in a context of genuine nuclear disarmament. That would require anti-nuclear political elites and leaders of the calibre of Mikhail Gorbachev and Barack Obama, who are not expected to hold sway in the foreseeable future.

Be that as it may, for political tensions and conflicts in Europe to be reliably resolved through diplomacy, as they were in the 1970s and 1980s, curtailing plans for using tactical nuclear arms would be highly desirable, if not necessary. That, in turn, may be feasible through an agreement to remove all such weapons from forward bases co-located with conventional forces (including dual-purpose delivery systems) to centralised storage facilities in US and Russian national territories.[35] This implies a milder verification regime that simply ensures that forward depots are empty and unguarded. In the long run, more restrictive regimes might be achievable.[36]

Dealing with emerging technologies

Sea- and air-based disposable uninhabited (that is, robotic) long-range weapons systems, including those equipped with artificial intelligence, should be controlled like all strategic weapons: according to the class of delivery vehicle and maximum tested range, rather than their guidance systems. For instance, Russia's *Poseidon* uninhabited underwater vehicles can be verifiably controlled just like sea-launched ballistic missiles. Their limitation would be determined by a political decision on whether to continue the programme, the utility of which is quite dubious, or to cancel or limit it in exchange for some concessions by the other side.[37]

The subject of space weapons is not a new one; it has been around for decades. At present, China, India, Russia and the US have already tested anti-satellite weapons that incorporate non-nuclear missiles and electronic warfare. It is still unclear how exactly they could be banned, but it is possible to mitigate the threat by prohibiting further tests of any anti-satellite systems against real targets in space.[38] This would significantly increase the survivability of key US and Russian space-based missile-attack early-warning systems, as well as slowing down the dangerous proliferation of space debris.

Agreeing and verifying prohibitions on cyber-war systems seems an unreachable goal at this time. Cyber-war-fighting assets have a potentially destabilising effect, but it is not at all clear what particular military impact they may have. In any case, the most that can be hoped for now is a dialogue between the United States and Russia on a mutual commitment (even if unverifiable, like the past commitment to refrain from targeting missiles on each other) not to launch cyber attacks on each other's strategic-information and command-and-control systems. There is a mutual interest in preventing an inadvertent exchange of nuclear strikes, as well as in jointly coping with the threat of provocation by third countries or cyber terrorists.

Deterrence, disarmament diplomacy and diplomatic conflict resolution are the three principal means of war prevention. Arms control cannot directly affect operational modes of weapons employment, such as counter-force conventional strikes ('sub-nuclear deterrence') or limited ('selective') use of nuclear weapons. However, it can limit the relevant weapons and capabilities on mutually acceptable terms and provide transparency and predictability regarding such weapons. This puts political constraints on their employment to threaten or conduct war.

The proposed model of a START follow-on would not address a number of potentially destabilising weapons systems and technologies: anti-missile defence, space arms, cyber warfare, directed-energy weapons, tactical nuclear weapons and a range of drones with artificial intelligence. Those systems and technologies cannot be addressed immediately, either technically or diplomatically. But that does not mean that there is no sense in tackling those weapons and technologies that may be immediately managed by arms control under the follow-on START treaty for the sake of salvaging strategic stability. Future negotiations might cover the exotic weapons, and taking steps to prevent the collapse of arms-control regimes safeguards that prospect.

Engaging China in arms control

Traditionally, nuclear arms control has been based on a bipolar world order and a rough balance of power between Soviet military forces and those of the United States and its allies. Now a multipolar world is emerging with asymmetrical balances of power. Yet, during the three decades since the end of the Cold War, changes in the global nuclear balance have not been revolutionary. During this time, the share of the two nuclear superpowers in the aggregate quantity of the world's nuclear weapons was only reduced from 98% to 91% (while the whole arsenal was cut from 46,000 to 14,000 weapons).[39]

It would be wonderful if other nuclear states also adopted restrictions on and subsequent reductions of nuclear weapons. But good intentions are not enough to achieve such an outcome; practical reasons need to be compelling. A state would adopt such obligations only if they led to tangible security improvements through comparable limitations and reductions undertaken by adversaries. In addition, no state would agree to legally validate the opponent's military advantage. Further, only comparable classes and types of weapons systems may feasibly be subject to agreements. Finally, trust cannot serve as a basis of arms-control treaties, but rather arises from reliably verified agreements.

All these considerations bear directly on the present US position on engaging China in limiting medium-range and strategic arms. There is no way of frightening China into arms-control treaties, especially when Russia is unwilling to join in applying pressure. Hence, it is up to the United States to develop a proposal that would interest China. The parties may also have to engage the UK and France, since Russia and China would certainly demand their inclusion. In view of the obligations of the five nuclear-weapons states under the Nuclear Non-Proliferation Treaty's Article VI, there would be no reason to exclude them.

So far, Beijing has categorically rejected Washington's proposals. Its attitude is seemingly determined by the slow-moving and highly conservative position of the Chinese Communist Party and military establishments, which operate without meaningful domestic opposition.[40] Evidently, the Chinese government is also reluctant to disclose information about its nuclear forces, which could indicate more significant nuclear potential than its propaganda suggests and outside parties estimate.[41] Beijing asserts that it can be transparent on this issue once the United States and Russia commit to no-first-use of nuclear weapons. This condition has no basis in strategic logic, since information on nuclear forces pertinent to arms control cannot be used to improve the first-strike counterforce targeting of an opponent. Otherwise, the US and Russia would never have exchanged such data.

Beijing has rejected Washington's proposals

If China were persuaded to change its stance, though, the United States might find itself in an awkward situation. The United States claims that China has about 2,000 high-precision medium- and short-range conventional missiles, which are capable of striking US aircraft carriers and sites in Guam, Japan, South Korea and Taiwan.[42] Many of these missile types fall into the range category covered by the INF Treaty. Having withdrawn from that treaty, Washington is considering deploying non-nuclear intermediate-range ballistic or cruise missiles in Asia.[43]

Logically, this means that the US is insisting on a new treaty that should limit or prohibit both nuclear and non-nuclear ground-launched missiles.

The US estimate of China's missile numbers clearly includes conventional systems just like the American missiles planned for deployment in Asia after the renunciation of the INF Treaty. (In fact, that treaty did not specify nuclear missiles as subject to prohibition, and Russian 9M729 missiles – which allegedly violate the treaty – are not considered nuclear either.) Accordingly, any new talks on this subject would supposedly deal with nuclear, conventional or dual-purpose systems of agreed range. Since the parties would be able to agree only on a final ceiling, it could be set at any level, from China's present 2,000 ground-launched missiles, as counted by the US, down to zero. But China would not gain anything in exchange for limiting or radically reducing the number of its deployed missiles. Hence China is unlikely to agree to such an unequal deal, especially in view of the huge superiority of the two nuclear superpowers in strategic weapons.

If China agrees to participate in negotiations, it would probably propose an overall equal ceiling for intermediate-range missiles, to include both ground- and sea-launched cruise missiles (air-launched cruise missiles are deployed on heavy bombers, which are subject to START treaties). The United States has more than 5,600 sea-launched cruise missiles in all of its fleets,[44] and Russia apparently possesses many hundreds of them as well.[45] Verifying the total number of sea-based missiles, as mentioned above, would present an enormous challenge. Moreover, unlike ground-launched intermediate-range missiles, mobile sea-launched systems are not restricted to a particular region, so China would certainly insist on global ceilings.

Nevertheless, this hypothetical position for China would be quite reasonable from the standpoint of arms control, and would put the United States (and, to some degree, Russia) in an uncomfortable position. China would score major political points, even if the negotiations were a failure. If a way to include and verify sea-based medium-range missiles were found, reaching an agreement on equal limitation of ground- and sea-based medium-range missiles might be a strategic victory for Beijing, while such a deal would hardly be welcomed in Washington.

Chinese participation in the next START treaty, on which the White House is also insisting, could create even greater problems for the two superpowers. Parity in strategic weapons for China would require a five- to tenfold reduction in the New START ceilings. Alternatively, China could insist on leeway to build up its weapons to START follow-on-treaty levels observed by Russia and the United States. Both options would be unacceptable to Washington and Moscow.

The severe asymmetries in both ground-based medium-range missiles and strategic arms between China, on the one hand, and the United States and Russia, on the other, are unconducive to arms-control agreements. Waiting until China builds up its strategic forces closer to the levels of the other two powers, or until those powers build up their medium-range missiles to Chinese levels, would be the worst possible approach in view of the dangers and costs of a trilateral arms race. But a compromise is theoretically feasible by integrating elements of the START and INF treaties. For instance, a trilateral treaty could establish some overall ceiling for deployed weapons close to the next START treaty, but with different counting rules than those of the current New START.[46] It might count land-based intermediate- and short-range ballistic, boost-glide and cruise missiles in addition to strategic land- and sea-based ballistic and boost-glide missiles, as well as bombers with air-launched missiles and nuclear gravity bombs. It should also include anticipated future land-based intercontinental cruise missiles and underwater drones. All these systems should be limited if they have a range in excess of 500–600 km (the lower bracket established by the INF Treaty). Just as now, the treaty would not distinguish between nuclear and non-nuclear missiles of various classes, which would make verification much easier.

China would be allowed to increase its strategic forces (currently around 150 delivery vehicles), while reducing the intermediate-range systems that worry the United States. The two nuclear superpowers would have some latitude in deploying intermediate- and short-range missiles, conditioned on corresponding reductions of strategic systems. All three parties would thus have sufficient flexibility in planning their strategic and intermediate-range forces. To prevent the rapid build-up of Chinese strategic arms, a sub-ceiling of 500–600 on strategic delivery vehicles (missiles and bombers), and some other structural and qualitative limitations, might be introduced. Under such an agreement, China would gain recognition of its right to parity and stable strategic relations with the other two powers, while addressing its specific geostrategic and technical priorities. The US and Russia would gain transparency, predictability and projected limits on Chinese strategic and theatre weapons deployment.

The legacy and urgency of arms control

These proposed schemes for bilateral and trilateral arms-control agreements should not be seen as refined blueprints of future practical treaties. Rather, they are possible ways of sorting out the pile of strategic troubles accumulated during the last decade owing to the national policies of the United States, Russia and China, and of accommodating military–technological developments. These objectives may not jibe with the evolved mentality of actual policymakers. Robert Legvold has vividly characterised this mentality, writing that

> the lethargy and false sense of safety that had set in when defense planners stopped worrying about global nuclear war and shifted their attention to other anxieties, such as nuclear terrorism and the spread of nuclear weapons, left them not only unprepared when the shadow of nuclear war reappeared, but also oblivious to the ways in which its context had shifted, producing dangers they had forgotten and some they had little imagined.[47]

Indeed, current state leaders and defence- and foreign-policy elites came to positions of influence at the beginning of the new century (or even later), and inherited for free the legacy of an arms-control system built during the preceding decades. They have taken it for granted and treated it as a pawn in the game of foreign and domestic politics. They have only a vague idea of a world without such a system, and do not know or credit the history of dangerous crises and wasteful cycles of the nuclear arms race during the Cold War.

Neither the changing world order nor innovative military technologies are the reason for the present crisis in arms control, although they are certainly making it more vexing and intricate. The crisis is rooted in the myopia of present national leaders and political elites. It is not certain that they would accept the solutions offered here, or other reasonable proposals. But it is quite clear that the continuation of the present course of major powers will lead to an uncontrolled, multifaceted and multilateral arms race, and potentially to catastrophe.

What is equally certain is that fastidious, granular and pragmatic arms-control negotiations cannot be replaced by recently proposed surrogates, such as discussion forums on 'strategic stability and predictability' and 'creating an environment for nuclear disarmament'. The advocates of this method do not understand that it was the ceilings, sub-ceilings and qualitative limits of the past INF and SALT/START treaties that served as concrete guarantees of stable mutual deterrence, transparency and predictability. Arms-control negotiations that do not focus on specific types of weapons and verification methods are doomed to be merely scholastic exercises.

In this connection, William Perry and Tom Collina point out:

> Arsenal limits backed by good information are the cure for a dangerous arms race. If both sides are confident that they have rough parity, then they can stop building more. And once we establish parity, we can move together to lower levels … A smaller arsenal is cheaper to maintain, easier to keep track of, less threatening to the other side, less polluting to the environment, and would show the rest of the world that the United States and Russia are working to disarm, which supports efforts to stop the spread of nukes to other nations.[48]

In fact, 'field tests' of the proposed non-traditional methods of arms control were conducted during the previous decade through official consultations on strategic stability between the US and Russia, China and the United States, at the 'Big Five' forums and in the United Nations, while practical negotiations on arms limitations were put on hold.[49] No progress has resulted, and the arms race is gaining momentum, with concurrent threats of confrontation and escalation to actual nuclear war fighting.

In order to stop this dangerous slide, the United States and Russia should urgently start negotiations on the START follow-on treaty after extending

New START by five years (or fewer if the new treaty is concluded earlier) and after agreeing on a verifiable moratorium on intermediate-range-missile deployment in Europe. This would provide a solid basis for starting arms-control talks with China. In parallel, the effort should be made to sign up the UK and France to unilateral nuclear-limitation obligations and transparency procedures.

A trilateral arms-control format is challenging but possible. However, advocates of this idea must realise that it requires more than simply revising the current positions of China or other third states. The two nuclear superpowers would have to make much bigger sacrifices, both strategically and politically. So far, it is not at all clear whether or when they will be ready to make such concessions for the sake of transitioning to a multilateral arms-control format.

*   *   *

No doubt arms-control agreements have their limits. In the past, for strategic or technical reasons, the parties could not limit the accuracy of nuclear weapons, their yield and speed, anti-submarine and air-defence systems, space weapons, sea-launched cruise missiles and tactical nuclear arms. Even so, despite certain gaps and failures, the arms-control process has scored a number of historic victories during the past 50 years, and made the world a much safer place until the last few. It should remain at the core of international security, even if many problems cannot be resolved quickly or easily. It would be possible to find ways to control the newest instruments of war using the framework of arms control, and unthinkable to do so in its absence. Likewise, it would be feasible to engage third countries in the nuclear-disarmament process if strategic dialogue between the United States and Russia continued, and implausible if that dialogue were terminated.

It is far from obvious that COVID-19, a new threat to humankind, will encourage international unity behind an important common cause. Despite salutary early signals, this did not happen after 9/11. Following initial cooperation in Afghanistan, the 'war on terror' became yet another subject of bickering and mistrust, as demonstrated in Iraq, Syria and elsewhere.

At the moment, the pandemic looks to be deepening the split, rather than forging unity, among the great powers. The lesson may be that robust cooperation against a common threat cannot be achieved by ignoring previous conflicts and rivalries, but requires bold decisions to calm them as a basis for jointly addressing new security priorities. Great powers must arrive at such decisions not only to redress the outbreak of a new disease, but also to prevent the collapse of an arms-control regime that has served humankind remarkably well.

Notes

1   US Secretary of State Michael R. Pompeo, 'On the Treaty on Open Skies', press statement, US Department of State, 21 May 2020, https://www.state.gov/on-the-treaty-on-open-skies/.

2   'Statement from Ernest J. Moniz and Sam Nunn on U.S. Withdrawal from the Open Skies Treaty', NTI.org, 27 May 2020, https://www.nti.org/newsroom/news/statement-ernest-j-moniz-and-sam-nunn-us-withdrawal-open-skies-treaty/.

3   Steven Pifer, 'How COVID-19 Might Affect US Nuclear Weapons and Planning', Brookings Institution, 18 May 2020, https://www.brookings.edu/blog/order-from-chaos/2020/05/18/how-covid-19-might-affect-us-nuclear-weapons-and-planning/.

4   See Alexey Arbatov, 'Mad Momentum Redux? The Rise and Fall of Nuclear Arms Control', *Survival*, vol. 61, no. 3, June–July 2019, pp. 7–38; and Jessica T. Mathews, 'The New Nuclear Threat', *New York Review of Books*, vol. 67, no. 13, pp. 19–21.

5   William J. Perry and Tom Z. Collina, *The Button: The New Nuclear Arms Race and Presidential Power from Truman to Trump* (Dallas, TX: BenBella Books, 2020), pp. 138–9.

6   'Colonel-General Viktor Yesin: "If the Americans Do Start to Deploy Their Missiles in Europe, We Will Have No Choice but to Abandon the Counter-strike Doctrine and Switch to the Preemptive Strike Doctrine"', *Zvevda Weekly*, 8 November 2018, https://zvezdaweekly.ru/news/t/2018117102-oiaAI.html.

7   Valery Gerasimov, 'The General Staff Is Planning Strikes', *Voenno-Promyshlennyi Kur'er*, no. 9, 12–18 March 2019, p. 6.

8   See Neil MacFarquhar, 'Russia Shows Off New Cruise Missile and Says It Abides by Landmark Treaty', *New York Times*, 23 January 2019, https://www.nytimes.com/2019/01/23/world/europe/russia-inf-cruise-missile.html.

9   This jaunty insight is credited to veteran arms-control negotiator Edward Ifft. He shared it in a talk given at the Soviet Mission in Geneva in November 1989, on the occasion of the 20th anniversary of the beginning of the SALT negotiations.

10   Vladimir Putin, 'Speech and the

Following Discussion at the Munich Conference on Security Policy', President of Russia, 10 February 2007, http://en.kremlin.ru/events/president/transcripts/24034.

11 Government of the Russian Federation, 'Prime Minister Vladimir Putin Meets with Experts in Sarov to Discuss Global Threats to National Security, Strengthening Russia's Defenses and Enhancing the Combat Readiness of Its Armed Forces', 24 February 2012, http://archive.government.ru/eng/docs/18248/.

12 'Joint U.S.–Russian Statement on the Treaty on the Elimination of Intermediate-range and Shorter-range Missiles at the 62nd Session of the UN General Assembly', US Department of State Archive, 25 October 2007, https://2001-2009.state.gov/r/pa/prs/ps/2007/oct/94141.htm.

13 See, for example, Paul Sonne and John Hudson, 'Trump Orders Staff to Prepare Arms-control Push with Russia and China', *Washington Post*, 25 April 2019, https://www.washingtonpost.com/world/national-security/trump-orders-staff-to-prepare-arms-control-push-with-russia-and-china/2019/04/25/c7f05e04-6076-11e9-9412-daf3d-2e67c6d_story.html.

14 President of Russia, 'Plenary Session of the Eastern Economic Forum', 15 September 2019, http://kremlin.ru/events/president/news/61451.

15 Although China keeps details of its current nuclear strategic forces secret, most foreign experts estimate their number at around 150 land- and sea-based ballistic missiles (China does not have heavy bombers) and slightly more warheads, since some of the missiles are equipped with MIRVs.

16 'The Importance of the New START Treaty', Hearing Before the Committee on Foreign Affairs, House of Representatives, 116th Congress, First Session, 4 December 2019, testimony of Pranay Vaddi, https://fas.org/irp/congress/2019_hr/newstart.pdf.

17 See Rose Gottemoeller, 'The New START Verification Regime: How Good Is It?', *Bulletin of the Atomic Scientists*, 21 May 2020, https://thebulletin.org/2020/05/the-new-start-verification-regime-how-good-is-it/.

18 See 'Operationalizing the Creating an Environment for Nuclear Disarmament (CEND) Initiative', Preparatory Committee for the 2020 Review Conference of the Parties to the Treaty on the Non-Proliferation of Nuclear Weapons, working paper submitted by the United States of America, 26 April 2019, https://undocs.org/NPT/CONF.2020/PC.III/WP.43; 'Creating the Conditions for Nuclear Disarmament (CCND)', Preparatory Committee for the 2020 Review Conference of the Parties to the Treaty on the Non-Proliferation of Nuclear Weapons, working paper submitted by the United States of America, https://undocs.org/NPT/CONF.2020/PC.II/WP.30; and Sergey Karaganov and Dmitry Suslov, 'How to Strengthen Multilateral Strategic Stability', *Russia in Global Affairs*, no. 4, July–August 2019, https://globalaffairs.ru/number/Sderzhivanie-v-novuyu-epokhu-20174.

19 Examples include US *Tomahawk* ship-launched (BGM-109) cruise missiles and air- and ground-launched missiles

(AGM-84, AGM-158B, JASSM-ER, ARRW). Russian analogues are non-nuclear 3M-14 *Kalibr* sea-launched missiles, Kh-55SM, Kh-555 and Kh-101 air-launched missiles, and 9M728 *Iskander* and 9M729 Novator ground-launched missiles.

20 James M. Acton, *Silver Bullet? Asking the Right Questions About Conventional Prompt Global Strike* (Washington DC: Carnegie Endowment for International Peace, 2013).

21 The US is testing such systems under its Prompt Global Strike programme. They include the army's Long-Range Hypersonic Weapon, the navy's Conventional Prompt Strike and the air force's Air-Launched Rapid Response Weapon. In addition, the US is testing the X-51A *WaveRider* hypersonic missile for heavy bombers. Russia is ahead of the United States in developing a nuclear-powered intercontinental cruise missile, namely the *Burevestnik* (*Skyfall*). It is also deploying the *Avangard* hypersonic boost-glide vehicle that is carried by the UR-100UTTKh (SS-19), deployed in 2019.

22 Steven E. Miller, 'The Rise and Decline of Global Nuclear Order?', in Steven E. Miller, Robert Legvold and Lawrence Freedman, *Meeting the Challenges of the New Nuclear Age: Nuclear Weapons in a Changing Global Order* (Cambridge, MA: American Academy of Arts & Sciences, 2019), pp. 25–6, https://www.amacad.org/sites/default/files/publication/downloads/2019_New-Nuclear-Age_Changing-Global-Order.pdf.

23 This is true of *Poseidon*, a Russian nuclear-powered and nuclear-armed intercontinental torpedo, as well as US long-range uninhabited aerial vehicles.

24 Examples include Russian *Nudol* missile-defence systems and the S-400 and S-500 missile-defence systems, and the US ship-based *Aegis* SM-3 missile-defence system.

25 'Sergey Shoygu Told How the Russian Army Was Saved', MKRU, 22 September 2019, https://www.mk.ru/politics/2019/09/22/sergey-shoygu-rasskazal-kak-spasali-rossiyskuyu-armiyu.html.

26 For instance, the US is developing *Trident* II submarine-launched ballistic missiles with low-yield warheads (W-76-2), aircraft-launched long-range cruise missiles (LRSO type), guided variable-yield gravity bombs (B-61-12) and new sea-launched nuclear-armed cruise missiles. See US Department of Defense, 'Nuclear Posture Review', February 2018, https://dod.defense.gov/News/SpecialReports/2018NuclearPostureReview.aspx.

27 'Soviet–United States Joint Statement on Future Negotiations on Nuclear and Space Arms and Further Enhancing Strategic Stability', 1 June 1990, https://www.presidency.ucsb.edu/documents/soviet-united-states-joint-statement-future-negotiations-nuclear-and-space-arms-and.

28 See Joint Chiefs of Staff, 'Nuclear Operations', Joint Publication 3-72, 11 June 2019, pp. III-3, V-3, https://fas.org/irp/doddir/dod/jp3_72.pdf; Yevgeny Akhmerov, Marat Valeev and Dmitry Akhmerov, 'The Balloon Is a Friend of "Sarmat"', *Military–Industrial Courier*, 12 October 2016, https://vpk.name/news/165525_aerostat__drug_sarmata.html; and

Elbridge Colby, 'If You Want Peace Prepare for Nuclear War', *Foreign Affairs*, vol. 6, no. 97, November/December 2018, pp. 25–32, https://www.foreignaffairs.com/articles/china/2018-10-15/if-you-want-peace-prepare-nuclear-war.

29   For instance, a discussion on creating an environment for nuclear disarmament took place in Washington on 1–2 July 2019. It attracted participants from 34 countries, including high-ranking officials from Russia and the United States. See Daryl G. Kimball, 'U.S. to Host Disarmament Working Group', *Arms Control Today*, July/August 2019, https://www.armscontrol.org/act/2019-07/news/us-host-disarmament-working-group; 'Operationalizing the Creating an Environment for Nuclear Disarmament (CEND) Initiative'; and Karaganov and Suslov, 'How to Strengthen Multilateral Strategic Stability'.

30   Alexey Arbatov, 'The Vicissitudes of Russian Missile Defense', *Bulletin of the Atomic Scientists*, 28 June 2018, https://thebulletin.org/2018/06/the-vicissitudes-of-russian-missile-defense/.

31   The 600 km range was set to define strategic air-launched cruise missiles and heavy bombers equipped with such weapons for the SALT II (1979) and START I (1972) treaties.

32   Only the 2010 New START adopted liberal counting rules for each bomber – one delivery vehicle = one warhead – although in reality, it could carry up to 20 missiles.

33   These criteria were established in the SALT I and START I (1991) treaties.

34   Alexey Arbatov, 'Why the US Withdrawal from the Intermediate-Range Nuclear Forces Treaty Is Dangerous for Russia', Carnegie Moscow Center, 22 October 2018, https://carnegie.ru/commentary/77543.

35   One of the challenges would be to agree on what 'centralised facilities' means, since the US and Russia have different approaches to the maintenance of such sites.

36   See Edward Ifft, 'Dealing with the INF Crisis', Commentary, European Leadership Network, 13 March 2020, https://www.europeanleadershipnetwork.org/commentary/dealing-with-the-inf-crisis/; and Steven Pifer and Michael E. O'Hanlon, *The Opportunity: Next Steps in Reducing Nuclear Arms* (Washington DC: Brookings Institution Press, 2012).

37   Alexey Arbatov, 'Doomsday Dialectics: Arms Race with Arms Control', *Polis. Political Studies,* no. 3, 2019, pp. 27–48.

38   Alexey Arbatov, 'Arms Control in Outer Space: The Russian Angle, and a Possible Way Forward', *Bulletin of the Atomic Scientists*, 27 June 2019, https://thebulletin.org/2019/06/arms-control-in-outer-space-the-russian-angle-and-a-possible-way-forward/.

39   The calculations are based on *SIPRI Yearbook 1990: World Armaments, Disarmament and International Security* (Oxford: Oxford University Press, 1991), pp. 3–54; and *SIPRI Yearbook 2018: Armaments, Disarmament and International Security* (Oxford: Oxford University Press, 2019), pp. 235–87.

40   Zhao Tong, 'No Magic in Nuclear Buildup', China–US Focus, 19 May 2020, https://www.chinausfocus.com/peace-security/

no-magic-in-nuclear-buildup.

[41] Such information could include details about hardened tunnels, several thousand kilometres long, which may host ground-mobile missiles.

[42] See Ambassador Jonathan Cohen, 'Remarks at a UN Security Council Briefing on Threats to International Peace and Security', 22 August 2019, https://usun.usmission.gov/remarks-at-a-un-security-council-briefing-on-threats-to-international-peace-and-security/; and Jacob Cohn et al., 'Leveling the Playing Field: Reintroducing US Theater-range Missiles in a Post-INF World', Center for Strategic and Budgetary Assessments, 2019, p. 5, https://csbaonline.org/uploads/documents/Leveling_the_Playing_Field_web_Final_1.pdf.

[43] 'Under Secretary Thompson's Statement for the Record: Testimony Before the Senate Committee on Foreign Relations, "The Future of Arms Control Post-Intermediate-Range Nuclear Forces Treaty"', 15 May 2019, https://www.foreign.senate.gov/imo/media/doc/051519_Thompson_Testimony.pdf. Thompson was then under-secretary of state for arms control and international security affairs.

[44] They are deployed on four modified *Ohio*-class missile submarines (154 cruise missiles on each, for a total of 616), and on 20 *Virginia*- and *Seawolf*-class attack submarines (500 cruise missiles), as well as on 22 *Ticonderoga*-class cruisers and

76 *Arleigh Burke*-class destroyers (4,560 cruise missiles). See Eugene Miasnikov, 'The Air–Space Threat to Russia', in Alexey Arbatov, Vladimir Dvorkin and Natalia Bubnova (eds), *Missile Defense: Confrontation and Cooperation* (Moscow: Carnegie Moscow Center, 2013), p. 131, https://carnegieendowment.org/files/Missile_Defense_book_eng_fin2013.pdf.

[45] Vladimir Putin, 'Presidential Address to the Federal Assembly', President of Russia, 1 March 2018, http://en.kremlin.ru/events/president/news/56957.

[46] According to New START, the warheads ceiling is 1,550 weapons, but taking into account the actual loading of nuclear cruise missiles and gravity bombs on heavy bombers, the force levels of the two parties are in fact around 2,100–2,200 weapons. See Vince Manzo, 'Nuclear Arms Control Without a Treaty? Risks and Options After New START', Deterrence and Arms Control Paper No. 1, CNA, April 2019, pp. 52–3.

[47] Robert Legvold, 'The Challenges of a Multipolar Nuclear World in a Shifting International Context', in Miller, Legvold and Freedman, *Meeting the Challenges of the New Nuclear Age*, p. 28.

[48] Perry and Collina, *The Button*, pp. 138–9.

[49] Regular talks on nuclear disarmament have been conducted among China, France, Russia, the UK and the US since 2007, but have not produced any agreement on any possible multilateral limitations on nuclear arms.

Battalions to Brigades: The Future of European Defence

Sven Biscop

There is no lack of initiatives to further defence cooperation between European states, but there might be a lack of ambition. Permanent Structured Cooperation (PESCO), the new European Union mechanism launched in December 2017, could probably be described as the most promising scheme, but the participating states have so far explored only a fraction of its potential. The risk is that it will yield but a small step forward, when much more is needed. Achieving inter-operability between Europe's limited existing capabilities should not be the only goal: Europe's defence effort must be truly integrated so as to increase capability. That means thinking big, including in terms of operations. Brigades, not companies or battalions, must be the building blocks of European defence.

Thinking small

During the Cold War, when European allies focused on territorial defence, the basic unit of NATO's combined force structure was the army corps. Even the smaller allies, such as the author's native Belgium, contributed a self-sufficient corps. Each national corps was pre-positioned in Germany, taking its place along the Iron Curtain. The corps were supported by the multinational NATO command structure and by specific multinational assets (such

Sven Biscop, an honorary fellow of the EU's European Security and Defence College, is the director of the Europe in the World programme at the Egmont – Royal Institute for International Relations in Brussels and a professor at Ghent University. He has been awarded the cross of Officer of the Order of the Crown (Belgium, 2020) and the Grand Decoration of Honour (Austria, 2017).

Survival | vol. 62 no. 5 | October–November 2020 | pp. 105–118   DOI 10.1080/00396338.2020.1819654

Units and formation strength

While the composition of military formations can vary by country and over time, this article assumes formations of the following approximate strengths:

Company   100–200
Battalion   500–1,000
Brigade   3,000–5,000
Division   15,000–20,000
Corps or Army 50,000–100,000

as the Airborne Warning and Control System, or AWACS). After the Cold War, the focus shifted to expeditionary operations outside Europe, until the Russian invasion of Ukraine in 2014 put territorial defence firmly back on the agenda of a much expanded NATO. Expeditionary operations have never ended, however, and are bound to continue, in particular in North Africa and the Middle East, in either a NATO, EU, United Nations or coalition framework. Several European states have also deployed their armed forces at home to support the security services in the fight against terrorism, or to assist in the fight against COVID-19.

Today, having in most cases abolished conscription and reduced defence budgets and force sizes, many European states find themselves hard put to reconcile all these commitments. Units tend to be available for homeland security; even signals or logistics personnel can sometimes find themselves patrolling the streets. When it comes to expeditionary operations, however, most European states already count a mere infantry battalion – if not a company or half-company – as a major deployment. Only the largest European states can deploy as much as a brigade abroad, and even then only if other European states or, in most cases, the US provide support. For the defence of the national territory, it is natural for a significant portion of a nation's forces to be employable. But the forward deployment of forces, such as NATO's Enhanced Forward Presence (EFP) in the Baltic states and Poland, in practice amounts to an expeditionary operation, and thus for most allies the same constraints apply.

To increase the readiness, deployability and sustainability of their forces, European states cooperate in various bilateral formats, as well as through NATO and the EU's Common Security and Defence Policy (CSDP). But even as they do so, they often think too small. For many, the most visible aspect of the CSDP, for example, is the multinational EU battlegroups, two of which are always on standby on a rotational basis. But each battlegroup is only a battalion-size force plus support units, and useable only in very specific scenarios. Furthermore, within many battlegroups inter-operability remains limited, and each one is only a temporary formation that is dissolved after its standby phase.

I am not proposing to reintroduce conscription (though some countries have done so), nor to recreate the 1st Belgian Corps and its sister units in other European states. It is clear to me, however, that the battalion cannot be the unit of measure for the defence effort of European states. Instead, this should be the brigade. A brigade is the largest army unit that every European state (except the very smallest ones) is able to field, and that is capable of independent operations. Belgium, for example, fields one motorised brigade and one special-operations regiment. It is also clear that national brigades will only be fully employable if they are permanently anchored in multinational corps or division structures, within which the contributing states will not just create technical inter-operability between the national force elements, but effectively integrate them. Finally, such military integration will be most effective under the aegis of the EU, which has developed a new range of instruments to support it. PESCO is precisely meant to promote military integration, whereas NATO does not have any specific mechanism in place. The increasingly integrated forces of the EU member states could obviously still be employed in a NATO framework; they would constitute the European pillar of NATO.

Brigades as building blocks

While many European states count one or more brigades in their armies, only a very few still possess the full range of support units that should buttress a brigade's manoeuvre units. As a result, regardless of the quality of the troops, these brigades are not employable in all operational scenarios. A brigade without an air-defence unit, for example, is unsuited to nearly every expeditionary scenario, as even irregular opponents now have access to commercial drones that are easily weaponised. And when it comes to the strategic enablers for force projection (transport, command and control, intelligence, field hospitals), hardly any European states have significant capabilities.

The key to enhancing the employability of Europe's armies lies in the creation of permanent multinational force packages, with national brigades serving as the building blocks. This approach would consist of three elements. Firstly, in the framework of a multinational army corps or division, a combination of integration and specialisation would be organised in the various support functions. In areas where some, or all, of the contributing states had only limited capabilities, these would be integrated into a single multinational support unit. In areas where contributing states had no capabilities at all, a division of labour would be established, with the national support units of some countries supporting the brigades of the others. Thus, all brigades would be more useable, in more scenarios, than in cases where they had to rely on national support only. This approach would also be much more cost-effective.

Belgian–Dutch naval cooperation is an example of this approach in the maritime domain. In this case, the national building blocks are frigates and minehunters. Ships sail under a national flag with a national crew, but most other functions have either been merged into binational capabilities (such as a single naval-operations school), or are provided by one nation for both navies. The Netherlands, for example, provides crew training and maintenance for all frigates, and Belgium for all minehunters. The same model could be applied to an army corps or division, or to an air wing, with the squadron as the basic national unit.

A second element of this approach is that, in the framework of a multinational corps or division, the participating states would harmonise doctrine as well as weapons and equipment. This would allow for maximum interoperability between all constitutive units, make integration or a division of labour much more feasible, and generate synergies and effects of scale. If all brigades were to use the same vehicles, for example, that would drastically reduce the logistics tail on operations, while making procurement simpler and more cost-effective.

Thirdly, the multinational corps or divisions would serve as the benchmark to quantify the need for strategic enablers. The states that made up a multinational formation would acquire the necessary strategic enablers without having recourse to the assets of others. Taken together, these three elements would allow European states to greatly improve the readiness of their forces and increase their capacity to generate larger-scale deployments, be it for expeditionary operations or for the forward deployment of troops in the context of territorial defence. Such an ambitious objective could give coherence and focus to Europe's defence effort.

The role of PESCO

There is, in fact, an EU project to build such a multinational force package: the EUFOR Crisis Response Operation Core (CROC), which falls under the PESCO mechanism.[1]

So far, PESCO has mostly focused on projects to develop new platforms and systems – 47 projects have been approved. If the 25 EU member states that participate in PESCO (only Denmark and Malta have not joined) use it to collectively procure equipment for their national forces, they will surely save money. But that in itself will not remedy a lack of support units and strategic enablers, and therefore will not automatically render their forces more employable. Moreover, many of these projects are only ideas without confirmed budgets, and very few address the shortfalls in European arsenals. In other words, even if the participating EU members were somehow able to accomplish all 47 projects, they would still not be that much more capable than they are today.

PESCO is much more than equipment projects, however: it entails 20 legally binding commitments. The most tangible of these is an obligation to address the common capability shortfalls that the EU has identified through collaborative projects. But the participating states have also committed to make available 'strategically deployable formations' in addition to the battlegroups, in order to achieve the EU's military level of ambition. The overall purpose of PESCO, therefore, 'could be to arrive at a coherent full spectrum force package'. That is how the participating states worded their 'long term vision' for PESCO in the notification document in which they announced, on 13 November 2017, their intention to activate the mechanism.[2] Unfortunately, this statement of purpose was later dropped from the

Council of the European Union decision that formally launched PESCO on 8 December 2017.[3]

A clear sense of purpose will be essential to give coherence and substance to PESCO and, ultimately, to achieve the EU's military level of ambition (or 'headline goal'), which was fixed by the European Council in 1999, and to fulfil the 2016 EU Global Strategy. The headline goal focuses on expeditionary operations and is defined as the ability to deploy and sustain for at least one year an army corps of up to 60,000 troops. EU member states have been claiming to be pursuing this goal for 20 years now. In reality, many have come to see it as an unrealistic level of ambition, though why that should be so, given that the EU members pay nearly 1.5 million men and women to wear a military uniform, is not clear. Even taking into account the need for a rotation of forces on expeditionary operations, these numbers should allow for the implementation of the headline goal without affecting the capacity for territorial defence and homeland security. This is where the CROC project comes in.

The role of CROC

CROC was among the first batch of PESCO projects announced in 2017. Its aim is to 'decisively contribute to the creation of a coherent full spectrum force package, which could accelerate the provision of forces … It should fill in progressively the gap between the EU Battlegroups and the highest level of ambition within the EU Global Strategy'.[4] In line with this view, which enjoys the support of the EU Military Staff, an initial food-for-thought paper released in September 2017 proposed to create a force package of one division or three brigades plus the required strategic enablers as a first step towards the headline goal, which would ultimately require a corps headquarters, three divisions and 9–12 brigades.[5]

CROC could become the central PESCO project and serve as a guiding framework for the other projects. It would represent the achievement of the headline goal, according to which all other PESCO projects could be tailored. The building blocks of CROC would be national brigades. Its objective should be to maximally harmonise all future equipment of these brigades, as well as to ensure that, at the level of CROC, all required combat support and combat service support is present. This would become the focus of the other PESCO projects.

There is, for example, space for only one future main battle tank in Europe, which should at the very least equip all armoured brigades in CROC. At a bilateral summit in summer 2017, France and Germany announced their intention to build the next main battle tank together. The two countries, together with a few more states, could define the requirements for the tank. In a next step, the tank could become a PESCO project, open to all other states that participate in PESCO. States outside the core main-battle-tank group would accept not having a say on the requirements, which could not reasonably be negotiated by 25 states. Nor would such negotiations be necessary – one can safely assume that the specifications that suit France and Germany would suit Belgium as well. In return for their commitment to procure the main battle tank, however, the relevant industries of the other states would be included in the consortium that would design and produce it.[6]

In addition to equipping the manoeuvre and support units of CROC, another layer of PESCO projects would need to address the shortfalls in strategic enablers, in order to make sure that CROC can be put to use whenever and wherever necessary, and be sustained. These projects too could lead to the creation of permanent multinational units. Suppose the current Eurodrone project delivers a new platform, for example: would it not make sense to operate the resulting drones as one fleet, with single structures for command and control, training, logistics and maintenance, rather than dividing them up between the states that financed them? For accounting purposes, drones could still be the property of individual countries (which could even paint their national flags on them), but for practical purposes they would constitute a European drone fleet. The same model could be applied to other enablers or even, in the future, to platforms such as the envisaged next-generation fighter aircraft, the Future Combat Air System. The European Defence Fund established by the European Commission can co-finance up to 30% of this kind of PESCO project by supporting the European defence firms designing and building the chosen platforms.

CROC brings together Cyprus, France, Germany, Italy and Spain, the defence ministers of which approved an implementation study in January

2019. The current plan is to start from the illustrative scenarios of the EU Military Staff – that is, the typology of operations the EU can undertake – and develop force-element lists with detailed military-capability needs for specific subsets of these scenarios. The participating states would have to report the capabilities they possess that fulfil these requirements. The aim would not be to create a standby force or to maintain a certain state of readiness, but to pre-identify capabilities. That should accelerate force generation when a decision is made to mount an actual operation. Furthermore, as a future step, command-and-control options would also be pre-identified.

The original food-for-thought paper did not propose to identify and assign units to CROC. But under the existing headline-goal process, the EU's force catalogue already lists theoretically available capabilities without identifying units, which renders an assessment of their actual readiness impossible. Force-element lists of pre-identified units would thus be an important improvement. It should be noted, however, that the implementation study dropped the level of ambition and, as a first step, envisaged no more than a brigade-size force plus enablers. That is far too modest an ambition to have a significant impact. As a first step, CROC could aim at generating brigade-size *operations*. But even in the first phase, CROC as a whole surely needs to count at least three brigades, as originally proposed by France and Germany. Even Belgium already has a brigade – it does not need the EU or CROC to create one.

The role of complementary schemes

Fortunately, other schemes exist, alongside CROC and outside the EU framework, that might yet help the EU to achieve a more serious level of ambition. Certain European states have already made the step towards deeply integrated multinational formations. The German–Netherlands Corps, created as far back as 1995, is an example of far-reaching integration between land forces. The corps' headquarters is binational, with a staff-support battalion and a communication and information-systems (CIS) battalion with mixed German and Dutch personnel. Among the units assigned to the corps is the German 1st Panzer Division, which comprises one Dutch brigade (the 43rd Mechanised Brigade). This brigade in turn comprises one mixed German–Dutch tank battalion that operates the only tank capacity in the Dutch army.

On 8 November 2018, Belgium and France signed an intergovernmental agreement on the Capacité Motorisée (CaMo) project, bringing together the Belgian Motorised Brigade and the French Armée de Terre. Belgium will acquire French vehicles,[7] but more than this, Belgium and France are jointly developing the doctrine for the use of the new platforms. The objective is deep inter-operability, down to platoon level, so that the Belgian brigade would mirror its French counterparts in everything except uniforms. In theory, Belgian and French crews should be able to swap vehicles and operate them immediately. The next step could be to anchor the Belgian brigade more firmly in one of the French divisional or corps structures, and to realign the support units into a coherent whole.

These are two examples of states using brigades as a building block and setting down a path of ever-increasing integration. This is exactly the spirit and the scale that should inform CROC, which could certainly be constructed on the foundation of these two binational projects.

The countries involved, Belgium, Germany and the Netherlands, also participate in France's European Intervention Initiative (EI2), launched in 2018 with the aim of increasing the capacity of the initiative's now 13 members to act together.[8] Participating states opt to join one or more working groups (such as on the Sahel, the Caribbean, power projection or terrorism) in order to forge a prior common understanding of the joint action that they might potentially undertake if a crisis were to occur in one of these areas. Put differently, France hopes via the EI2 to create a pool of able and willing partners to build ad hoc coalitions for French-led military interventions.

The link with CROC is obvious: the understanding on likely intervention scenarios forged by the EI2 members ought to inform the force-element lists for CROC. The EI2 scenarios are much more ambitious than the scenarios that the CROC implementation study proposes to focus on: humanitarian assistance, non-combatant evacuation and conflict prevention with battle-group-size forces only. (Arguably the most ambitious scenario discussed in the study is protecting lines of communication and critical resources.) Governments may hope that they will only ever face these less threatening scenarios, but the composition of a coherent, full-spectrum force package should be determined by the scenarios that Europeans may well be *obliged* to deal with, not those that they would *like* to deal with.

The logical step, therefore, would be for all EI2 participants to join CROC with at least a brigade. They could thus collectively shape a force package capable of undertaking the types of operations required by the scenarios that they have elaborated in the framework of the EI2. Eventually, the EI2 and CROC could be merged into a single initiative, under the aegis of PESCO.[9]

CROC, NATO and the EU

Creating CROC using German–Dutch and Franco-Belgian cooperation as a starting point does not mean merging the two initiatives. Within CROC, there can be more than one core, each with a specific orientation.

Indeed, neither the EI2 nor even PESCO is exclusively about expeditionary operations or the EU. The Baltic focus of one of the EI2 working groups, and the launching of PESCO projects on intra-European military mobility and on artillery and missiles, clearly serve territorial defence and NATO. Previous EU defence schemes addressed only those capabilities EU member states had declared to be theoretically available to the CSDP, for expeditionary operations only. The initial focus of PESCO too naturally remains the EU level of ambition. But at the same time, without there having been any great debate about it, most capitals effectively understand PESCO as covering the armed forces of the participating states in their entirety, with the aim of achieving the NATO, EU and national levels of ambition in an integrated manner, for both territorial defence and expeditionary operations. That is a breakthrough in itself, which would have been impossible before the activation of PESCO.

Ideally, the European states would build on this breakthrough to further tear down the NATO and EU stovepipes. NATO planning envisages three army corps. Could not CROC be one of those? It would be the corps on which the EU objective of 'strategic autonomy' would centre.[10] On the one hand, CROC would be ready to take its place alongside the non-EU NATO allies in case of an Article V collective-defence scenario. On the other, CROC formations could be readily generated for expeditionary operations outside NATO/EU territory, relying only on the assets held by participating states. CROC could also be called upon to defend Europe and deter aggressors should the mutual-defence guarantee of Article 42.7 of the Treaty on European Union be activated instead of NATO's Article V.[11]

CROC could thus comprise both heavy armoured formations and more rapidly deployable motorised and air-mobile formations, organised into multinational divisions with national brigades as the building block. There could be divisions that focus primarily on territorial defence and others oriented primarily towards expeditionary operations.[12] This would allow all participants in the EI2 – both EU member states and others, including the formally neutral states – to join a core within CROC that fits their national-defence orientation. All could thus benefit from the synergies and effects of scale that integration into CROC would entail, while preserving maximal discretion regarding the type of operations in which they would participate.

CROC could also incorporate some of the existing corps headquarters to provide a force headquarters and ensure command and control for all operations that it might undertake. The Eurocorps headquarters in Strasbourg is an obvious candidate for this. Multinational strategic enablers could be organised around the various CROC divisions, such as a drone fleet, an air-transport fleet and so on.

CROC and defence planning

In order to achieve more synergies between states and their various initiatives, and between NATO and the EU, Europeans could also revise the way they do multinational defence planning. Today, the NATO Defence Planning Process sets binding capability targets for individual allies. In many key areas, notably strategic enablers, however, the European allies individually lack the scale to meet these targets in a cost-effective way, if at all. Many targets will thus likely never be met. On the EU side, the Capability Development Plan and the Coordinated Annual Review on Defence focus more on cooperation between states, but the Capability Development Plan does not set binding targets, and its impact on national defence planning is therefore limited. Instead of running the two processes in parallel, could they not be joined up?

Within the NATO Defence Planning Process, one possibility would be to insert a collective EU/European level of ambition between the national targets and the target for NATO as a whole. In addition to binding individual targets for all NATO allies, binding *collective* targets could be set for the group of NATO allies and partners that make up the EU (plus any European state that might wish to associate with it, such as Norway). Those collective targets could focus especially on enablers, which today are very unevenly spread across the Alliance, and are in fact mostly American. NATO and the EU would have to establish these collective targets together, the former deriving its input from the overall NATO level of ambition, the latter from its own level of ambition for autonomous operations, in line with the EU Global Strategy. The existing headline goal would, of course, be a minimum.

It would be up to the states within such a 'European pillar' to determine how to meet their collective targets. They could notably make full use of EU instruments such as PESCO and the European Defence Fund, and would, by embracing CROC, constitute a coherent, full-spectrum force package.

Joining up EU and NATO defence planning would serve three aims. Firstly, it would permit the European allies and partners to meet their capability targets in a much more cost-effective way, thanks to the collective approach. Secondly, it would make the EU targets, much like NATO targets, binding on participants. Thirdly, it would create a capability mixture within the European group that would permit it to undertake expeditionary operations without needing any assets from outside the group.

Resisting PESCO pessimism

Moving towards NATO and EU 'co-decision' on defence planning may seem politically unfeasible today, though it may well become easier, if not imperative, if President Donald Trump is re-elected and the US adopts an ever more 'transactional' stance within the Alliance. If the Europeans are forced to assume more responsibilities, they may no longer be able to afford the luxury of maintaining parallel processes. Meanwhile, integration is ongoing, as the German–Dutch and Franco-Belgian examples, among others, demonstrate. States with ambitions in the field of defence should grasp this opportunity by defining the responsibilities that they are willing to assume in the EI2 and providing themselves with the means of achieving their ambitions through CROC. Thinking on CROC currently focuses on land forces and the required enablers, but it is clear that similar schemes are possible – and necessary – for Europe's naval and air forces as well, and could easily be incorporated into CROC.

Those who want European defence to advance should be truly ambitious. There is no point in announcing grand multinational initiatives that, in terms of the level of ambition, do not look beyond what individual members should already be capable of today. Similarly, every initiative that brings together a subset of the EU's 27 members should be truly integrative from the start. Otherwise, one might as well stay within the purely intergovernmental framework of the CSDP and NATO. Yielding to pessimism is easy, but also dangerous. Do Europeans really need more convincing of the fact that nobody, not even the US, will defend their interests for them? In the context of European defence, the realists must be optimists.

Finally, a serious initiative should have a serious name. During the Second World War, Winston Churchill issued a directive to his commanders urging them to avoid 'names of a frivolous character' for operations, noting that it would be unseemly for 'some widow or mother to say that her son was killed in an operation called "Bunnyhug" or "Ballyhoo"'.[13] Likewise, would any soldier be keen to deploy as part of the EUFOR CROC? (Croque-monsieur? Croque-madame? Crocs footwear?). Better to call it the EUROFORCE, to forcefully express that the EU and its European partners want to be a force in international politics.

Acknowledgements

The author warmly thanks Brigadier-General (Retd) Jo Coelmont, Dr Bastian Giegerich, and the other officers from various nations and institutions without whose expert military advice this article could not have been written.

Notes

1   See Sven Biscop, 'European Defence: Give PESCO a Chance', *Survival*, vol. 60, no. 3, June–July 2018, pp. 161–80.

2   Participating States, 'Notification on Permanent Structured Cooperation (PESCO) to the Council and to the

High Representative of the Union for Foreign Affairs and Security Policy', Brussels, 13 November 2017.

3   Council of the European Union, 'Council Decision Establishing Permanent Structured Cooperation (PESCO) and Determining the List of Participating Member States', Brussels, 8 December 2017.

4   PESCO Secretariat, 'EUFOR Crisis Response Operation Core (EUFOR CROC)', https:// pesco.europa.eu/project/ eufor-crisis-response-operation-core/.

5   'Food for Thought Paper on the CROC', prepared by France and Germany, September 2017.

6   Further consolidation of the European defence industry is inevitable, however, notably in the land sector.

7   Specifically, Belgium will acquire 382 *Griffon* multi-role armoured vehicles and 60 *Jaguar* armoured reconnaissance and combat vehicles.

8   The members are Belgium, Denmark, Estonia, Finland, France, Germany, Italy, the Netherlands, Norway, Portugal, Spain, Sweden and the UK.

9   The precondition is that the EU member states participating in PESCO agree on a rule for third-country participation, so that the UK can stay involved. The UK may be reticent to join the more integrative parts of the scheme, certainly in the first stage. But it could ensure that its own expeditionary forces are interoperable with CROC, along the lines of its current cooperation with France in the Combined Joint Expeditionary Force, and with Denmark, Estonia, Finland, Latvia, Lithuania, the Netherlands, Norway and Sweden in the Joint Expeditionary Force.

10 Introduced by the 2016 EU Global Strategy, the EU has yet to formally define 'strategic autonomy'. Arguably, the headline goal already defines the minimum degree of autonomy the EU member states should achieve. As far back as 1999, the objective was to enable expeditionary operations without the need to have recourse to assets of non-EU member states.

11 This has happened once, at the request of France, following the 2015 terrorist attacks in Paris by the Islamic State (ISIS).

12 The capabilities required for these would certainly overlap.

13 Winston S. Churchill, *The Second World War*, Volume 5: *Closing the Ring* (London: Cassell, 1952), p. 583.

The Strategic Implications of China's Weak Cyber Defences

Greg Austin

China has raced ahead in quantum-communication technology, with remarkable achievements in teleportation of the electronic properties of remote subatomic particles.[1] In 2015, it had its first mainland-resident Nobel Prize winner in a scientific discipline (medicine).[2] Yet the innovation picture for the country is a mixed one. China publicly promotes the indigenisation of advanced technologies, including cyber capabilities, but more candid assessments do not bear out its technological nationalism. In particular, the country's leaders consider its cyber defences weak, as reflected in its continued reliance on US-based corporations for basic, front-line cyber security.[3] In 2016, for instance, President Xi Jinping complained that foreign corporations controlled China's core technologies.[4] In 2019, the Bank of China – China's leading international bank – and IBM announced a partnership in developing new cyber architectures for the bank, which has offices around the world.[5]

Western assessments confirm the weakness of China's cyber defences, although mostly in passing. The IISS's *Asia-Pacific Regional Security Assessment 2019* concluded that the country 'continues to encounter a range of challenges and potential vulnerabilities in this new domain, including the relative insecurity of its own information-technology ecosystem'.[6] US sources, often prone to exaggerating China's strengths, have begun to recognise the weaknesses in China's cyber defences.[7] According to the International Telecommunications Union's most recent cyber-security index, China ranks 27th in the world

Greg Austin is IISS Senior Fellow for Cyber, Space and Future Conflict.

Survival | vol. 62 no. 5 | October–November 2020 | pp. 119–138   DOI 10.1080/00396338.2020.1819648

in overall cyber capability, behind countries such as Croatia, Denmark, Egypt, Germany, Italy, Russia and Turkey.[8] China and Turkey have among the highest rates of malware infections. An industry website, Comparitech, has ranked China 23rd out of 76 countries based on 2019 data.[9] The World Economic Forum's 'Global Information Technology Report' ranked China 59th in network readiness in the several years up to 2016, when it was discontinued.[10] The Global Innovation Index (GII) for 2019, compiled by a consortium of reputable international organisations and not confined to cyber, ranks China 14th. China has not been in the top ten in any year since the GII was established, that range being dominated by the US and its allies.[11]

According to a report from China's National Internet Emergency Response Center in 2018, phishing cases in China decreased by 72.5% from 2016 to 2017. The number of active control terminals launching distributed denial-of-service (DDoS) attacks decreased by 46%, and the number of controlled sources launching DDoS attacks decreased by 37%.[12] But although the proportion of backdoors installed in Chinese websites decreased significantly, the volume of webpage-tampering incidents increased by 20% across all sectors, and by 30% for government websites. The annual growth rate of the number of new security vulnerabilities discovered exceeded 20%. DDoS attacks against China became more powerful, with the number of high-volume attacks (exceeding one terabyte per second) reaching 68 in 2018. The number of malicious sniffing and cyber attacks on industrial facilities, systems and platforms increased significantly. The National Internet Emergency Response Center also reported that the top three foreign sources for malicious software in China in 2018 were Canada, Russia and the United States, and that the three top ones for hosting control servers distributing this software were Germany, Japan and the US.

Leadership perceptions

In 2013, two public events demonstrated to the Chinese leadership how weak their cyber defences had been. In February of that year, the private US company Mandiant (since subsumed by FireEye) was able to penetrate one of the People's Liberation Army's (PLA) most secretive cyber-espionage teams, Unit 61398, reportedly even acquiring video footage of activity inside its operations centre. The company publicly documented its success, which was amplified by *New York Times* reporter David Sanger in his 2018 book *The Perfect Weapon*.[13] Mandiant's infiltration revealed significant Chinese vulnerability.

In June 2013, Edward Snowden revealed widespread successful penetration of Chinese systems by the National Security Agency (NSA). Snowden claimed that the NSA had been hacking the majority of Chinese government and private systems since 2007, relying on routers provided by the US firm Cisco Systems.[14] American agencies also had been closely tracking supposedly secret cyber operations by China for several years.[15] In his State of the Union address in February 2013, president Barack Obama suggested that the US had substantial knowledge of China's cyber-intelligence operations, stating that 'our enemies are also seeking the ability to sabotage our power grid, our financial institutions, our air traffic control systems'.[16]

Chinese leaders were concerned about the security of their own high-level communications. In 2012, when Xi Jinping was assuming leadership of the country, two Western news outlets revealed explosive details of the personal wealth of the families of Xi and outgoing premier Wen Jiabao.[17] Most likely, hacks into Chinese systems produced some of the information. By 2013, electronic documents from two tax havens (the Cook Islands and the British Virgin Islands), almost certainly leaked by a Western intelligence agency,[18] led to publication of a thorough investigative report on corrupt Chinese offshore investments by the International Consortium of Investigative Journalists.[19] Intensifying leadership concerns was the constant flow of secret Chinese Communist Party documents about censorship and public security into the hands of Western analysts.[20]

To Chinese leaders, they and China's security sector seemed almost defenceless in cyberspace. The public response came in February 2014 when Xi announced his country's intent to become a cyber power and set in motion a raft of institutional reforms.[21] He explicitly linked cyber defence to national security, noting that there can be no national security without cyber security.[22] His government saw cyberspace defence as the front line of international security, reflected in a statement in China's Military Strategy 2015 that 'outer space and cyberspace have become the new commanding heights in strategic competition among all parties'.[23]

Foundations of China's national cyber security

China still has only a modest domestic cyber-security industry, a fraction of the size of its American counterpart. According to a recent report by an authoritative industry alliance, the 'overall scale of the industry is still small', around RMB39 billion (about $6bn) in 2018.[24] (The estimate does not appear to include two state-owned corporations included in the Global Fortune 500 that have cyber-security divisions.) The report notes rapid growth in the sector in recent years (18% from 2017 to 2018, and a projected annual growth rate of 20% to the end of 2021). The sector should reach RMB66.8bn ($10bn) by 2021. For comparison, in 2018 the security-related income of IBM alone, the leading US cyber-security company, grew by 55%, and revenues may have reached $4bn.[25] The report indicates that in China the 'proportion of investment allocated to cyber security within informatisation projects is still low, demonstrating an evident gap with the more developed countries in Europe and the United States'.[26]

A recent report from Tencent Security Response Centre – part of the Chinese company Tencent, one of the world's largest internet firms – offered additional explanations for the weak position of the country's cyber-security sector.[27] These included a focus on profit instead of security; high cost; a general lack of talent; concentration of the sector in Tier 1 and Tier 2 cities such as Beijing, Guangdong and Shanghai; poor cyber-security-threat technology; reliance on foreign imports for basic information infrastructure; lack of national control in core technologies; weak capability to track hostile activity (especially advanced persistent threats); reliance on out-of-date methods of protecting data; limited legal foundations for countering and tracking illegal access of data; and underdeveloped identity-authentication systems. The report observed that Chinese firms' cyber-security investment as a share of total investment (1.78%) was far lower than that in the US (4.78%) and the rest of the world (3.75%).[28]

Although China's cyber-security companies' global footprint is improving, it remains underdeveloped. Consequently, they do not benefit from internationalisation in the same way as firms such as NortonLifeLock, IBM and even Kaspersky have done. More broadly, the Chinese government has not been able to elevate its educational system to meet the cyber-power ambition set in 2014.[29] The workforce deficit is massive. One Chinese corporation recently noted that 'the current supply of cyber security talent is approximately 100,000 while demand is expected to reach 1.4 million in 2020'.[30] Further distorting the labour market, less developed areas of China 'suffer from a lack of educational resources, hence causing poor cybersecurity practices and awareness in those regions'.[31] The massive over-concentration of trained people in a small number of cities makes the problem even worse.

The quality of cyber-security education has caught the government's attention. It has launched a number of initiatives to remedy the problem, but not on a scale that matches the shortfall in numbers or quality. For example, in its annual ranking of the country's educational institutions by discipline, the Chinese Universities Alumni Association includes none of China's universities at world-class level (nine stars) or the next level (eight stars).[32] Only two universities are graded at seven stars. By 2019, China was able to report a 16% increase in enrolments in its five undergraduate cyber-security degrees compared with the previous year, though the total numbers (fewer than 10,000) were still small relative to the need. Enrolment growth in master's degrees from 2017 to 2018 was more impressive, at 44% for a total of just over 30,000. The years between 2014 and 2018, since China declared its cyber-power ambition, had not seen such impressive growth.[33]

According to Li Aidong, deputy director-general of the Cyber Security Coordination Bureau of the Cyberspace Administration of China, the country's use of 5G 'introduces new security risks, making it possible for the network to be more infiltrated and attacked'.[34] These risks will be tougher for a country like China to handle, given its poorly developed talent pool, than for a country like the United States.

As indicated in Table 1, Western corporations (the so-called 'US alliance') hold by far the most 5G security patents, with the US company Qualcomm in the lead. It is worth noting that overall there is a surprisingly low number of patents dealing with 5G security. There will probably be more inherent security vulnerabilities in 5G technology than any intentionally created by the Chinese intelligence services, and there is no solid evidence in the public domain of gaps created specifically for Chinese spying purposes. They arise more from the nature of the technology than from the malign intent of the

Table 1: **Number of European Patent Office patents mentioning '5G' and 'security'**

Total patents mentioning '5G' and 'security'	29,934
Mentioning Qualcomm	2,066
Mentioning Huawei	1,387
Mentioning AT&T	1,233
Mentioning Ericsson	694
Mentioning ZTE	223

Source: European Patent Office, as of December 2019.

corporation designing the software and firmware. If Huawei's participation in national 5G networks creates vulnerabilities for Western cyber security, China itself would face reciprocal vulnerabilities that are probably more daunting: leading Western intelligence agencies can exploit Huawei technology at least as easily as Chinese agencies can.[35]

Cyber-defence weaknesses in the civil domain carry over to the military sector to a considerable degree. All countries' militaries depend in part on non-military organisations to provide cyber defences for military forces and national security. For instance, the US Department of Defense has a large civilian cyber-security workforce drawn largely from educational and training institutes in the civilian sector. So it is in China. While the country has made impressive breakthroughs in niche areas, such as quantum communications, these do not depend as much on distributed capabilities and mass interventions as cyber defence does. The cyber-defence task for the PLA is gargantuan, involving the personal security habits of hundreds of thousands of uniformed personnel as well as a large number of civilian employees and external contractors supporting PLA systems.[36]

The PLA has several major professional military-education institutions at university level that produce graduates in cyber-defence areas. The most important one now is the PLA Information Engineering University (IEU) in Zhengzhou, subordinate to the Strategic Support Force. This university is the only officially designated national cyber-security personnel-training base for the PLA.[37] It has more than 2,000 teaching and research staff, including 153 doctoral supervisors and 447 master's supervisors. The overall size of the IEU disguises its intense concentration of resources in teaching cyber defence. It takes a multidisciplinary approach that integrates

Table 2: **Number of planned IEU places by major for 2013, 2018 and 2019**

Major	2013	2018	2019
Communications engineering (communications techniques and application)	30	10	17
Communications engineering (communications-equipment research and protection)		10	14
Information engineering (signal analysis and treatment)	25	40	30
Artificial intelligence (treatment of artificial-intelligence data, research and development of equipment)	0	0	30
Information-confrontation techniques (cyber defence and attack)	0	20	20
Information security (cyber defence and attack)	89	24	20
Information security (information management)		0	64
Electronic science and technology (information-equipment techniques and protection)	0	35	20
Management science and engineering (information management)	0	30	85
Confidentiality management	0	0	85
Microelectronics science and engineering (information-equipment techniques and protection)	0	20	20
Computer science and techniques (cyberspace security, techniques and command)	17	20	40
Computer science and techniques (computer-equipment research, development and protection)		0	14
Internet engineering (cyberspace security, techniques and command)	35	30	45
Cyberspace security (cyberspace security, techniques and command)	0	70	60
Cryptography engineering (information research)	93	0	41
Cryptography (information management)	37	25	20
Electronic-information engineering (information-equipment techniques and protection)	0	0	11
Electronic-information engineering (information techniques and command)	0	20	11
Big-data engineering (data protection)	0	30	45
Target engineering (data protection)	0	20	45
Totals	**326**	**402**	**737**

Sources: Huangpu No. 1 Military Academy Information, '2019 Military Academy Admissions Guide 24th Station: Information Engineering University', China Military Network, 21 June 2019, http://www.chinamil.com.cn/201311jxjjh/2019-06/21/content_9535184.htm; Information Engineering University of the Strategic Support Force of the Chinese People's Liberation Army, 'Strategic Support Force Information Engineering University 2018 Recruitment Program for General High School Graduates', Qian Ye Wang website, 8 July 2018, https://www.zjut.cc/article-130162-1.html; and 'China People's Liberation Army Information Engineering University Admissions Plan 2013', BaiduWenku, 3 July 2013, https://wenku.baidu.com/view/6844bf552b160b4e767fcf31.

science, engineering, military affairs, culture and management. It has 78 distinct undergraduate programmes, though some have little to do with cyber defence. Table 2 shows a list of the majors for 2013, 2018 and 2019, and the number of students planned for recruitment in each year.[38] It appears that four new majors may have been created for 2019: artificial intelligence (AI), information security (information management), confidentiality management and electronic-information engineering. In 2019, the total number of student places for all listed cyber disciplines was 737. This accounts for 64% of the places available at the IEU. The percentage of IEU students undertaking the cyber-related majors for 2019 is double the share for 2013, which was 34%. The number of students represents around 8% of the total number of all military-academy places available in 2019. There has been a 15% increase in overall numbers recruited for the IEU between 2013 and 2019, as well as a dramatic shift in the share of places going to the cyber disciplines. However, higher student throughput may still be too low for a country aiming to produce fully informatised armed forces by 2035. For comparison, US cyber-security education for military and national-security purposes has been the subject of concern and a succession of presidential initiatives over more than a decade. US President Donald Trump declared an arms race in cyberspace workforces in May 2019.[39] But the quality of cyber-security education in the United States is far richer than China's at every level.[40]

Based on open-source information, there is not yet a sufficient Chinese educational infrastructure to allow widespread diffusion of knowledge about cyber defence in the officer corps. Public reporting about cyber military exercises suggests a similar lack of diffusion of ideas and policies among lower-ranking personnel.

Implications of China's cyber-defence weakness

There are few probative public documents or statements from the Chinese government on different approaches to the use of force involving cyber-strike assets. Articles in military journals such as *China Military Science* (published by the PLA Academy of Military Science) or *Military Technology* (published by the National University of Defense Technology) offer some guidance, but it is impossible to determine what weight opinions published in such journals carry in leadership circles, or in formal doctrine and planning. No doubt US and allied intelligence agencies have greater insights into that question than are available in the public domain. We can, however, draw considered inferences on the basis of Chinese strategic policy.

One is that China has no intention of provoking a war, or even a short armed conflict, with the United States. This stance is unlikely to change during the next decade. China is prepared, however, to use force against the US if needed to prevent a permanent separation of Taiwan from the mainland.[41] It would also do so to defend its current positions on disputed parts of the Spratly Islands. Of these two different scenarios, only the Taiwan crisis would be likely to involve large-scale use of cyber attacks on military targets.

Chinese leaders almost certainly believe that the United States and its allies possess overwhelming military power for most contingencies involving China, and they see superior cyber capability as underpinning that power. Partial confirmation emerges from the political, strategic and military reforms begun in 2014, which were manifested most directly in 2015 in both China's Military Strategy and its creation of the Strategic Support Force to lead and coordinate cyberspace and related information-warfare activities for the armed forces.[42] China sees itself as in the early stages of the military reforms required to be competitive in military cyberspace operations in future war, a position evidenced in part by three military goals: basic mechanisation and progress on informatisation by 2020; modernisation (including informatisation) by 2035; and top-tier global war-fighting capability by 2049.[43] Beijing also presumably envisages an AI-enabled warfare plan as part of the latter objective.[44]

Chinese planners apprehend the threats and opportunities in military uses of cyberspace in much the same way as their US counterparts. The main goal of both is information dominance. An authoritative PLA analysis, *The Science of Military Strategy*, specifically cites coordinated space, cyber and electronic warfare as strategic means to 'paralyze enemy operational system of systems and to sabotage the enemy's military command system of systems'.[45] Another source identifies targets in information warfare as including 'the enemy's information detection sources, information channels, and information-processing and decision-making systems'.[46] In a 2016 paper, Adam Segal quotes from *The Science of Military Strategy*:

> The side holding network warfare superiority can adopt network warfare to cause dysfunction in the adversary's command system, loss of control over his operational forces and activities, and incapacitation or failure of weapons and equipment – and thus seize the initiative

> within military confrontation, and create conditions for … gaining
> ultimate victory in war.[47]

Notwithstanding the visibility of such doctrinal views and of some organisational changes in cyber military capability, as James Johnson notes, 'far less ink has been spilled on Chinese thinking in the development of the critical support architecture, which enables and enhances China's war-fighting capabilities'.[48] In the public domain, China's military cyber-exercise scenarios and its perceptions of US target selection against China in the event of a military confrontation or related political crisis remain opaque. A recent Chinese article does suggest, however, that planners' focus has shifted from offence and early cross-domain engagement to defence and cross-domain deterrence.[49] Unsurprisingly, the author attributes the shift to 'US perceptions and practice of cyberwar'.[50]

Military academics at the PLA Air Force Engineering University have assessed that China is lagging in its development of cyber warfare compared to the United States and Russia, which have established specialised cyber-combat units with actual cyber offensive and defensive training.[51] Non-Chinese analyses are equally critical. A 2015 RAND Corporation study described China as losing out to the United States in a number of net assessments for cyber-dominated conflicts in the Taiwan Strait and in the Spratly Islands.[52] For cyber-dominated conflict, the study observed that by 2015 and looking forward to 2017, even though China had reduced the US advantage, it was still palpable.[53] Another 2015 assessment that canvassed Chinese military writings on cyberspace and asymmetric warfare concluded that 'the United States dominates cyberspace and its hegemony there is even more significant than in the real world'.[54] In a probing and significant recent contribution to understanding relative cyber military power, the authors argued that Chinese military and political leaders' dream of catching up with the US could not be achieved merely by following technological leaders, and therefore was unlikely to be realised without massive improvements in national scientific and innovation capability.[55]

Chinese political leaders probably have only a general understanding of cyber's military potential and the cyber superiority of the US alliance.

But that would be enough for them to be very cautious about approving any moves that might bring down a cyber storm on China. It is unknown whether Chinese political leaders have insisted at any stage on a position that the United States adopted in 2012, whereby only the president could authorise offensive cyber operations against other countries in peacetime. But as a result of the diplomatic tensions over cyber activities against the United States, beginning in 2013 and escalating in 2018, it is a safe assumption that Chinese leaders require a very high level of political authority in China to initiate such operations, and that they have not yet assessed, as the United States did with the Cyber Deterrence Initiative in 2018, that this authority should be passed down the chain of command. It is also unlikely that China is in a position to devolve decision-making on wartime cyber options to every level of command, as the US did in 2015.[56] In all probability, any Chinese cyber attack against the United States would require high-level political authorisation that cannot be delegated.

Nevertheless, China's political leaders do face pressure. They know that the United States and its Five Eyes allies (Australia, Canada, New Zealand and the United Kingdom) have been conducting 'active defence' operations (non-espionage attacks) in cyberspace as part of the Cyber Deterrence Initiative to disrupt China's cyber-espionage and -reconnaissance operations, and its emplacement of militarily significant malware. The United States has also been conducting a trade war and a technology war, both launched in March 2018 and prompted in part by China's malicious activity in cyberspace. These moves threaten China's economic prosperity.[57]

As for the military leaders, the first two commanders of the Strategic Support Force have not had a solid background in cyber-warfare planning. The second of these and current commander was appointed in 2019, and had spent most of his military career in the PLA Air Force Airborne Corps. The most cyber-literate person in the command hierarchy may be one of the deputy commanders, Lieutenant-General Zheng Junjie, who has been director of the Network Systems Department since 2016, having served as president of the IEU and director of the General Staff Technical Reconnaissance Department, an intelligence-collection unit relying on cyber operations.[58]

Table 3: **Probable Chinese list of assets subject to US cyber attacks on China in a military crisis, in order of priority**

1. Strategic nuclear-missile command and control
2. Medium-range-missile command and control
3. Strategic Support Force command and control
4. Naval headquarters
5. Eastern Theatre Command headquarters, opposite Taiwan, with primary responsibility for Taiwan contingencies
6. Electric grids around key naval and air bases
7. Satellite-navigation systems used by Chinese forces
8. Naval weapons systems and platforms
9. On-board combat systems of military aircraft
10. Chinese intelligence, surveillance and reconnaissance capabilities

Chinese military planners surely would have compiled a list of cyber assets that are critical to national military operations in various contingencies and vulnerable to cyber attacks. The list would be a long one given the weaknesses in China's civil- and military-sector cyber defences, and its late start in planning for civil defence in cyberspace.[59] The top targets would probably include the ten listed in Table 3, many of which would also be susceptible to some form of classic electronic-warfare attacks. This list would not be highly dependent on any particular scenario.[60]

Unlike the US, China probably has not developed elaborate, computer-simulated scenarios for specific target sets. Nevertheless, China's Military Strategy 2015 indicates that the government anticipates widespread cyber disruption of its forces.[61] At the same time, Chinese military planners probably would not expect to have substantial strategic warning about where the disruptions would occur or how serious they would be for different types of units, systems and platforms.

From China's perspective, the upshot is that any armed hostilities with the United States or its allies must be as contained and brief as is politically feasible. There is clearly some tension between this imperative and China's overarching strategic priority – the use of all necessary force against Taiwan and its supporters to prevent its permanent separation from China, recognising that this may involve attacks on US military targets. To harmonise these objectives, and for other domestic political reasons, China wants to put off for as long as possible any use of force against Taiwan.[62] Thus, China sees the need for a range of coercive and subversive, but non-kinetic, measures. The crucial question it faces is whether it can apply such measures against Taiwan without provoking the US into unleashing its substantial cyber capabilities against the Chinese armed forces and economy. While Beijing probably assesses – accurately – that the United States would seek to preserve its most advanced and secret cyber capabilities for higher-level conflict, it would be prudent for China also to judge that the US would use low- and mid-level cyber assets in a non-kinetic contingency to deter Beijing from escalating.

Segal believes that 'both the United States and China have an incentive to use cyber attacks early in a military confrontation. In addition, there are strong incentives to use the attacks broadly for denial and punishment. Every network that can support military operations is likely to be targeted.'[63] It is sensible to conclude that every such network could be targeted, but Chinese leaders would be unlikely to do so except in the most extreme circumstances. China has far less incentive than the United States to conduct the sort of military campaign in which its overall military success depends heavily on success in cyber defence.

*　　*　　*

All countries, including the United States, have appreciable weaknesses in their cyber defences. But China's are greater than those of its strategic rivals. It has a much weaker cyber-industrial base than the US, far lower levels of nationwide informatisation, a less advanced and fertile educational system, and a smaller global industrial and economic footprint. In these circumstances, new technologies such as 5G exacerbate threats. Most importantly, China has no cyber military allies, whereas the United States leads an unmatchable cyber military-alliance network.

These constraints will shape how China conducts any war with the United States and its allies. China's cyber-defence weaknesses are not likely to be manifested in asymmetric warfare across domains, involving cheap offensive cyber weapons to degrade superior US weapons platforms and systems that China cannot match. Rather, those weaknesses will probably be most salient in the balance Beijing chooses among military assets, subversion, sabotage, disruption and political pressure to push forward its strategic agenda. In particular, China appears likely to avoid reliance on cyber strikes to disable US military assets and civilian infrastructure in favour of its better-developed assets of subversion and political warfare. In a war with the United States in the next decade, at least, China's weak cyber defences will compel it to minimise both large-scale kinetic engagements and large-scale cyber attacks on US military forces.

Acknowledgements

The author would like to acknowledge the assistance of Kai Lin Tay of the IISS in research for this article, and to thank Franz-Stefan Gady, Arthur Laudrain and Meia Nouwens for critical reviews.

Notes

[1] One of the latest quantum-communication achievements from China (working with Australian physicists) was the teleportation of multidimensional states of photons. See 'Quantum Teleportation Moves into the Third Dimension', *Physics World*, 7 August 2019, https://physicsworld.com/a/quantum-teleportation-moves-into-the-third-dimension/.

[2] There are eight other Chinese Nobel laureates, but those in science (four) earned their awards either as Taiwanese (two in the 1950s) or as non-Chinese citizens (two).

[3] In 2017, China had to walk away from its indigenisation plan for an operating system in favour of continued reliance on a special edition of Microsoft Windows developed for the Chinese government in a joint venture between Microsoft and a state-owned Chinese partner. See Iain Johnson, 'Redmond Puts Wall Around Windows 10 for Chinese Government Edition', 23 May 2017, *Register*, https://www.theregister.co.uk/2017/05/23/redmond_puts_wall_around_windows_10_for_chinese_government_addition/. Windows 10 is one of several US-designed software systems in common use in China providing security packages.

[4] See 'President Xi Says China Faces Major Science, Technology "Bottleneck"', Xinhua, 1 June 2016, http://en.people.cn/n3/2016/0601/c90000-9066154.html.

[5] See 'Bank of China Expands Relationship with IBM for Digital Transformation', IBM News Room, 27 September 2019, https://newsroom.ibm.com/2019-09-27-Bank-of-China-Expands-Relationship-with-IBM-for-Digital-Transformation.

[6] IISS, 'China's Cyber Power in a New Era', *Asia-Pacific Regional Security Assessment 2019* (London: IISS, 2019), p. 90, https://www.iiss.org/publications/strategic-dossiers/asiapacific-regional-security-assessment-2019/rsa19-07-chapter-5.

7   See, for example, U.S.–China Security and Economic Review Committee, *2019 Report to Congress of the US–China Economic and Security Review Commission*, 116th Congress, 1st Session, November 2019, p. 135, https://www.uscc.gov/sites/default/files/2019-11/2019%20Annual%20Report%20to%20Congress.pdf. The report says: 'China has made great strides in key defense technologies related to cyber, space, advanced computing, and AI, and is a world leader in hypersonic weapons. Nevertheless, Beijing believes China is still lagging behind the United States, noting in its most recent defence white paper that China's military is "confronted by risks from technology surprise and a growing technological generation gap".' On p. 287, the report continues: 'Central to Beijing's new military modernization goal is the view of top civilian and military leaders that the PLA continues to lag behind the United States and other leading militaries in many elements of military power.' Also reflecting this assessment is China's own 2019 defence White Paper, which notes that although China has made 'great progress' in improving its military capabilities, the PLA has yet to complete the task of mechanisation, urgently needs to improve informatisation and 'still lags far behind the world's leading militaries'. See State Council Information Office of the People's Republic of China, 'China's National Defense in the New Era', July 2019, http://english.www.gov.cn/archive/whitepaper/201907/24/content_WS5d3941ddc6d08408f502283d.html.

8   ITU Publications, 'Global Cybersecurity Index (GCI) 2018', p. 62, https://www.itu.int/dms_pub/itu-d/opb/str/D-STR-GCI.01-2018-PDF-E.pdf.

9   Paul Bischoff, 'Which Countries Have the Worst (and Best) Cybersecurity?', Comparitech, updated 3 March 2020, https://www.comparitech.com/blog/vpn-privacy/cybersecurity-by-country/.

10 Silja Baller, Soumitra Dutta and Bruno Lanvin (eds), *Global Information Technology Report 2016: Innovating in the Digital Economy* (Geneva: World Economic Forum, 2016), p. 16, http://www3.weforum.org/docs/GITR2016/WEF_GITR_Full_Report.pdf.

11 Cornell University, INSEAD and the World Intellectual Property Organization, 'Global Innovation Index 2019', https://www.wipo.int/publications/en/details.jsp?id=4434.

12 See China Legislation Standard, 'China Cyber Security Research Report 2018', 18 July 2019, http://www.cnstandards.net/index.php/china-cyber-security-report-2018/.

13 See Mandiant, 'APT1: Exposing One of China's Cyber Espionage Units', FireEye, 2013, https://www.fireeye.com/content/dam/fireeye-www/services/pdfs/mandiant-apt1-report.pdf; and David E. Sanger, *The Perfect Weapon: War, Sabotage, and Fear in the Cyber Age* (New York: Crown, 2018). Scholar and cyber analyst Thomas Rid doubted that the Mandiant team could have pulled off such a brazen 'hackback', and publicly questioned the accuracy of Sanger's account. FireEye issued a press release stating that Sanger had mischaracterised

the operation, clarifying that it had only exploited consensual third-party security monitoring, and Sanger acknowledged that the company's clarification sounded reasonable and that he may have misunderstood key details. See Thomas Rid, 'An Imperfect Weapon', *Survival*, vol. 60, no. 5, October–November 2018, pp. 230–1; and Morgan Chalfant, 'US Cyber Firm Denies Claim It Breached Chinese Military Hackers', *Hill*, 25 June 2018, https://thehill.com/policy/cybersecurity/393994-us-cyber-firm-denies-claim-it-breached-chinese-military-hackers.

14 See Glenn Greenwald, *No Place to Hide* (New York: Metropolitan Books, 2014); and Sean Gallagher, 'Photos of an NSA "Upgrade" Factory Show Cisco Router Getting Implant', Ars Technica, 14 May 2014, https://arstechnica.com/tech-policy/2014/05/photos-of-an-nsa-upgrade-factory-show-cisco-router-getting-implant/.

15 See Office of the National Counter Intelligence Executive, 'Foreign Spies Stealing US Economic Secrets in Cyberspace: Report to Congress on Foreign Economic Collection and Industrial Espionage 2009–2011', Homeland Security Digital Library, October 2011, https://www.hsdl.org/?abstract&did=720057. The US government had been tracking Chinese cyber espionage since 2003, as reflected in annual reports of the National Counter Intelligence Executive, but by 2011 the United States had radically upgraded its assessment of the scale and impact of the activity.

16 'Remarks by the President in the State of the Union Address', Obama White House, 12 February 2013, https://obamawhitehouse.archives.gov/the-press-office/2013/02/12/remarks-president-state-union-address.

17 See 'Xi Jinping Millionaire Relations Reveal Fortunes of Elite', Bloomberg News, 29 December 2012, https://www.bloomberg.com/news/articles/2012-06-29/xi-jinping-millionaire-relations-reveal-fortunes-of-elite.

18 The document trove was on a hard drive left in a journalist's post box.

19 The completed report was released in 2014, but details had been available on the ICIJ website since April 2013. See 'Secrecy for Sale: Inside the Global Offshore Money Maze', ICIJ, https://www.icij.org/investigations/offshore/.

20 For a summary, see Greg Austin, *Cyber Policy in China* (Cambridge: Polity Press, 2014), chapter four.

21 See 'Xi Jinping Leads Internet Security Group', *China Daily*, 27 February 2014, https://www.chinadaily.com.cn/china/2014-02/27/content_17311358.htm.

22 See 'Xi Jinping: Build China from a Big Network Power to a Strong Network Power', Xinhuanet, 27 February 2014, http://news.xinhuanet.com/politics/2014-02/27/c_119538788.htm.

23 State Council Information Office of the People's Republic of China, 'China's Military Strategy', China Military Online, May 2015, http://english.chinamil.com.cn/news-channels/2015-05/26/content_6507716.htm.

24 China Cybersecurity Industry Alliance, 'China's Cyber Security Industry Analysis Report 2019', December 2019, p. 2, http://www.

china-cia.org.cn/AQLMWebManage/
Resources/kindeditor/attached/file//20
191219/20191219092355_6832.pdf.

25 According to IBM, the 'company's
key differentiators are built around
three pillars – innovative technology,
industry expertise, and trust and
security'. IBM Security is described
as the 'world's largest cybersecurity
enterprise', with '8,000 subject matter
experts serving more than 17,000
clients in more than 130 countries'.
IBM, '2018 Annual Report', https://
www.ibm.com/annualreport/
assets/downloads/IBM_Annual_
Report_2018.pdf.

26 'China's Cyber Security Industry
Analysis Report 2019', p. 2.

27 Tencent Cyber Security Research Centre,
'Research Report on China's Industrial
Internet Security Development', July
2019, p. 19, https://max.book118.com/
html/2019/1011/6043232152002112.shtm.

28 Ibid., p. 22.

29 See Greg Austin and Wenze Lu, 'Five
Years of Cyber Security Education
Reform in China', in Greg Austin (ed.),
Cyber Security Education: Principles and
Policies (Abingdon: Routledge, 2020),
pp. 173–93.

30 Tencent Cyber Security Research
Centre, 'Research Report on
China's Industrial Internet Security
Development', p. 23.

31 Ibid., p. 19.

32 Chinese University Alumni
Association, 'Alumni Association
2019 China's Top Computer Majors
Ranking', 2019, http://www.
cuaa.net/paihang/news/news.
jsp?information_id=135786.

33 See 'Director of the Development
Planning Department of the Ministry

of Education: Should Explore the
Dual-Mentor System for Training
Cyber Security Talents', Paper, 17
September 2019, http://www.sohu.
com/a/341380535_260616.

34 Lu Yuanzhen, 'Respond to Challenges
and Build a Good Network Security
Ecosystem', Guangming Daily, 26
August 2019, http://www.xinhuanet.
com/2019-08/26/c_1124920850.htm.

35 Exploitation of 5G for cyber intru-
sions does not depend significantly
on the country of origin of the
vendor. According to the US-based
Information Technology Industry
Council, country of origin is only
one of more than 100 potential risk
factors to be considered in supply-
chain security for 5G. See Information
Technology Industry Council, 'ITI's
5G Policy Principles and 5G Essentials
for Global Policymakers', June 2020,
p. 18, https://www.itic.org/policy/
ITI_5G_Full_Report.pdf.

36 According to one military source, 'the
heavy use of civilian personnel has
become a common practice in modern
military forces and is the only way
to adapt to the new military changes
in the world. From the perspective of
the military of developed countries
in the world, the number of civilian
personnel generally reaches more than
half of the active duty.' 'Recruitment
Announcement of the Academy of
Electronic Warfare of the National
University of Defence Technology in
2020', 19 October 2019, http://www.
offcn.com/jzg/2019/1019/33384.html.

37 See 'The 24th Station of the 2019
Military Academy Admissions
Guide: Information Engineering
University', China Military Network,

21 June 2019, http://www.chinamil.
com.cn/201311jxjjh/2019-06/21/
content_9535184.htm.

38 See *ibid.*; Information Engineering
University of the Strategic Support
Force of the Chinese People's
Liberation Army, 'Strategic Support
Force Information Engineering
University Enrollment Plan for
General High School Graduates in
2018', Qianzhiwang, 8 July 2018,
https://www.zjut.cc/article-130162-1.
html; and 'China People's
Liberation Army Information
Engineering University Admissions
Plan 2013', Baidu Library, 3 July
2013, https://wenku.baidu.com/
view/6844bf552b160b4e767fcf31.

39 'Statement from President Donald J.
Trump on America's Cybersecurity
Workforce', White House, 2 May
2019, https://www.whitehouse.
gov/briefings-statements/
statement-president-donald-j-trump-
americas-cybersecurity-workforce/.

40 See Austin (ed.), *Cyber Security
Education*.

41 Trends in political relations between
Taiwan and the authorities in Beijing
are negative from China's point of
view, especially in light of the re-
election of the pro-independence
President Tsai Ing-wen in January 2020.
They have been deteriorating since a
high point when Xi Jinping met with
Ma Ying-jeou, then the nationalist
president of Taiwan, in November 2015
– the first such meeting since China's
civil war ended and the People's
Republic of China was established in
1949. See Brendan Taylor, *Dangerous
Decade: Taiwan's Security and Crisis
Management*, Adelphi 470 (Abingdon:

Routledge for the IISS, 2019).

42 See, for example, Rachel Burton and
Mark Stokes, 'The People's Liberation
Army Strategic Support Force:
Leadership and Structure', Project
2049 Institute, 25 September 2018,
https://project2049.net/wp-content/
uploads/2018/09/180925_PLA_SSF_
Leadership-and-Structure_Stokes_
Burton.pdf.

43 See 'The Full Text of the Report of the
19th National Congress of Xi Jinping
(record)', Sina Finance, 18 October
2017, http://finance.sina.com.cn/china/
gncj/2017-10-18/doc-ifymvuyt4098830.
shtml; and US Department of Defense,
'Annual Report to Congress: Military
and Security Developments Involving
the People's Republic of China 2019', 2
May 2019, p. 14, https://media.defense.
gov/2019/May/02/2002127082/-
1/-1/1/2019_CHINA_MILITARY_
POWER_REPORT.pdf. The Pentagon
notes that these goals appear regularly
in PLA documents.

44 See 'With the Tide of Intelligence
Coming, How Can Artificial
Intelligence Subvert Future Wars?',
China Science Communication,
13 August 2018, http://www.
kepuchina.cn/mil/news/201808/
t20180813_684798.shtml; and Yuan
YiWei and Guo Yonghong, 'How to
Integrate and Develop Mechanized
Information and Intelligence? "Three
in One" Compatibility', Chinmil.
com, 12 September 2019, http://
www.81.cn/jmywyl/2019-09/12/
content_9619072.htm.

45 Peng Guangqian and Yao Youzhi
(eds), *The Science of Military Strategy*,
3rd edition (Beijing: Military Science
Press, 2013), p. 164.

46 Zhang Yuliang (ed.), *The Science of Military Campaigns* (Beijing: National Defense University Press, 2006), p. 155, cited in Larry M. Wortzel, 'The Chinese People's Liberation Army and Information Warfare', Strategic Studies Institute and US Army War College, March 2014, p. 3, https://publications.armywarcollege.edu/pubs/2263.pdf.

47 Adam Segal, 'U.S. Offensive Cyber Operations in a China–US Military Confrontation', SSRN, 15 June 2016, p. 2, https://papers.ssrn.com/sol3/papers.cfm?abstract_id=2836203.

48 James S. Johnson, 'China's Vision of the Future Network-centric Battlefield: Cyber, Space and Electromagnetic Asymmetric Challenges to the United States', *Comparative Strategy*, vol. 37, no. 5, 2018, pp. 373–90.

49 Tianjiao Jiang, 'From Offense Dominance to Deterrence: China's Evolving Strategic Thinking on Cyberwar', *Chinese Journal of International Review*, vol. 1, no. 2, August 2019, pp. 1–23.

50 *Ibid.*, p. 16.

51 See Ren Meili and Du Na, 'Analysis of Network Offensive and Defensive Actions Based on Lanchester Type Equation', *National Defense Science and Technology*, no. 4, 2019, http://mall.cnki.net/magazine/article/GFCK201904021.htm.

52 Eric Heginbotham et al., *The US–China Military Scorecard: Forces, Geography, and the Evolving Balance of Power, 1996–2017* (Santa Monica, CA: RAND Corporation, 2015), https://apps.dtic.mil/dtic/tr/fulltext/u2/a621618.pdf.

53 *Ibid.*, pp. 281–3.

54 Andrzej Kozłowski, 'The "Cyber Weapons Gap": The Assessment of China's Cyber Warfare Capabilities and Its Consequences for Potential Conflict over Taiwan', in D. Mierzejewski and K. Żakowski (eds), *On Their Own Paths: Japan and China Responses to the Global and Regional Challenges* (Łódź: Łódź University Press, 2015), pp. 161–72.

55 Andrea Gilli and Mauro Gilli. 'Why China Has Not Caught Up Yet: Military–Technological Superiority and the Limits of Imitation, Reverse Engineering, and Cyber Espionage', *International Security*, vol. 43, no. 3, Winter 2018/19, pp. 141–89.

56 See US Cyber Command, 'Beyond the Build: Delivering Outcomes Through Cyberspace: The Commander's Vision and Guidance for US Cyber Command', Homeland Security Digital Library, 2015, https://www.hsdl.org/?view&did=787006.

57 See Cyberspace Administration of China, 'National Cyberspace Security Strategy', translated by China Copyright and Media, December 2016, https://chinacopyrightandmedia.wordpress.com/2016/12/27/national-cyberspace-security-strategy/.

58 See Adam Ni and Bates Gill, 'The People's Liberation Army Strategic Support Force: Update 2019', *China Brief*, vol. 19, no. 10, 29 May 2019, https://jamestown.org/program/the-peoples-liberation-army-strategic-support-force-update-2019/; and Wang Jun, 'Meng Xuezheng, Head of a Certain Department of the General Staff, Succeeded Zheng Junjie as the President of PLA Information Engineering University', *Paper*, 6

May 2015, https://www.thepaper.cn/newsDetail_forward_1328391.

59 See Munish Sharma, 'India and China: Warnings Ignored?', in Greg Austin (ed.), *National Cyber Emergencies: The Return to Civil Defence* (Abingdon: Routledge, 2020), pp. 60–75.

60 See Admiral Phil Davidson, 'Transforming the Joint Force: A Warfighting Concept for Great Power Competition', speech delivered in San Diego, CA, on 3 March 2020, US Indo-Pacific Command, https://www.pacom.mil/Media/Speeches-Testimony/Article/2101115/transforming-the-joint-force-a-warfighting-concept-for-great-power-competition/. Admiral Davidson notes that the US military goal in a war with China, and therefore the foundation of the US deterrence posture, would be 'penetration and then disintegration of an adversary's systems and decision-making, thereby defeating their offensive capabilities'.

61 This is reflected in the statement: 'In response to security threats from different directions and in line with their current capabilities, the armed forces will adhere to the principles of flexibility, mobility and self-dependence so that "you fight your way and I fight my way".' State Council Information Office of the People's Republic of China, 'China's Military Strategy'.

62 See You Ji, 'Making Sense of War Games in the Taiwan Strait', *Journal of Contemporary China*, vol. 6, no. 5, June 1997, pp. 287–305.

63 Segal, 'U.S. Offensive Cyber Operations in a China–US Military Confrontation', p. 13.

The Great Hype: False Visions of Conflict and Opportunity in the Arctic

Øystein Tunsjø

In recent years there has been an abundance of studies, reports, articles and statements presenting the Arctic as a new frontier for resource extraction and sea lanes of communication.[1] These studies claim that the receding Arctic ice provides not just commercial opportunities, but also security challenges that could fuel great-power rivalry and conflict.[2] Yet, despite the hype, there is little likelihood of a shipping bonanza or a natural-resource boom in the Arctic.[3] This does not mean that climate change is unimportant for the region – we can expect more shipping activity, investment and competition as the ice cap recedes. But it is important to maintain a balanced view of the opportunities and challenges presented by the 'new Arctic'.[4]

Equally important, the stakes in a changing Arctic are not high enough to warrant a great-power conflict. As in the past, it remains unlikely that military force will be used to resolve a conflict originating in the Arctic. It is more likely that any potential great-power competition in the High North between Russia and NATO will reflect the more consequential sources of competition and conflict in Eastern or Southern Europe – in other words, that conflict might spill over into the High North from somewhere else.[5] Developments in the Arctic appear to have caused some observers to forget that Russia's recent naval build-up is primarily focused on safeguarding traditional Russian security interests, such as maintaining its sea-based

Øystein Tunsjø is a professor and head of the Asia programme at the Norwegian Institute for Defence Studies at the Norwegian Defence University College. His most recent book is *The Return of Bipolarity in World Politics: China, the United States and Geostructural Realism* (Columbia University Press, 2018).

Survival | vol. 62 no. 5 | October–November 2020 | pp. 139–156   DOI 10.1080/00396338.2020.1819649

nuclear deterrent and contesting sea lanes of communication in the North Atlantic. Thus, it is a familiar security challenge – Russia's rivalry with the United States and NATO over the European security order – that has the highest potential for creating conflict in the Arctic.

Similarly, the recent focus on China's Arctic ambitions minimises the importance of the changing balance of power in East Asia as the primary source of US–China competition. Beijing's foremost security concern is the US response to China's activities in its own maritime periphery, but Chinese behaviour will also determine the United States' global strategic priorities. Sino-American competition will compel the US to prioritise the Asia-Pacific, and thus to draw down its commitments to other regions. This will constrain its options in the High North.

Since European states are unprepared to substitute for American power, Russian advancements in Europe and the Arctic will primarily reflect US retrenchment and European inertia, rather than improved Russian capabilities. Moreover, heightened US–China competition in the Arctic, much like heightened competition with Russia, will be a spillover effect of US–China rivalry in East Asia.

The new Arctic: land of opportunity?

One of the leading champions of the new Arctic has been the Norwegian government. It defined the region as a national priority in 2005 and launched an international diplomatic offensive to increase international awareness of its supposedly vast potential. In a speech in 2006 at the Center for Strategic and International Studies in Washington, Norway's then-minister for foreign affairs Jonas Gahr Støre declared that 'in the years to come … the High North will be one of the most important strategic areas in the world'.[6] In 2014 Oslo released 'Norway's Arctic Policy', which stated that 'the Arctic is the Norwegian Government's most important foreign policy priority', adding that 'access to energy resources and other natural resources is becoming easier, and new trade routes are opening up in the north. All this is creating new opportunities.'[7] Such claims have been echoed in other countries too. US Secretary of State Michael Pompeo, for example, emphasised in a speech to the Arctic Council in May 2019 that the Arctic is at the forefront of opportunity and abundance. It houses 13 percent of the world's undiscovered oil, 30 percent of its undiscovered gas, and an abundance of uranium, rare earth minerals, gold, diamonds, and millions of square miles of untapped resources ... Steady reductions in sea ice are opening new passageways and new opportunities for trade.[8]

This kind of public diplomacy, along with exaggerated media reporting, appears to have contributed to the circulation of imprudent claims and unfounded assumptions about the opportunities presented by the new Arctic – and about the likelihood of conflict in the region.[9]

Limits on hydrocarbon production

In 2008, the US Geological Survey estimated that 400 oil and gas fields north of the Arctic Circle accounted for 'almost 10 percent of the world's known conventional petroleum resources (cumulative production and remaining proved reserves)'. It also noted that 'the extensive Arctic continental shelves may constitute the geographically largest unexplored prospective area for petroleum remaining on the Earth', with an estimated '90 billion barrels of oil, 1,669 trillion cubic feet of natural gas, and 44 billion barrels of natural gas liquids' yet to be discovered. Most of these undiscovered resources (84%) were 'expected to occur in offshore areas'.[10]

'Offshore' does not necessarily mean 'up for grabs', however. Most of these undiscovered resources are thought to be located within the littoral states' exclusive economic zones or in non-disputed continental shelves in the Arctic Ocean.[11] The few petroleum reserves that might be in the seabed outside of coastal-state control will not be extractable for decades to come due to the high costs involved and the difficulties posed by 'severe cold, drifting ice, violent weather, darkness and remote location from infrastructure and markets of destination', as Katarzyna Zysk points out in her contribution to *International Order at Sea*.[12] Environmental concerns are also a constraint in a region with minimal capacity for spill responses.[13] All this suggests that the likelihood of energy-related conflicts erupting in the Arctic has been overstated.[14]

If anything, interest in petroleum extraction in the Arctic has cooled rather than intensified in recent years. The Shtokman field in the Barents

Sea was shelved in 2012, and the Prirazlomnoye field in the Kara Sea, the only Russian hydrocarbon-production project implemented on the Arctic shelf, produced only 3.2 million tons of oil in 2018, representing about 0.5% of Russian oil production.[15] The major Russian oil- and gas-production sites in the Arctic are located onshore, such as those on the Yamal Peninsula. Moreover, developments in the global petroleum market, such as fracking, oil-sand production and expectations of decreased global demand for oil, will undermine the profitability of drilling in the Arctic. Global natural-gas consumption is still expected to grow over the coming decades, but the shale-gas revolution has made offshore extraction in the Arctic less competitive compared to other production areas. Finally, growing concern about climate change is compelling governments and investors to shift funding away from fossil fuels and into renewable energy.

These trends suggest that a hydrocarbon-exploration and -production boom in the new Arctic might never take place. Moreover, any major future petroleum production is likely to be cooperatively developed and based on joint ventures.[16] Thus, there are few grounds for contending that there will be a 'race' or a 'scramble' to explore and develop petroleum resources in the new Arctic.

Limits on shipping

Increased interest in the Arctic and wariness about the potential for confrontation has also focused on the possibility of new shipping routes. Avoiding maritime piracy and cutting costs by using shorter routes between Asia and Europe – which are also touted as an alternative for ships that are unable to transit the Suez Canal due to their size – are often cited as potential commercial and strategic benefits of the new Arctic.[17] Yet the Northeast and Northwest passages are not economically viable or competitive in the short term, and are unlikely to become so in the long term.[18] Major trading ports in South China offer a shorter route to southern Europe and the Atlantic Ocean through the Suez Canal than through the Northeast Passage. The Northern Sea Route and the Northwest Passage are, at best, only useable during parts of the summer season, and even then, ships have to contend with floating ice, a lack of infrastructure and limited search-and-rescue capabilities. Winter darkness, strong currents, narrow passages and shallow waters make it challenging for large tankers to transit the Bering Strait or make full use of the new sea routes. Icebreakers will be needed for many years to come when transiting Arctic waters, even in the summer months, thereby driving up costs. Double-hull vessels are needed to take advantage of new Arctic sea routes, requiring shipping companies to pay a premium for insurance. Even with insurance, bankruptcy is a likely outcome should there be an accident or oil spill.

Since seasonal variations and floating ice will remain a problem, the Arctic routes cannot provide the degree of punctuality and reliability upon which the business model of many container ships and bulk carriers depends. The top priority of any shipping firm is that its goods arrive when scheduled and agreed upon with customers. If a shipment is delayed due to environmental conditions or limited icebreaker capacity along the Northern Sea Route, that will undermine the company's business interests. Some shipping companies are willing to take the risk, but most have concluded that for now, sending ships through the Northern Sea Route is not advantageous compared to traditional routes. The situation might change if the entire ice cap in the Arctic Ocean melts, but that remains only a distant possibility.

Between 2011 and 2015, 207 vessels transited through the Northern Sea Route. In 2018, only 18 ships made the Arctic journey between Europe and Asia, compared to the roughly 17,500 vessels that transit through the Suez Canal annually.[19] These numbers suggest that the Northern Sea Route is unlikely to become commercially viable any time soon, and that there is little reason to fear heightened confrontation in the new Arctic over sea lanes.

Minerals and fishing

Much like the Arctic's petroleum reserves, the region's minerals are mostly located onshore or in the exclusive economic zones of coastal states. Currently, there is little interest in mining activities outside these states' sovereign waters, and it is widely accepted that Arctic coastal states have the authority to develop laws and procedures for managing the natural resources within their borders. The littoral states can also shape the rules of international cooperation to facilitate and enhance search-and-rescue capabilities to promote commercial activity. As the ice continues to diminish and more areas on land and at sea become accessible for mining development, there is likely to be increased interest among states and commercial actors, though it remains to be seen whether mining and resource extraction in the new Arctic will be profitable. Moreover, the prospect for managing competing interests in the Arctic's onshore and offshore mining sector is strong, since the areas are already under the sovereign control of regional states.

The Arctic coastal states are seeking to defuse any potential confrontation or rivalry over unregulated fishing as well. In July 2015, Canada, Denmark/Greenland, Norway, Russia and the US signed a statement declaring that their fishing vessels will refrain from entering a 1.1m-square-mile (2.8m-square-kilometre) zone in the central Arctic Ocean.[20] Given that fishery agreements were achieved even amid the tension and rivalry of the Cold War, there is little reason to think that fishing activities will spark conflict today.[21]

China: an Arctic power?

Hype about emerging opportunities in the new Arctic has generated misguided claims about a 'new great game' and alarmist views about rivalry and conflict on the new frontier.[22] A stream of official reports, strategy papers and news articles has promoted the view that the region is ripe for conflict.[23] A report from the French Ministry for the Armed Forces, for example, referred to the Arctic as the 'new Middle East', while US Secretary of State Pompeo has asked, 'do we want the Arctic Ocean to transform into a new South China Sea, fraught with militarization and competing territorial claims?'[24]

The fact that non-polar countries, including China, India, Japan, South Korea and members of the European Union, have expressed interest in securing access to the new Arctic has only increased concern that the 'North Pole could become the world's next battlefield', as commentator Conn Hallinan put it.[25] China's growing interest in the Arctic and its supposed status as a 'polar great power' has been particularly alarming for littoral states, China's Asian neighbours and indeed the wider world.[26] Despite

China's self-styled 'near Arctic' status, however, its power in the region is limited, and its behaviour towards coastal states has been largely coopera- tive and free from challenges to their sovereignty.[27]

China has no military presence in the Arctic, and it is difficult to see how it could fulfil Eleanor Ross's prediction that 'China's Arctic empire will upset the global balance of power'.[28] Beijing has enhanced its mili- tary, economic, technological and diplomatic cooperation with Russia, but it is unlikely that Moscow will allow China to develop military bases in the Arctic region any time soon. China has sought a stronger presence in Greenland, but this is hardly enough to shift the global balance of power. Denmark, supported by the US, has pushed back against China's initiative. Chinese researchers have been critical of Norway's imposition of new con- ditions regarding research activities at the Ny-Ålesund research station on the island of Spitsbergen, but again, this is hardly a step towards a new great game or a conflict in the Arctic.

Small encroachments by China, a new superpower with growing global interests, could challenge the interests of smaller coastal states and the overall stability of the new Arctic. However, Canada, Denmark and Norway are capable of managing any conflicts arising from competing interests. Canada has effectively managed its dispute with the United States over the Northwest Passage, and Norway has similarly managed its maritime dis- putes with the Soviet Union/Russia.

Strategic and military investments in the new Arctic could potentially affect the balance of power in the region: China and Russia's collaboration on missile defence, early-warning systems, telecommunication and satel- lites is particularly worthy of attention. At the same time, however, Russia remains wary of any potential Chinese military presence in the Arctic. Meanwhile, China remains preoccupied with pressing challenges at home and in East Asia, meaning that it can give only secondary attention to its interests in the Arctic.

In its 2019 annual report to Congress on Chinese military and security developments, the US Department of Defense stated that 'civilian research could support a strengthened Chinese military presence in the Arctic Ocean, which could include deploying submarines to the region as a deterrent against nuclear attacks'.[29] However, Chinese power projection into the Arctic Ocean would necessitate sailing through the first island chain in East Asian waters and the narrow and shallow Bering Strait, heightening the risk that US and allied forces might detect any Chinese submarine activity. Once a Chinese submarine arrived in the Arctic Ocean, it would need to rely on cooperation with Russia to sustain its presence. It is unlikely that Russia would agree to such cooperation. It is far more likely that Chinese submarines will operate in the relatively secure, deeper waters of the South China Sea. Such patrols would be closer to home and protected by the People's Liberation Army's growing military capabilities. From these relatively secure waters, China could deploy its new JL-3 submarine-launched ballistic missile, a capability that could allow it to potentially hit the continental United States with a nuclear warhead.[30]

A legal and diplomatic framework for stability

Rather than hosting the kind of rivalry and conflict anticipated by some commentators, the Arctic region is actually characterised by a high degree of international cooperation.[31] Past disputes have been settled peacefully, and future differences are likely to be settled in accordance with international legal principles.[32] The Arctic's coastal states agree that the Law of the Sea is the appropriate legal framework for solving outstanding legal claims.[33] When non-Arctic coastal states have become observers in the Arctic Council, they have also agreed to abide by the UN Convention on the Law of the Sea (UNCLOS) and to not challenge the sovereignty of the littoral states in the Arctic Ocean.[34] China, an observer at the Arctic Council, has confirmed its adherence to international law for maintaining order and stability in the region. In 2015, China's Vice Foreign Minister Zhang Ming emphasised in a speech at the third Arctic Circle Assembly that 'the territorial sovereignty over the Arctic continent and islands belong to the Arctic states. They enjoy territorial seas, exclusive economic zones and continental shelves in the Arctic.'[35] China's official Arctic policy reaffirms this position.[36]

The Arctic is an area of regime-building and diplomatic cooperation rather than confrontation.[37] The Arctic Council is an important arena for managing environmental, scientific, societal, commercial and safety issues, and for advancing normative standards for managing disputes among regional states. In addition, NATO coastal states in the Arctic have sustained cooperation with Russia despite heightened competition outside the Arctic. Norway and Russia have consolidated cooperation over natural-resources management and coastguard operations in the High North, despite Russia's military intervention in Ukraine and involvement in the war in Syria. In collaboration with the International Maritime Organization, Arctic coastal states have approved the International Code for Ships Operating in Polar Waters – commonly known as the Polar Code. The Ukraine crisis of 2014 did not affect scientific cooperation in the Arctic.

While the effects of climate change are being felt in the Arctic region, the problem originates elsewhere. Moreover, the limited resource extraction, commercial activity and military operations taking place in the region are not a major contributor to global warming. This means that the challenges created by climate change will not be addressed through policies and developments in the new Arctic.

Challenges from Russia and China

Scholars and policymakers who are focused on the overhyped challenges and opportunities related to petroleum, shipping routes, military competition, mining and fisheries in the new Arctic may be overlooking the real challenge to the region: Russia's military modernisation and the country's re-emergence as a great power in Europe and the North Atlantic. Developments in the Arctic have prompted the reopening of bases in the Russian Arctic, and Russia has increased the number of flights of its long-range bombers in the High North.[38] The country's renewed emphasis on developing anti-access and area-denial capabilities challenges US dominance in the North Atlantic, especially given the US Navy's increasing preoccupation with China's growing military capabilities in East Asia.

Russian economic growth in the first decade of the new millennium, combined with fiscal and organisational stability, has allowed the country to modernise its Northern Fleet, which is tasked with preserving, defending and promoting Russia's interests in the Arctic region.[39] The Northern Fleet primarily focuses on 'bastion defence', a Russian defence concept from the Cold War era that aims to ensure the survival of Russia's strategic ballistic-missile submarines. Recently, the fleet has also taken up other traditional tasks, such as projecting power to other regions, and has improved its capacity to interdict sea lanes in the Atlantic, and to support Russian armed forces on the European continent and in the Middle East.[40]

The aircraft carrier *Admiral Kuznetsov*, which had not operated in the Mediterranean since winter 1995–96, has deployed to the Mediterranean on an almost annual basis since 2007–08. In 2016–17, it led a flotilla of naval ships to support Russian military actions in Syria. The cruiser *Peter the Great* and two *Udaloy*-class guided-missile destroyers have also increased their operations since 2007. Similarly, over the past ten years, Russian ballistic-missile submarines have been more active outside Russian waters.[41] By 2016, due to the decommissioning of older ships, the Russian fleet was more modern and at its strongest since the end of the Cold War.[42]

Nonetheless, recent declines in defence budgets and an emphasis on the Russian army in defence spending have left the Northern Fleet with limited capabilities and insufficient readiness. As one study on trends in Russia's armed forces notes, 'in the area of capacity, the Russian Navy simply does not have enough high-quality platforms to challenge the U.S. Navy and its allied NATO navies in a long, high-intensity naval war'. The study describes Russia's navy as 'a long way away from being proficient in the remaining mission areas of open ocean sea denial, sea control, and power projection from the sea'. It has few large surface combatants to accomplish these mis-sions, and *Admiral Kuznetsov*, its only aircraft carrier, will likely spend the next three years in dry dock for maintenance and repairs.[43]

NATO still lacks a coherent response to the Russian military build-up on the Alliance's northern flank and in the maritime domain.[44] Rolf Tamnes has noted that NATO's air- and ground-centric phase in the 1970s was followed by a maritime strategy in the early 1980s, and argues that today's challenges demand a similar, maritime-oriented response that builds on the air and ground measures implemented since 2014.[45] However, power shifts and new challenges could undermine NATO's response to more assertive Russian policies, including naval operations that can target NATO's bases and critical infrastructure in Europe with long-range, high-precision guided missiles, and that could undermine the security of sea lanes of communication and the strategic link between North America and Europe.

Meanwhile, China, while not equal to the United States in aggregate power, has narrowed the gap significantly and is emerging as the only peer competitor of the US.[46] In recognition of this, the US is gradually rebalancing its forces towards the Indo-Pacific region, a shift that is likely to constrain the US from strengthening its presence in Europe and the High North in the years to come. US–China rivalry will primarily be in the maritime domain, and will require a strong US air and naval presence in maritime East Asia.

In the European theatre, by contrast, the maritime domain remains secondary to the continental theatre, in which the primary challenge comes from Russian ground forces. Thus, the US Army might sustain a light footprint in Europe, but US naval and air forces are likely to be concentrated in the Indo-Pacific theatre. The US is unlikely to abandon Europe or NATO altogether, but global power shifts and US–China bipolarity suggest that a US forward presence to counter Russia's activities in the North Atlantic is likely to be, at best, a secondary priority for the US Navy.

As Russia modernises its military and China emerges as a peer competitor of the United States, it is highly unlikely that the US will continue to bear the lion's share of responsibility for maritime security in the North Atlantic. While NATO is aware of the Russian Navy's enhanced capabilities, it is unlikely that the Alliance will shift its focus to the Arctic region, or that European NATO allies will establish a strong maritime presence in the High North. US preoccupation with East Asia might provide Russia with more manoeuvrability and opportunities in the Arctic, but any conflict between NATO and Russia there is almost certain to originate elsewhere. Likewise, any clashes between the US and China in the Arctic are more likely to be a continuation of conflict elsewhere, rather than the product of any competition over natural resources or sea lanes in that region. Thus, traditional security challenges from Russia and the emerging US–China rivalry are more serious threats than any developments in the Arctic region itself.

Notes

1   See, for example, Jo Inge Bekkevold
     and Uttar Kumar Sinha (eds), *Arctic:
     Commerce, Governance and Policy*
     (London: Routledge, 2015); James
     Kraska (ed.), *Arctic Security in an
     Age of Climate Change* (Cambridge:
     Cambridge University Press, 2011);
     Heather A. Conley et al., *A New
     Security Architecture for the Arctic: An
     American Perspective* (Washington DC:
     Center for Strategic and International
     Studies, 2012); Rose E. Gottemoeller
     and Rolf Tamnes (eds), *High North,
     High Stakes: Security, Energy, Transport,
     Environment* (Bergen: Fagbokforlaget,
     2008); and Sven G. Holtsmark and
     Brooke A. Smith-Windsor (eds),
     *Security Prospects in the High North:
     Geostrategic Thaw or Freeze?* (Rome:
     NATO Defence College Research
     Division, 2009).

2   See, for example, US Department
     of Defense, 'Report to Congress:
     Department of Defense Arctic
     Strategy', June 2019; Chief of Naval
     Operations, 'Strategic Outlook for
     the Arctic, the United States Navy',
     January 2019; United States Coast
     Guard, 'Arctic Strategic Outlook',
     April 2019; French Ministry for
     the Armed Forces, 'France and the
     New Strategic Challenges in the
     Arctic', 2019; French Ministry of
     Foreign Affairs and International
     Development, 'The Great Challenge
     of the Arctic: National Roadmap for
     the Arctic', June 2016; Hal Brands,
     'America Is Losing the Battle of the
     Arctic', Bloomberg, 30 July 2019;
     and Neil Shea, 'A Thawing Arctic Is
     Heating up a New Cold War', *National

     Geographic*, September 2019.

3   See Oran R. Young, 'The Future of the
     Arctic: Cauldron of Conflict or Zone
     of Peace?', *International Affairs*, vol.
     87, no. 1, 2011, pp. 185–93; and Rolf
     Tamnes and Kristine Offerdal (eds),
     *Geopolitics and Security in the Arctic:
     Regional Developments in a Global World*
     (London: Routledge, 2014).

4   The term 'new Arctic' refers to the
     changes, opportunities and challenges
     that are emerging in the Arctic region
     as the ice cap shrinks.

5   See Svein Efjestad, 'Norway and
     the North Atlantic: Defense of the
     Northern Flank', in John Andreas
     Olsen (ed.), *NATO and the North
     Atlantic: Revitalising Collective Defense*
     (London: RUSI, 2017), pp. 59–74,
     65–6. The term 'High North' is not
     self-explanatory: it was introduced
     by the Norwegian government in
     the mid-1980s as a synonym for the
     Norwegian term *nordområdene* (that is,
     the 'northern areas'). It was adopted in
     official discourse when the Norwegian
     government launched its 'High North
     Strategy' in 2006. The term was then
     presented as a dynamic concept: 'The
     High North is a broad concept both
     geographically and politically. In
     geographical terms, it covers the sea
     and land, including islands and archi-
     pelagos, stretching northwards from
     the southern boundary of Nordland
     county in Norway and eastwards
     from the Greenland Sea to the Barents
     Sea and the Pechora Sea. In political
     terms, it includes the administrative
     entities in Norway, Sweden, Finland
     and Russia that are part of the Barents

Cooperation. Furthermore, Norway's High North policy overlaps with the Nordic cooperation, our relations with the US and Canada through the Arctic Council, and our relations with the EU through the Northern Dimension.' Accordingly, there are linkages between the High North and the Arctic, but we can still distinguish between three main areas in the latter: the European Arctic, which correlates with the High North; the Russian Arctic in Siberia and the Far East; and the North American Arctic in Alaska and Canada. This study primarily focuses on developments in the European Arctic or the High North. See Norwegian Ministry of Foreign Affairs, 'The Norwegian Government's High North Strategy', 2006, p. 13, https://www.regjeringen. no/globalassets/upload/UD/Vedlegg/ strategien.pdf.

6   Cited in the introduction to Tamnes and Offerdal (eds), *Geopolitics and Security in the Arctic*, p. 1.

7   Norwegian Ministry of Foreign Affairs, 'Norway's Arctic Policy', 2014, pp. 3, 11, https://www.regjeringen. no/globalassets/departementene/ud/ vedlegg/nord/nordkloden_en.pdf.

8   US Secretary of State Michael R. Pompeo, 'Looking North: Sharpening America's Arctic Focus', speech delivered at Rovaniemi, Finland, 6 May 2019, https://www.state.gov/ looking-north-sharpening-americas- arctic-focus/.

9   See, for example, Martin Breum, 'Cold, Hard Facts: Why the Arctic Is the World's Hottest Frontier', *Global Asia*, vol. 8, no. 4, 2013, pp. 92–7.

10   US Geological Survey, 'Circum-Arctic Resource Appraisal: Estimates of Undiscovered Oil and Gas North of the Arctic Circle', Fact Sheet 2008- 3049, 2008, https://pubs.usgs.gov/ fs/2008/3049/fs2008-3049.pdf.

11   See the introduction to Holtsmark and Smith-Windsor (eds), *Security Prospects in the High North*, p. 14.

12   Katarzyna Zysk, 'Maritime Security and International Order at Sea in the Arctic Ocean', in Jo Inge Bekkevold and Geoffrey Till (eds), *International Order at Sea* (London: Palgrave, 2016), p. 145. See also Kristine Offerdal, 'High North Energy: Myths and Realities', in Holtsmark and Smith- Windsor (eds), *Security Prospects in the High North*, pp. 151–78; and Betsy Baker, 'Oil, Gas, and the Arctic Continental Shelf: What Conflict?', *Oil, Gas & Energy Law Intelligence*, vol. 10, no. 2, 2012.

13   In 2012, France's Total and Russia's Lukoil pulled back from drilling in the Arctic over concern for potential oil spills in the frozen northern reaches.

14   See Dag Harald Claes, 'Arctic Petroleum Resources in a Regional and Global Perspective', in Tamnes and Offerdal (eds), *Geopolitics and Security in the Arctic*, p. 98.

15   Gazprom, 'Prirazlomnoye Field', https://www.gazprom.com/proj- ects/prirazlomnoye/. Russian oil output reached 555.838 million tonnes in 2018. Vladimir Soldatkin, 'Russian Oil Output Reaches Record High in 2018', Reuters, 2 January 2019, https://www.reuters. com/article/us-russia-oil-output/ russian-oil-output-reaches-record- high-in-2018-idUSKCN1OW0NJ.

16   Sanctions imposed on Russia in

2014 prevented cooperation with Western petroleum companies. Instead, Russian companies turned to China for investment and joint ventures. See Tom Røseth, 'Russia's Energy Relations with China: Passing the Strategic Threshold?', *Eurasian Geography and Economics*, vol. 58, no. 1, 2017, pp. 23–55.

17 It is estimated that the maritime route between Asia and Europe can be reduced by almost 40% using the Northeast Passage or the Northwest Passage. The distance between Rotterdam and Yokohama via Panama is 23,470 kilometres, and 21,170 km via the Suez Canal. By contrast, the distance via the Northwest Passage is 13,950 km, and 13,360 km via the Northern Sea Route north of Russia. See Frédéric Lasserre, 'Arctic Shipping Routes: From the Panama Myth to Reality', *International Journal*, vol. 66, no. 4, Autumn 2011, pp. 793–808; and Linda Jakobson, 'China Prepares for an Ice-free Arctic', SIPRI Insight on Peace and Security, no. 2, March 2010.

18 See T. Mitchell and R. Milne, 'First Chinese Cargo Ship Nears End of Northeast Passage Transit', *Financial Times*, 6 September 2013; Andreas Raspotnik and Kathrin Stephen, 'The Myth of Arctic Shipping: Why the Northern Sea Route Is Still of Limited Geo-economic Importance', Arctic Institute, 8 September 2013, http://www.thearcticinstitute.org/the-myth-of-arctic-shipping/; Arild Moe, 'The Northern Sea Route: Smooth Sailing Ahead?', *Strategic Analysis*, vol. 38, no. 6, 2014, pp. 784–802; and Expert Commission on Norwegian Security and Defense Policy, 'Unified Effort',

2015, p. 23.

19 For data on shipping traffic, see the website of the Center for High North Logistics (CHNL) at https://arctic-lio.com/category/statistics/. As of October 2019, there had been five transits in 2019.

20 Yereth Rosen, '5 Nations Sign Declaration to Protect Arctic "Donut Hole" from Unregulated Fishing', *Alaska Dispatch News*, 16 July 2015.

21 See Rolf Tamnes, 'The Significance of the North Atlantic and the Norwegian Contribution', in Olsen (ed.), *NATO and the North Atlantic*, p. 15; and Rolf Tamnes and Sven G. Holtsmark, 'The Geopolitics of the Arctic in Historical Perspective', in Tamnes and Offerdal (eds) *Geopolitics and Security in the Arctic*, pp. 36–42.

22 See, for example, Keith Johnson and Dan De Luce, 'U.S. Falls Behind in Arctic Great Game', *Foreign Policy*, 26 May 2016; Steven Lee Myers, 'U.S. Is Playing Catch-up with Russia in Scramble for the Arctic', *New York Times*, 29 August 2015; Scott G. Borgerson, 'The Great Game Moves North', *Foreign Affairs*, 29 March 2009; Scott G. Borgerson, 'The Coming Arctic Boom: As the Ice Melts, the Region Heats Up', *Foreign Affairs*, July–August 2013; Scott G. Borgerson, 'Arctic Meltdown: The Economic and Security Implications of Global Warming', *Foreign Affairs*, March–April 2008; David Fairhall, *Cold Front: Conflict Ahead in Arctic Waters* (London: I.B. Tauris, 2010); Richard Sale and Eugene Potapov, *The Scramble for the Arctic: Ownership, Exploitation and Conflict in the Far North* (London: Frances Lincoln, 2010),

Margaret Blunden, 'The Problem of Arctic Stability', *Survival*, vol. 51, no. 5, 2009, pp. 121–42; James R. Holmes, 'The New Great Game: The Arctic Ocean', *Diplomat*, 7 November 2012; and 'The Race for the Arctic', a collection of articles published by Spiegel Online, https://www.spiegel.de/thema/the_race_for_the_arctic_en/.

23 See, for example, US Department of Defense, 'Report to Congress: Department of Defense Arctic Strategy', June 2019; United States Navy, 'Chief of Naval Operations Strategic Outlook for the Arctic', January 2019; and United States Coast Guard, 'Arctic Strategic Outlook', April 2019.

24 French Ministry for the Armed Forces, 'France and the New Strategic Challenges in the Arctic', 2019; and Pompeo, 'Looking North'. See also Robinson Meyer, 'The Next "South China Sea" Is Covered in Ice', *Atlantic*, 15 May 2019; and Jeffrey Mazo, 'Who Owns the North Pole?', *Survival*, vol. 56, no. 1, February–March 2014, pp. 61–70.

25 Conn Hallinan, 'How the North Pole Could Become the World's Next Battlefield', *Nation*, 14 November 2014. See also Peter Giraudo, 'Forget the South China Sea: China's Great Game in the Arctic Draws Near', *National Interest*, 4 August 2014.

26 Anne-Marie Brady, *China as a Polar Great Power* (Cambridge: Cambridge University Press, 2017). See also Shiloh Rainwater, 'Race to the North: China's Arctic Strategy and Its Implications', *Naval War College Review*, vol. 66, no. 2, Spring 2013, pp. 62–82; Linda Jakobson and Jingchao Peng, 'China's

Arctic Aspirations', SIPRI Policy Paper 34, 2011; Vijay Sakhuja, 'Arming the Arctic', *South Asia Defence & Strategic Review*, 18 May 2011; Linda Jakobson, 'Northeast Asia Turns Its Attention to the Arctic', National Bureau of Asian Research analysis brief, 17 December 2012; Raja Murthy, 'China, India Enter Heating-up Arctic Race', *Asia Times*, 25 January 2012; and Per Erik Solli, E.W. Rowe and Wrenn Y. Lindgren, 'Coming into the Cold: Asia's Arctic Interests', *Polar Geography*, July 2013, pp. 1–18.

27 See Ingrid Lundestad and Øystein Tunsjø, 'The United States and China in the Arctic', *Polar Record*, vol. 51, no. 4, 2015, pp. 392–403; Christopher Weidacher Hsiung, 'China and Arctic Energy: Drivers and Limitations', *Polar Journal*, vol. 6, no. 2, 2016, pp. 273–90; and Tom Røseth, 'Russia's China Policy in the Arctic', *Strategic Analysis*, vol. 38, no. 6, 2014, pp. 841–59.

28 Eleanor Ross, 'How China's Arctic Empire Will Upset the Global Balance of Power', *Newsweek*, 14 July 2017.

29 US Department of Defense, 'Annual Report to Congress: Military and Security Developments Involving the People's Republic of China 2019', pp. v, 114, https://media.defense.gov/2019/May/02/2002127082/-1/-1/1/2019_CHINA_MILITARY_POWER_REPORT.pdf.

30 David Axe, 'China's New Missile Submarines Could Nuke America (or Not)', *National Interest*, 15 January 2020, https://nationalinterest.org/blog/buzz/chinas-new-missile-submarines-could-nuke-america-or-not-114211.

31 See Tamnes and Offerdal (eds),

Geopolitics and Security in the Arctic; Leif Christian Jensen and Geir Hønneland, *Handbook of the Politics of the Arctic* (Cheltenham: Edward Elgar Publishing, 2015); Oran R. Young, 'Whither the Arctic? Conflict or Cooperation in the Circumpolar North', *Polar Record*, vol. 45, no. 232, 2012, pp. 73–82; Timo Koivurova, 'Limits and Possibilities of the Arctic Council in a Rapidly Changing Scene of Arctic Governance', *Polar Record*, vol. 46, no. 237, 2010, pp. 146–56; Caitlyn L. Antrim, 'The Next Geographical Pivot: The Russian Arctic in the Twenty-first Century', *Naval War College Review*, vol. 63, no. 3, Summer 2010, pp. 15–38; Ian G. Brosnan, Thomas M. Leschine and Edward L. Miles, 'Cooperation or Conflict in a Changing Arctic?', *Ocean Development & International Law*, vol. 42, nos 1–2, 2011, pp. 173–210; and Andreas Kuersten, 'The Battle for the Arctic', *National Interest*, 3 November 2016.

32 In 2010, for example, Norway and Russia signed a treaty on maritime delimitation and cooperation in the Barents Sea and the Arctic Ocean. For an overview of the legal landscape in the Arctic, see Michael Byers, *Who Owns the Arctic? Understanding Sovereignty Disputes in the North* (Vancouver: Douglas & McIntyre, 2010); Alf Håkon Hoel, 'The Legal–Political Regime in the Arctic', in Tamnes and Offerdal (eds), *Geopolitics and Security in the Arctic*, pp. 49–72; and Ted L. McDorman and Clive Schofield, 'Maritime Limits and Boundaries in the Arctic Ocean: Agreements and Disputes', in Jensen

and Hønneland, *Handbook of the Politics of the Arctic*, pp. 207–26.

33 The five coastal states – Canada, Denmark/Greenland, Norway, Russia and the United States – stated this explicitly in the 'Ilulissat Declaration' of the Arctic Ocean Conference in Ilulissat, Greenland, 27–29 May 2008.

34 The criteria for admitting observers to the Arctic Council are available on its website, http://www.arctic-council.org/index.php/en/about-us/arctic-council/observers.

35 Zhang Ming, 'Keynote Speech by Vice Foreign Minister Zhang Ming at the China Country Session of the Third Arctic Circle Assembly', 17 October 2017, http://www.fmprc.gov.cn/mfa_eng/wjbxw/t1306858.shtml.

36 People's Republic of China State Council Information Office, 'China's Arctic Policy', January 2018, http://english.www.gov.cn/archive/white_paper/2018/01/26/content_281476026660336.htm.

37 See Olav Scram Stokke, 'International Environmental Governance and Arctic Security', in Tamnes and Offerdal (eds), *Geopolitics and Security in the Arctic*, pp. 121–46.

38 See Malte Humpert, 'New Satellite Images Reveal Extent of Russia's Military and Economic Build-up in the Arctic', *High North News*, 3 May 2019, https://www.highnorthnews.com/en/new-satellite-images-reveal-extent-russias-military-and-eco-nomic-build-arctic.

39 See Expert Commission on Norwegian Security and Defense Policy, 'Unified Effort', p. 18; US Office of Naval Intelligence, 'The Russian Navy: A Historic Transition', December

2015, p. xix; Kathleen H. Hicks et al., *Undersea Warfare in Northern Europe* (Washington DC: Center for Strategic and International Studies, July 2016); and Michael Kofman and Jeffrey Edmonds, 'Why the Russian Navy Is a More Capable Adversary than It Appears', *National Interest*, 22 August 2017. Kofman and Edmonds point out that the Russian Navy's principal missions are defence of Russia's maritime approaches and littorals; long-range precision strike with conventional and nuclear weapons; power projection via the submarine force; defence of Russia's sea-based nuclear deterrent; and naval diplomacy. See also Roger Howard, 'Russia's New Front Line', *Survival*, vol. 52, no. 2, 2010, pp. 141–56.

40 According to Vice-Admiral Clive Johnstone, former commander of NATO's Allied Maritime Command, Russian submarine activity in the Northern Atlantic is returning to Cold War levels. See Nicholas de Larrinaga, 'Russian Submarine Activity Topping Cold War Levels', *IHS Jane's Defence Weekly*, 2 February 2016; and Katarzyna Zysk, 'The New Normal: Russia to Increase Northern European Naval Operations', *Jane's Navy International*, vol. 121, no. 7, 2016. It remains to be seen whether Russia can sustain relatively high defence spending and maintain a strong emphasis on defence modernisation, patrols and power projection. Figures released by the Russian Treasury have confirmed that Russia's defence budget was cut by 25.5% in 2017. See Craig Caffrey, 'Russia Announces Deepest Defence Budget Cuts Since 1990s', *IHS Jane's Defence Weekly*, 16 March 2017. The

Russian economy is likely to struggle from sanctions, low oil prices and a lack of reforms for years to come.

41 See Hans M. Kristensen, 'Russian SSBN Fleet: Modernizing but Not Sailing Much', Federation of American Scientists, 3 May 2013; Hans M. Kristensen, 'Russian Strategic Submarine Patrols Rebound', Federation of American Scientists, 17 February 2009; and Kristian Åtland, 'Militarization of the Russian Arctic', in Mats-Olov Olsson (ed.), *Encyclopedia of the Barents Region*, Volume 1 (Oslo: Pax Forlag, 2016), pp. 475–81.

42 See de Larrinaga, 'Russian Submarine Activity Topping Cold War Levels'; and Zysk, 'The New Normal'. An assessment of the Russian Navy's ability to contest littoral waters and carry out anti-access/area-denial actions in the North Atlantic was not included in Barry Posen's seminal article on US command of the commons. However, compared to Russia's Northern Fleet, the navies of countries such as China, Iran and Iraq were less capable of contesting littoral waters in the 1990s and the first years of the new millennium. See Barry Posen, 'Command of the Commons: The Military Foundations of US Hegemony', *International Security*, vol. 28, no. 1, Summer 2003, pp. 5–46.

43 See Keith Crane, Olga Oliker and Brian Nichiporuk, 'Trends in Russia's Armed Forces: An Overview of Budgets and Capabilities', RAND Corporation, 2019, pp. 41, 44, https://www.rand.org/pubs/research_reports/RR2573.html.

44 NATO's response to Russian aggression in Ukraine established that the

Alliance remains committed to collective security: NATO has boosted its ground and air forces in Eastern Europe. This includes the rotational presence of four multinational battalions in the three Baltic states and Poland; rotational deployment of a US armoured-brigade combat team, headquartered in Poland; and the formation of the Very High Readiness Joint Task Force. See Tamnes, 'The Significance of the North Atlantic and the Norwegian Contribution', p. 27.

45 *Ibid.*, pp. 9, 27.

46 China's GDP and defence spending are roughly as large as all other East Asian countries combined. Even if India and Russia are added to the equation, China can match all these states' aggregate power. Russia's GDP, on the other hand, is roughly equal to that of Spain. Germany alone has a GDP that is almost three times larger than Russia's. If Germany had committed itself to spending 2% of its GDP on defence, which is the goal set by NATO, then its spending would have easily surpassed Russia's. GDP data from International Monetary Fund, 'World Economic Outlook Database', October 2019, https://www.imf.org/external/pubs/ft/weo/2019/02/weodata/index.aspx. It should be noted that the Soviet Union was never as powerful as the United States during the Cold War, which shows that power parity is not a requirement for bipolarity.

Iran's Grand Strategic Logic

Kevjn Lim

The spectre of armed conflict is haunting the Persian Gulf for the fourth time in as many decades. In response to the United States' withdrawal from the Joint Comprehensive Plan of Action (JCPOA) – that is, the Iran nuclear deal – and reinstatement of economic sanctions in 2018, the Islamic Republic has gradually scaled down its nuclear commitments under the deal and dialled up its use of force. It has downed a US drone, seized foreign vessels and allegedly attacked six foreign oil tankers as well as major energy facilities in Saudi Arabia, the latter through Yemen's Houthi rebels. In January 2020, following rising tensions between the US and Iran in Iraq, the US abruptly assassinated Islamic Revolutionary Guard Corps Quds Force Commander Major-General Qasem Soleimani, bringing both countries to the brink of war. This was the United States' first targeted killing of a top-ranking Iranian official; Soleimani was widely regarded as Iran's second-most powerful figure after Supreme Leader Sayyid Ali Hosseini Khamenei. Iran responded with calibrated barrages of ballistic missiles on US forces deployed at two Iraqi air bases, causing traumatic brain injury to more than 100 US military personnel.

Iran then announced the removal of all restrictions on its uranium-enrichment programme. While it stopped short of resuming 20% enrichment,

Kevjn Lim is a doctoral researcher at the School of Political Science, Government and International Affairs at Tel Aviv University, a research fellow at Tel Aviv University's Alliance Center for Iranian Studies (ACIS), and a Middle East and North Africa consultant analyst for IHS Markit. This article draws on elements of his doctoral dissertation, *Between Crusade and Crisis: Power, Perception and Politics in the Making of Iranian Grand Strategy, 1988–2017*.

Survival | vol. 62 no. 5 | October–November 2020 | pp. 157–172   DOI 10.1080/00396338.2020.1819651

the nuclear agreement's three European signatories responded by triggering the dispute-resolution mechanism before indefinitely suspending the deadline to refer Iran back to the UN Security Council. While the COVID-19 pandemic temporarily diverted attention, tensions continued to rise. In August, after failing to press other Security Council members into extending the arms embargo on Iran, which is scheduled to expire in October 2020, the United States triggered the sanctions-snapback mechanism, intensifying the showdown between the two countries.

Revisiting shaky assumptions

At the eye of the storm is Iran's grand strategy. There are two commonly held assumptions about it. Firstly, Khamenei, who has been Iran's Supreme Leader for the past three decades, has the final word in decision-making.[1] According to this view, the strategic orientations and external policies of individual elected presidents vary only in style rather than substance. Secondly, Iran's resources, capabilities and particularly its oil revenues drive its intentions and therefore its foreign activism.[2] The Trump administration has elevated this view to the level of gospel. The more funds Iran has access to, the thinking goes, the more aggressive and expansionist it becomes, starting in its immediate region. Both assumptions warrant re-examination.

The first assumption may be broadly true, but its corollary is highly questionable. Both of Iran's Supreme Leaders – Khamenei and before him the Islamic Republic's charismatic founder Ayatollah Ruhollah Mousavi Khomeini – have set broad national objectives and had the final say over external policy and strategy, which has ensured a consistency of purpose. Yet Iranian presidents – and, before 1989, prime ministers – alongside the political factions they embody have left unmistakable imprints on the country's grand strategy. In other words, changes in executive authority have accompanied substantive changes in grand strategy, under the same Supreme Leader and despite shared revolutionary boundaries.

On external if not internal policy, these factions generally split into two main camps over one central issue: the US and the international order it leads. Revisionists oppose the US outright and seek to revise the international order, placing a premium on confrontational diplomatic postures, military preponderance and a qualified degree of autarky. These revisionists comprise the hardliners, whether from the radical left of the 1980s, the traditional conservative camp with which Khamenei has often been associated or the neoconservative group that arose in the 2000s. Across the aisle, accommodationists prefer to tolerate the US-led status quo, if only temporarily and begrudgingly. They comprise the relatively moderate and pragmatic conservatives, as well as the reformists who had been the radicals of the 1980s. They favour playing by the rules of the existing international order and prioritise cooperation and diplomacy rather than force vis-à-vis the US and the West, with the higher aim of securing state and regime. None of this is to suggest that accommodationists do not compete, and revisionists cannot cooperate, with the US and the West, but in principle these are not typical opening positions.

The second assumption on means driving ends is an oversimplification. While an indicator of state power for any oil-rentier state, rising oil revenues often but not always correlate with assertiveness in foreign policy. Iranian regional activism was conspicuously on the rise, for instance, at a time when oil revenues plummeted and the country's GDP growth per capita contracted in 2012–13 and again in 2014–15 as a result of multilateral sanctions.[3] In fact, what crucially drives the strategic conduct of a state perennially lurching between crusade and crisis is perceptions of threat, especially from the outside, combined with factional preference. Indeed, variation in both – high vs low threat, and accommodationist vs revisionist dominance – has consistently produced four broad sets of strategic outcomes over time, with important implications for future behaviour.

Accommodationist dominance and threat perceptions

When accommodationist governments have coincided with low perceived external-threat environments, Iran has tended to prioritise engagement and, where necessary, some degree of retrenchment. At the start of his presidency in 1989, when threat perception had been significantly allayed with the end of the eight-year war with Iraq, Ali Akbar Hashemi Rafsanjani and the technocratic and relatively moderate, pragmatic government he led vigorously banked towards engagement with the West and even the US. At the same time, the war's destructiveness demanded domestic attention to economic reconstruction and military rehabilitation, the latter primarily to restore the country's earlier force levels.

A similar set of circumstances marked Sayyid Mohammad Khatami's first term in office from 1997 to 2001, when he went even farther than Rafsanjani by calling for a 'dialogue of civilisations', and by engaging directly with the Clinton administration and its European allies to reduce existing tensions. Facing low external threats at the time despite domestic economic problems, Khatami also pursued sociocultural liberalisation at home, over and beyond Rafsanjani's economic liberalisation, even as Iran continued to have a relatively light military footprint abroad.

Iran consistently advanced engagement

When accommodationist governments coincided with high perceived external threats, Iran still consistently advanced engagement. This tended to take defensive forms such as appeasement and bandwagoning, however, and did not exclude limited balancing involving military power. Unlike engagement under low threat conditions, bandwagoning and appeasement aim primarily to reduce threats rather than maximise opportunities. But they can have affirmative strategic dimensions: bandwagoning can occasionally seek profit, while appeasement might help defer conflict until it can be managed on more favourable terms, and is not necessarily capitulation.[4] Given their ideological commitments, revisionists are able to adopt such approaches only in extreme circumstances and at heavy political cost. Because reformists and pragmatic moderates are generally willing to accommodate the existing order, however, they can justify bandwagoning and appeasement as elements of broader strategic-engagement efforts.

For instance, when the 1990–91 Gulf War broke out, Rafsanjani's government remained neutral and reportedly even permitted the US to use its airspace, a move which in effect would have approximated a form of bandwagoning with the US against another adversary.[5] In 1995, Rafsanjani famously but unsuccessfully offered oil concessions worth $1 billion to US oil giant Conoco, originally slated for France's Total S.A. This was clearly an attempt at appeasement, since during that period the Clinton administration and especially Congress, then focused on the Middle East peace process, were aggressively intensifying sanctions against Iran.

Iran also continued to balance. After the collapse of the Soviet Union and the end of the bipolar international system in 1991, Tehran hedged against the United States' momentary unipolar dominance, and the ambiguity of relations with the George H.W. Bush administration, by pursuing external balancing through Russia and China. Having initiated arms purchases from these two powers to restock its war-depleted arsenal, Iran continued them to ramp up its internal-balancing efforts. Cut out of the Middle East peace process and isolated despite having once indicated that it would accept any peace the Palestinians agreed to (without necessarily recognising Israel), Rafsanjani's Iran shifted towards the role of a spoiler by backing Palestinian rejectionist factions, which was also a form of balancing and deterrence against Israel and the US.

During this period of Rafsanjani's presidency, then, Tehran favoured a defensive form of engagement and some rear-ground balancing. Given the rise in perceived threats posed by the Gulf War, the end of the Cold War and the emergence of the US as the sole superpower, Rafsanjani's earlier emphasis on proactive engagement and retrenchment justified by urgent domestic reconstruction was no longer tenable.

High external threats again confronted an accommodationist government at the start of Khatami's second term (2001–05), when the 9/11 terrorist attacks led to US military intervention in Afghanistan and Iraq. Tehran found itself increasingly hemmed in by a swelling American military presence along its eastern and western borders. Whereas Khatami could previously sell an engagement based on a 'dialogue of civilisations' alongside a greater focus on internal issues, once perceptions of the external threat changed – including those arising after the US bundled Iran into the 'axis of evil' and the disclosure of Iran's secret nuclear programme – so did the strategies required to meet the new circumstances.

Iran bandwagoned with Washington against the Taliban and al-Qaeda, and to a lesser extent against Saddam Hussein before the US invasion of Iraq, by cooperating on largely tactical security and intelligence matters. When the US seemed on the verge of targeting Iran for regime change in

2003, Khatami's government, with Supreme Leader Khamenei's knowledge, made the famous 'grand bargain' offer to resolve all outstanding bilateral issues with Washington. The Bush administration declined the offer. But it was clear that Iran had seriously considered a form of appeasement, which if accepted would have been the most consequential strategic adjustment by Tehran since 1979.

Still in Khatami's second term, following the controversy over the previously secret Natanz and Arak nuclear facilities, Iran not only agreed to negotiations with the EU3 (France, Germany and the United Kingdom) but offered what it considered voluntary concessions exceeding the requirements of existing agreements – appeasement by another name. These included temporarily suspending enrichment- and reprocessing-related activities, which exceeded existing Safeguards Agreement requirements, as a confidence-building measure, and provisionally implementing the Additional Protocol requiring increased information to and access for the International Atomic Energy Agency (IAEA). A 2007 CIA National Intelligence Estimate assessed that Iran had halted its nuclear-weapons programme in 2003. But the 'Atomic Archive' spirited out of Tehran by Mossad, if reliable, indicates that Iran also continued quietly pursuing internal balancing by maintaining some military aspects of its larger nuclear programme after 2003.[6]

In the following decade, amid elevated threat perceptions – crippling international sanctions, massive economic recession, diplomatic isolation, cyber attacks, assassinations and increasing prospects of a hot war – the pragmatic conservative and centrist Hassan Rouhani's election to the presidency in 2013 advanced negotiations that produced the JCPOA, which had begun with secret, Omani-mediated talks in 2012. While the US agreed to concede Tehran's key demand for an indigenous Iranian enrichment capacity, the short- and medium-term constraints Iran agreed to arguably amounted to appeasement.

Indeed, the JCPOA was ultimately about minimising Iran's losses more than maximising its gains. Iran had had an even bigger civilian nuclear programme lacking only pro forma recognition, and besides, India, Pakistan and Israel have attained military nuclear programmes with neither legal recognition nor the trauma of crippling sanctions. If Iran's objective was to produce a bomb, the JCPOA both pre-empted and significantly reversed its progress. If Tehran intended merely to secure a threshold capability, the JCPOA locked in its status as a threshold state. But if the nuclear programme was purely civilian in intent as Iran's leaders repeatedly assert – a matter of 'our honor, our independence and our progress'[7] and 'a leap … toward deciding our own destiny rather than allowing others to decide for us'[8] – it came at exorbitant economic and political cost. If the JCPOA collapses, given the uncertain legal status of Iran's civilian nuclear programme and that programme's ongoing economic non-viability, it is hard to imagine how the JCPOA could be a 'great victory', as former chief nuclear negotiator Abbas Araghchi put it, when Iran's fortunes differ little with or without the JCPOA.[9]

Nevertheless, having secured sanctions relief, Tehran could focus on the Arab world's uprisings and the emerging regional contest between the Shia 'Axis of Resistance' and the Saudi-led Sunni bloc. Tehran pursued a balancing strategy aimed at militarily defending its national-security interests and investments and minimising its losses in Syria and then Iraq. This combination of appeasement and balancing unfolded at the same time in different arenas. Over time, the balancing imperative morphed into what looked like expansionism, with Iranian military support extending not only to Bashar al-Assad's government in Syria and Iraq's Shia-majority government, but also to the Houthis in Yemen, where Tehran had relatively little skin in the game. Even so, the initial motivation behind Iran's intervention in Syria and Iraq was overwhelmingly defensive, not expansionist.[10]

Revisionist dominance and threat perceptions

The picture changes when revisionist factions dominate Iranian government. When they have perceived lower external threats, revisionist Iranian leaders have leaned towards a calibrated brand of expansionism prioritising political influence rather than military power, simply because the latter risked unnecessarily provoking a counterbalancing response. The most illustrative and indeed only example since 1979 is Mahmoud Ahmadinejad's first administration (2005–09), when the neoconservatives replaced the reformists in government. As Iran's own power and wealth grew and the United States' regional position weakened, neoconservatives abandoned their domestic rivals' earlier emphasis on bandwagoning and appeasement. Ahmadinejad's government instead embarked on a conspicuous campaign to maximise its political influence by showcasing its nuclear nationalism and scientific advancement, particularly its space programme. It also pursued comprehensive political, security, economic, religious and media influence inside neighbouring post-Saddam Iraq.

The Ahmadinejad government also sought to diplomatically enlist an international coalition including Latin American, African and Asian countries, even as it 'looked east' towards China, Russia and, to an extent, India.

Anti-Western radicals dominated Iran's external policy

This expansionism pivoted on the notion of Iran as the morally superior prime mover of a revolutionary resistance front and a reimagined international order opposed to the US and the West. Tehran in this period may still have sought to boost its military power and deterrence, particularly through fringe rejectionist Shia militias inside Iraq, including Kata'eb Hizbullah and Asaib Ahl al-Haq. But at a time when the external threat posed by the US was temporarily receding, military might was secondary to political influence.

When revisionist pre-eminence has coincided with high perceived threat, Iran has consistently preferred balancing strategies, again at times merging into military expansionism. Balancing was often accompanied by subversion or *astuce* – a lower-cost, lower-risk though potentially high-yield supplement to internal balancing through arms build-ups and external balancing through expanding alliances – especially salient when arms and allies were suboptimal or hard to come by. Subversion encompasses a wide array of measures including pay-offs or inducements, deception, covert operations and coercion through blackmail. What these measures share is the use of indigenous means to actively yet indirectly counter or blunt perceived threats, in a way that avoids open war.

For much of the 1980s – a time of domestic political flux and a brutal war initiated by Saddam – rabidly anti-Western radicals epitomised by prime minister Mir-Hossein Mousavi dominated Iran's external policy. To balance against Iraq, which had the backing of the US and other Western and Gulf governments, Iran acquired arms from external sources including China, and US-made weaponry from Israel, compensating for its lack of internal military–industrial capability and its unwillingness to seek alliances owing to its revolutionary rejection of dependence on foreign powers. In mid-1982, having recovered lost territory, Tehran decided to resort to total war to topple Saddam, thereby crossing the Rubicon from balancing to military expansionism.

During the same period, given Iran's relatively limited military power, the radicals also spearheaded ideologically based subversion efforts by exporting the revolution and expanding support for Islamic causes and armed groups. Under war conditions, subversion extended beyond ideational struggle to kinetic operations including terrorism, mainly through the Lebanese Shia militia Hizbullah, such as its suicide attacks in Beirut against US and French military personnel in 1983 and the US Embassy in 1984, as well as the abduction of foreign nationals, especially in Lebanon. Iran extended this form of subversion to Europe, as well as to Gulf states backing Saddam, notably Kuwait. Iran was also suspected of attempting to destabilise Saudi Arabia, especially in its Eastern Province and in Mecca during the hajj, and planning an outright coup in Bahrain in 1981.

About two decades later, around the start of the neoconservative Ahmadinejad government's second term in 2009, as sanctions, sabotage and the threat of war rose dramatically, Tehran again leaned more forcefully towards balancing and subversion. This was a shift from the Ahmadinejad administration's earlier emphasis on political expansionism, which it could afford at a time of relatively low threats. Between 2008 and 2012, China played the key enabling role in Iran's balancing efforts by maintaining arms sales to Iran.[11] During the same period, when Dmitry Medvedev was president of Russia, the other pillar of Iran's balancing strategy, Moscow downgraded ties with Tehran amid its own improving relations with the Obama administration, even refusing to honour an earlier contract to deliver the S-300 air-defence system to Iran. After officially applying for full membership in 2008, Iran placed even greater priority on the Shanghai Cooperation Organisation, which is co-led by China and Russia and hence often seen as a bulwark against NATO and the US. However, the bloc demurred, citing UN sanctions, just when Iran most needed an external, multilateral security guarantor. With arms and allies both uncertain during Ahmadinejad's second term, and having been the victim of the Stuxnet cyber attack and assassination attempts, both targeting the nuclear programme and its scientists, Tehran itself turned to various forms of subversion. These included cyber warfare, assassination attempts (mainly against Israeli targets across a sprawl of countries) and blackmail through increased arrests of foreigners and dual citizens in Iran.

Strategic adjustments

On only two occasions after the revolution did change occur simultaneously to both threat-perception levels and factional dominance. In both cases – Rafsanjani in 1989 after the Iran–Iraq War, and Ahmadinejad in 2005 with US regional power waning – the strategic adjustments were dramatic. More importantly, they produced 180-degree turnarounds in the way Iran interacted with the international community, especially the US and its allies.

Since the Trump administration withdrew from the JCPOA in May 2018, the relatively centrist Rouhani has again faced severe sanctions pressure and a spiralling risk of military conflict in the Gulf. Although increasingly constrained by its hardline conservative rivals and despite Supreme Leader Khamenei's objections, the Rouhani government has repeatedly left the door open to diplomacy. Rouhani's government has also occasionally hinted at a willingness to countenance certain concessions – appeasement if not bandwagoning – provided the US first removed its oil sanctions and returned to the JCPOA.[12]

At the same time, with US sanctions starting to bite, the IRGC has resorted to military measures, such as shooting down a US drone and attacking Saudi oil facilities, while Iran has revved up its nuclear programme before the time prescribed by the JCPOA. These moves are clearly intended to push back – that is balance – against the US and its allies, and to shape the terms of any subsequent negotiations with a White House so far unwilling to embroil itself militarily or otherwise in the region, with the apparently isolated exception of Soleimani's assassination. Tehran now has good reasons to count on Trump's defeat in the November US presidential election, and is therefore highly unlikely to seek appeasement in the interim, let alone another 'grand bargain', unless the US makes major concessions too.

Nevertheless, the United States' 'maximum pressure' policy has increased Iran's external-threat perceptions in the short term. Furthermore, widespread fuel-price-hike protests and tanking regime legitimacy – especially after Iran's inadvertent shoot-down of a Ukrainian airliner in January 2020 and its ineffective handling of the COVID-19 pandemic – have caused internal pressures to spike. For these reasons, change appears increasingly likely in the other key driver of Iranian strategic conduct: factional dominance.

By rejecting the JCPOA and attempting to force Tehran to negotiate a more comprehensive agreement covering its nuclear programme, ballistic missiles and regional activities, Trump has vindicated and empowered Iran's conservative hardliners. This has already had domestic consequences. In the 21 February 2020 parliamentary elections, backed by the Guardian Council's routine disqualification of dozens of accommodationist candidates including some incumbents, conservative hardliners swept the majority of seats in the first round of voting, taking back control of the legislature. While hardliners already traditionally controlled the security establishment and other key levers of domestic power and influence, including the judiciary and the media, a significant increase in their parliamentary representation lowers the bar for ministerial impeachments and vetoes against any presidential initiative in the final year of Rouhani's presidency. Indeed, hardline lawmakers have already attempted to summon for questioning the president as well as members of his cabinet, including Oil Minister Bizhan Namdar Zanganeh and Interior Minister Abdolreza Rahmani Fazli.[13]

US sanctions have given another political boon to hardliners. Sanctions continue to impede third parties from exporting drugs and medical equipment necessary to contain COVID-19.[14] US hawks including Secretary of State Mike Pompeo and National Security Advisor Robert O'Brien have reportedly sought to exploit Iran's beleaguerment from the disease by encouraging Trump to escalate military pressure. The proximate aim was to punish Iran for its support of Kata'eb Hizbullah, the Iraqi Shia militia behind ongoing rocket attacks on US assets in Iraq. The larger aim, however, was to force Tehran back to the negotiation table.[15] While Trump has demurred, the confluence of pressures could still prompt Iran to seek a diplomatic compromise.

It appears equally likely that Tehran will harden its position, however. Iran has rejected medical assistance offered by Washington. As a pretext, Khamenei has disingenuously speculated that US aid might be designed to prolong rather than mitigate the disease in Iran.[16] The real reason, however, is probably that the Soleimani assassination, on top of the United States' unrelenting maximum-pressure campaign, politically precludes Iran's accepting American charity. Hardliners have even pressured the health ministry to eject an emergency team from Médecins Sans Frontières, the Paris-based humanitarian organisation, which deployed in Isfahan with a 50-bed hospital.[17]

Future Iranian strategic adjustments

In Rouhani's first term, sanctions pressures together with the Obama administration's concession on Iranian indigenous enrichment paved the way for appeasement on the nuclear issue. Over the remainder of Rouhani's second term and beyond, for Iran to again countenance appeasement through some renegotiated or extended version of the JCPOA with supplementary constraints on its conduct, the Trump administration (or its successor) would almost certainly have to make 'meaningful' concessions. The only alternative is the credible and enforceable threat of a full invasion as in 2003, which appeared to prompt Iran's offer of a grand bargain.

Temporarily easing sanctions in a way that allows Iran's leadership to better deal with the pandemic at home may not make strategic sense to the Trump administration at the moment. But it would be the right moral decision. The administration has shown pragmatic flexibility on sanctions in other areas. Although it has now ended them, Washington previously renewed waivers allowing civilian nuclear cooperation between Iran and third parties, the idea being to maintain non-proliferation efforts that hinder Tehran from getting a nuclear weapon. And, though they have fluctuated, waiver extensions have also allowed an economically and politically fragile Iraq to import electricity and gas from Iran.

The Trump administration has claimed that it does not seek regime change in Iran. If that is the case, short of returning to the JCPOA altogether, relaxing sanctions (including those on oil exports) for the duration of the pandemic – which would relieve foreign suppliers of paralysing uncertainty[18] – might also be the most viable diplomatic off-ramp from military confrontation, as well as humanitarian disaster.[19] This could also be sufficiently short-term to continue, for now, deterring major commercial and financial concerns from the country. Other meaningful concessions to Tehran would be farther-reaching and likely unpalatable for Washington, at least as long as Trump is in office. These include acknowledging Iran's security interests and its status as a regional power; recognising the political legitimacy of the Islamic Republic; definitively accepting Iran's civilian nuclear programme and right to access peaceful nuclear technology; and providing US security guarantees against invasion and regime change so as to moderate Tehran's threat perceptions and reduce the urgency of relying on ballistic missiles and regional proxies. Conversely, a temporary lifting of sanctions could at least facilitate renewed negotiations, something Trump still claims he seeks.

* * *

During Khatami's second term, from 2001 to 2005, Washington rebuffed Tehran's reformist and hence accommodationist government despite its post-9/11 security cooperation and the unprecedented grand bargain that Iran proposed. That cold shoulder ultimately enabled the rise of the incendiary and reckless Ahmadinejad, who shared and reinforced the Supreme Leader's confrontational cast of mind. Ahmadinejad's was Tehran's first and, until now, only full-fledged revisionist government since 1989. In his first term, however, Iran assessed that the United States' power, influence and will, and hence the threat it posed in the Middle East, were declining due to its fraught Iraq intervention. This perception afforded Iran's leadership room to temper the military dimension of Iranian expansionism in favour of softer options.

If, however, perceptions of the present US threat remain elevated and propel the rise of another clearly revisionist, anti-US and anti-West president in June 2021, and especially if the JCPOA ultimately collapses despite the other world powers' efforts, Iran would be expected to bank hard towards a mixture of balancing, military expansionism and subversion. By then, as in 2005, Tehran would likely have little confidence in diplomacy as a first resort, having been scalded by the US. Iran's revisionists could still consider negotiations or detente. After all, although to little avail, Iran under Ahmadinejad offered direct talks with the Bush administration in 2006, actually brooked direct contacts the following year in Baghdad and again countenanced direct talks after Obama was elected. And in the Geneva round of nuclear talks in October 2009, Ahmadinejad accepted an IAEA proposal to transfer out four-fifths of Iran's low-enriched uranium stock, although the decision was taken on his own initiative and ultimately vetoed by Khamenei. But under renewed revisionist dominance, such moves would very likely come at a high cost. The Trump administration has in unpredictable ways deviated from decades of American foreign-policy practice. Iran, in comparison, might prove more consistent.

Notes

1   'Iran: How Ayatollah Khamenei Became Its Most Powerful Man', BBC, 9 March 2020, https://www.bbc.com/news/world-middle-east-29115464.

2   See Steven Erlanger, 'As U.S. Sanctions on Iran Kick In, Europe Looks for a Workaround', *New York Times*, 5 November 2018, https://www.nytimes.com/2018/11/05/world/europe/us-iran-sanctions-europe.html.

3   See International Crisis Group, 'The Illogic of the U.S. Sanctions Snapback on Iran', Briefing No. 64, 2 November 2018, https://www.crisis-group.org/middle-east-north-africa/gulf-and-arabian-peninsula/iran/b64-illogic-us-sanctions-snapback-iran.

4   See Randall L. Schweller, *Deadly Imbalances: Tripolarity and Hitler's Strategy of World Conquest* (New York: Columbia University Press, 1998), pp. 76–82.

5   Trita Parsi, *Treacherous Alliance: The Secret Dealings of Israel, Iran, and the U.S.* (New Haven, CT: Yale University Press, 2007), p. 142.

6   Ronen Bergman, 'Iran's Great Nuclear Deception', Ynet News, 23 November 2018, https://www.ynetnews.com/articles/0,7340,L-5412157,00.html.

7   'Revealed: Iran's 15 Deal Secrets', Iranwire, 13 August 2015, https://iranwire.com/en/features/1251.

8   Mohammad Javad Zarif, 'Iran's Message: There Is a Way Forward', YouTube.com, 19 November 2013, https://www.youtube.com/watch?v_Ao2WII6GDW24.

9   'Revealed: Iran's 15 Deal Secrets'.

10 See Hadi Ajili and Mahsa Rouhi, 'Iran's Military Strategy', *Survival*, vol. 61, no. 6, December 2019–January 2020, pp. 139–52.

11 Stockholm International Peace Research Institute, 'Importer/ Exporter TIV [Trend-Indicator Value] Tables', database, March 2019, http://armstrade.sipri.org/armstrade/page/values.php.

12 See 'Iran Rejects Suggestion Its Missile Programme Is Negotiable', BBC, 16 July 2019, https://www.bbc.com/news/world-middle-east-49011836; and Arshad Mohammed and Steve Holland, 'Iran Floats Offer on Nuclear Inspections; U.S. Sceptical', Reuters, 18 July 2019, https://www.reuters.com/article/us-mideast-iran-usa-zarif/iran-floats-offer-on-nuclear-inspections-us-skeptical-idUSKCN1UD310.

13 See Babak Dehghanpisheh, 'Hardline Iranian Lawmakers Back Off from Move to Impeach President', Reuters, 15 July 2020, https://www.reuters.com/article/us-iran-politics-rouhani/hardline-iranian-lawmakers-back-off-from-move-to-impeach-president-idUSKCN24G1VD; and Al-Monitor Staff, 'Iran's Hard-line Parliament Set to Impeach Two Rouhani Allies', *Al-Monitor*, 11 August 2020, https://www.al-monitor.com/pulse/originals/2020/08/iran-parliament-impeach-rouhani-allies-bijan-bangeneh.html.

14 Parisa Hafezi, 'Rouhani: U.S. Should Lift Sanctions If It Wants to Help Iran Fight Coronavirus', Reuters, 23 March 2020, https://www.reuters.com/article/us-health coronavirus-iran/rouhani-u-s-should-lift-sanctions-if-it-wants-to-help-iran-fight-coronavirus-idUSKBN21A0XJ.

15 Mark Mazzetti et al., 'As Iran Reels, Trump Aides Clash Over Escalating Military Showdown', *New York Times*, 21 March 2020, https://www.nytimes.com/2020/03/21/world/middleeast/trump-iran-iraq-coronavirus-militas.html.

16 See 'The Supreme Leader of the Revolution's Important Command to General Bagheri on Countering the Corona / Exercise to Counter the Possibility of a "Biological Attack"', Tasnim News Agency, 12 March 2020; and 'Following Khamenei's Remarks About Americans Reading the Coronavirus as American, an IRGC Commander Said that "A Specific Virus in the Iranian Nation's Gene May Have Been Made"', Radio Zamaneh, 23 March 2020, https://www.radiozamaneh.com/495446. Khamenei and other top officials have publicly suggested that the coronavirus's infiltration of Iran resulted from a biological attack by the US, perhaps one genetically customised for Iranians. This claim is obviously for domestic consumption. It is farcical to think that Iranian leaders actually believe it.

17 'An Official from the Ministry of Health Ruled out the Presence of Doctors Without Borders in the Isfahan Project', Radio Farda, 24 March 2020, https://www.radiofarda.com/a/the-team-of-msf-in-iran-has-been-canceled/30505015.html.

18 In January 2019, the EU established its Instrument in Support of Trade Exchanges (INSTEX) to support humanitarian trade with Iran, but only on 31 March 2020 – after 14 months

– did the first transaction take place, involving an Iranian purchase of medical equipment. Furthermore, while Switzerland and South Korea have either begun or are operationalising their own trade mechanisms with Iran in the form of the Swiss Humanitarian Trade Arrangement and the Korean Humanitarian Trade Arrangement, transactions remain highly sporadic and only for limited volumes.

19 See Mark Fitzpatrick, 'Sanctioning Pandemic-plagued Iran', *Survival*, vol. 62, no. 3, June–July 2020, pp. 93–102.

Worse than Nothing: Why US Intervention Made Government Atrocities More Likely in Syria

Richard Hanania

American leaders often portray foreign policy as a struggle between good and evil. Political science offers a more nuanced view. The literature on why governments engage in large-scale violations of human rights, including mass killing, demonstrates that violence is often a tool employed in pursuit of political goals, usually government survival and leaders' self-preservation. Mass killing is particularly likely to be employed in civil wars and insurgencies, in which governments face an existential threat from a domestic enemy. The greater the severity of the threat, the greater the scale of the repression. This has profound implications for US policy, which in recent years has pursued the overthrow of oppressive governments facing domestic uprisings. If the underlying power balance between the state and the rebels makes ultimate regime change unlikely, or undesirable because of concerns about what might come after, attempts by any outside power to boost rebels or deplete the economic strength of the state are likely to prompt a substantial increase in state-orchestrated mass killing. US support for rebels fighting Bashar al-Assad's government in Syria demonstrates this reality.

The United States' superior power emboldens Washington to pursue lofty objectives under the illusion that they can be cheaply attained. Among these objectives is the overthrow of dictators facing insurgencies through a

Richard Hanania is a Fellow at Defense Priorities and a Research Fellow at the Saltzman Institute of War and Peace Studies at Columbia University.

Survival | vol. 62 no. 5 | October–November 2020 | pp. 173–192   DOI 10.1080/00396338.2020.1819653

limited exercise of force along with economic pressure. The seeming imperative to do something about leaders whose forces commit atrocities relies on a logic that says, essentially, 'Why not? Things can't get worse.' This reasoning reflects a lack of imagination, especially in the context of civil war. By aiding the Syrian rebels and trying to strangle the government economically, the United States likely spurred worse abuses by President Assad's regime owing to its increasingly perilous position. That does not make Washington morally responsible for the crimes committed by the government in Damascus. It does, however, offer a stark lesson about unintended consequences and what not to do in the future.

Critics of the Obama administration's Syria policy often claim the United States 'did nothing' to stop the Assad government from slaughtering civilians to hold on to power. If Iraq and Libya show the dangers of regime change, these interventionists argue, Syria reveals what can happen when the US stands back and watches. According to the late Senator John McCain, writing in 2016, 'the name Aleppo will echo through history, like Srebrenica and Rwanda, as a testament to our moral failure and everlasting shame'.[1] Another observer similarly argued that in Syria 'President Obama serially failed to intervene – tarnishing his otherwise accomplished tenure in the White House'.[2] This argument is so entrenched that in 2016 the Brookings Institution published an article titled 'Why the United States Hasn't Intervened in Syria'.[3] The same year, Shadi Hamid of Brookings wrote that the fact that Barack Obama had not committed to doing more in Syria as the situation developed 'suggests an insularity and ideological rigidity rare among recent presidents', comparing him unfavourably to George W. Bush.[4] Last year, Paul Wolfowitz was given space in the op-ed pages of the New York Times to reflect on 'President Obama's failure … to support the Syrian opposition' when doing so could have led to successful regime change.[5]

This narrative is bizarre. It is true that the Obama administration felt acutely constrained from undertaking full-scale coercive regime change in Syria for fear of courting a political–military debacle on the scale of the Iraq invasion and occupation.[6] That said, the US not only intervened in a more limited way against Assad, but also worsened the humanitarian situation in Syria by doing so. From the earliest years of the war, the US imposed an economic embargo against the Syrian government and funded and supported rebels seeking to overthrow the regime. These actions accelerated the collapse of the Syrian economy and exacerbated a war that has killed more than 100,000 regime and allied forces, out of a total of around 585,000 dead.[7]

Moreover, the literature on mass killing indicates that the US not only did little to help the Syrian people, but also made atrocities more likely. The Obama administration faced a bad situation and made it worse, as indicated by the rising death toll after it began its intervention. Rather than seek to stop human-rights abuses through regime change when states face domestic uprisings, the United States should choose engagement and seek to end civil wars in ways that realistically take into account the power disparities between the various parties to the conflict.

The madman theory

Underlying the view that the US did nothing in Syria is an implicit belief about what causes atrocities. Those who think the US should have done more in Syria argue for a model of the world in which bad men do bad things because they are evil or crazy. In this narrative, little can be done to stop such actors short of removing them from power. Thus, even well-respected journalists and scholars call Assad a 'madman', 'sadistic' or 'crazy'.[8] He may be all these things. But this assumption leads to an unconstructive framing in which one cannot reason with such a person or change his incentives, and all that is required is the moral courage to face him down.[9]

Senior officials as well as pundits have promoted this perspective. According to former US Ambassador to Syria Robert Ford, Assad is 'evil'.[10] Before being expelled from Syria, Ford told his staff at the embassy that 'for once you are in a place where there is a huge morality play going on and you are on the right side of the issue and you can take satisfaction from that, that the sacrifices you are making are being made for the right reason'. When Victoria Nuland, then assistant secretary of state for European and Eurasian affairs, was asked whether Assad was a 'rational actor', she replied, 'I don't think anybody who … is guilty of the kinds of crimes against your own people that he's guilty of can be considered rational by any human sense of the word'.[11]

Certainly, the Assad regime has committed horrific atrocities. But while calling their perpetrators 'evil' may make US officials feel better and serve their political ends, doing so can also short-circuit sound analysis of their motives, leading to the premature conclusion that they cannot be reasoned or negotiated with, and counterproductively narrowing policy options. Once an actor is declared irrational, there is little hope of appealing to either his morality or self-interest to compel him to change his behaviour.

Scholars have investigated why governments engage in atrocities against civilians and reached more nuanced conclusions than those put forth by American officials. Among the most basic scholarly findings is that governments engage in widespread violations of human rights, including the murder of civilians, because they are seeking to achieve certain political goals, most notably self-preservation. In 2004, a landmark study showed that the key predictor of mass killing – defined as the deliberate killing of at least 50,000 civilians over five years – was civil war, and guerrilla warfare in particular.[12] The authors looked at 42 instances of mass killing between 1945 and the time of their paper, of which 30 (71%) occurred during civil wars. Mass killings, they found, are most common during guerrilla warfare, when states may lack the ability to differentiate between combatants and civilians, thus leading them to target broad swaths of the population. Other studies show that countries are also more likely to engage in mass killing when they are poor,[13] when regime elites are personally threatened[14] and when foreign states arm their enemies.[15]

Mass killing is rare

The literature consistently shows that mass killing is rare because states would rather not engage in it. A regime committing atrocities can find itself an international pariah, and it can lose whatever legitimacy it has among its own population. It also runs the risk that the military and other organs of state repression will refuse to carry out orders, potentially prompting the fall of the regime.[16] Poverty plays a role because mass killing is a relatively cheap way to deal with threats. Wealthier regimes can train their soldiers better and buy off potential enemies. They have the technology and resources to focus their repression on those who actually threaten the government through mechanisms such as smart bombs, intelligence gathering and well-functioning legal and judicial systems.[17]

The upshot is that governments commit atrocities at least in part because of their circumstances. Whether or not some leaders are deranged or evil, a humane US foreign policy would try to create conditions that make mass killing less likely, especially when a regime is well entrenched and there is no realistic replacement. Unfortunately, Washington's policies have had the opposite effect. The notion that Assad murders civilians merely because of who he is or the nature of his regime clashes with the fact he only began doing so in large numbers after the Syrian civil war began. There was no ongoing mass killing before the civil war started in 2011, but the number of deaths surged over the next few years as the United States more aggressively pursued a policy of regime change.

Even Saddam Hussein, who, like Assad, was accused of madness by Western analysts, behaved in a way consistent with the rational-actor model and academic findings.[18] The fall of the Iraqi regime in 2003 enabled researchers to obtain internal documents that shed light on the inner workings of Saddam's government. They generally found that the regime narrowly targeted the arrests and killings of its enemies when it could, using more widespread repression only during wartime and against communities that the regime could not penetrate due to linguistic or religious barriers, mainly Kurds and religious Shi'ites.[19] This result undercuts the view of supporters of the Iraq War who tended to treat Saddam's crimes as a matter of clinical psychology rather than an issue of incentives and political interests.[20]

Hafez al-Assad, father and predecessor of Bashar al-Assad, had his bloodiest month as Syria's dictator in February 1982, when putting down a rebellion led by the Muslim Brotherhood centred in the city of Hama. Elite troops killed as many as 40,000 people, thus ending the main domestic challenge to the regime.[21] Although the Syrian government has always violated human rights on a large scale, it has turned most brutal when directly threatened. It is also worth noting that for several decades, the most powerful domestic opponents of the regime have been Sunni Islamists, who consider the Alawite sect of the Assad family and many top officials to be heretical and worthy of annihilation, thus making unthinkable the idea that the ruling family and its allies would leave power voluntarily.[22]

How US intervention in Syria backfired

The literature on mass killing thus suggests that if the policy objective is to preserve life in a state facing internal rebellion, providing assistance to the opposition should be avoided. An external actor should instead try to make sure there is as little damage to the economy as possible, and lines of communication should remain open. In the case of Syria's civil war, the US did almost precisely the opposite.

While the US did not itself arrest or kill the leaders of the Syrian regime – as it did in Iraq and Libya – it did seek the removal of the government and armed its enemies. Widespread protests against the regime began in March 2011; by August of that year Obama had declared that 'Assad must go'.[23] This likely motivated the rebels to resist the government more actively, on the assumption that the US might repeat its intervention in Libya and militarily overthrow Assad's government. The US Embassy was closed, thus ensuring the diminution of Washington's influence over Damascus.

At that time, the US was seeking to refer the situation in Syria to the International Criminal Court at The Hague, a process that ultimately failed due to Chinese and Russian vetoes in the United Nations Security Council. Had the effort succeeded, it might have been less feasible for high-level regime officials to seek asylum abroad as part of any peace deal.[24] In the event, the threat of imprisonment or death due to American intervention was sure to have a large impact on the Assad regime's calculus. The US had already fought a war that led to the execution of Saddam and was in the process of bombing the government of Muammar Gadhafi, whom rebel forces would kill following NATO airstrikes on his convoy in October 2011.[25]

In 2012, the US began arming and training Syrian rebels directly. In theory, this was supposed to help only 'moderate rebels' rather than Islamists. According to the mass-killing literature, however, any armed threat to a regime makes atrocities against the civilian population more likely. Furthermore, the programme perhaps inevitably did end up helping Islamists, who have been the main force opposing the Assad regime for decades. US officials never provided a credible explanation of how rebels would be vetted, with CIA operatives telling journalists that it was practically impossible to do it.[26] The US ended up relying largely on Turkey, Qatar and Saudi Arabia – states known to support Sunni Islamist factions – to run US-supplied armaments to the rebels.[27] It was thus unsurprising when reports emerged that American weaponry had wound up in the hands of al-Qaeda and the Islamic State (ISIS), crucially aiding in the success of those organisations in Syria.[28] According to a 2017 report funded by the European Union, 'international weapon supplies to factions in the Syrian conflict have significantly augmented the quantity and quality of weapons available to [ISIS] forces', with one anti-tank guided-missile weapon having ended up in the hands of ISIS within two months of leaving a European factory via the American programme to send weapons to the conflict zone.[29] In August 2017, the US finally ended its effort to arm and train Syrian rebels.[30] By then, the project had been one of the costliest in the history of the CIA, at about $1 billion. Another $500-million Pentagon programme to train Syrian forces was cancelled in 2015 after producing no more than a few dozen fighters.[31]

Given that the United States could not build governments in Iraq and Afghanistan that could withstand pressure from non-state actors even after years of occupation, it is highly unlikely that a US-led effort could have overthrown the regime and produced a friendly new government in Damascus that could establish control over the entire country. After the US left Iraq in 2011, that nation's army lost territory to ISIS within a few years. American leaders to this day worry that a US withdrawal from Afghanistan would lead to a comprehensive Taliban victory. From this perspective, solutions like Kenneth Pollack's 2014 idea of training an army outside of Syria to overthrow a functioning state and establish control of the country seems like pure fantasy, especially in light of Iranian and Russian support for the Assad regime.[32] In a part of the world in which efforts at coercive regime change have been disastrous, Syria's large army, religious and ethnic divides, foreign allies, minority rule and history of Sunni-fundamentalist opposition made it perhaps the worst candidate of all.

Even officials within the Obama administration recognised the futility of their efforts. According to Ben Rhodes, General David Petraeus, then director of the CIA and one of the main backers of arming the rebels, did not believe that the American assistance programme would change the course of the civil war, but rather that it would allow the US to 'build relationships' with the opposition.[33] Why it was important to build relationships with a force that had no chance of winning remains a mystery. The humanitarian costs of intensifying a civil war without changing the results were overlooked or disregarded.

Concurrent with the 2011 announcement that Assad must go, the Obama administration froze all Syrian assets under US control, barred the importation of Syrian oil and largely prohibited any US citizen or company from doing business with or investing in Syria.[34] The EU followed suit by banning the importation of Syrian oil in September 2011. This was particularly damaging, as Damascus was then sending 95% of its oil exports to Europe.[35] Unlike the project to find and arm moderate rebels, the attempt to choke off the Syrian economy achieved its immediate aim. Between 2010 and 2015, the Syrian economy contracted by an estimated 57% in real terms, worse than the shrinkage of Japan's and Germany's economies over the course of the Second World War.[36]

To what end? Hillary Clinton, secretary of state during much of the period, promised that the sanctions imposed would 'strike at the heart of the regime' by eliminating its ability to fund its security forces.[37] Trying to eliminate a regime's ability to make war may make sense in the context of a great-power arms race, in which the two sides are in technological competition and one party can outspend the other. In the context of a civil war, however, the military costs are lower, and regime spending on repression will take priority over all else when the target state is confronted by existential threats, real and perceived.

Instead of becoming unable to defend itself, a government deprived of funds is likely to become more brutal and indifferent to the suffering of its people, and more willing to take extreme measures to survive and stay in power. In the mid-1990s, North Korea suffered a famine in which the death toll may have run into the millions, but the Kim dynasty did not face a serious threat.[38] Saddam was hit with some of the most crushing sanctions the world had ever seen, but he remained in power until his regime was directly overthrown by the US military in 2003.[39]

Governments facing civil war have been known to entice young men to fight by allowing them to plunder civilians and regime opponents – a policy that costs the state practically nothing.[40] This may have happened in the Syrian conflict, in which the regime relied on the shabiha militia, a pro-government force accused of widespread human-rights violations.[41] States with dwindling resources may find this kind of dispensation attractive, and it leads to greater abuse of the civilian population than a professional military would likely perpetrate. In addition, Iran and Russia increased their support for Syria as the US ramped up its anti-Assad efforts. This dynamic further invalidates the argument that sanctions could have ever led to the collapse of the Assad regime.[42] Alongside those who have been murdered, thousands of prisoners have died due to disease and malnutrition; some might still be alive if the government had been able to afford higher-quality facilities.[43]

The US has armed rebels

A country commits fewer atrocities when it is wealthier, foreigners do not arm rebels and the threat to the government is low. US policy, however, has worked to ensure that Syria stays as poor as possible and, until recent years, has armed rebels to increase the threat to the regime. In August 2011, an estimated 2,000 civilians had been killed in Syria. The total number of dead is now thought to be as high as 585,000.[44] Figure 1 suggests a positive correlation between Washington's efforts towards regime change, including supplying arms to rebels, and Syrian deaths.

The figure shows the total number of Syrians – including combatants and civilians – killed by year according to the Syrian Observatory for Human Rights.[45] In all of 2011, there were 7,841 deaths resulting from the Syrian civil war. The next year, the US adopted a policy of regime change and through a covert CIA-run programme known as 'Timber Sycamore' began arming and training rebels in coordination with other governments, including Saudi Arabia, Qatar, Turkey and Jordan. The programme was established in substantial part because the United States believed that the regional states would supply Syrian rebels in any event, and wanted to exercise control over the types of weapons supplied and which groups got them – and, in particular, to keep lethal arms out of the hands of jihadist groups.[46]

Figure 1: **Annual deaths in the Syrian civil war**

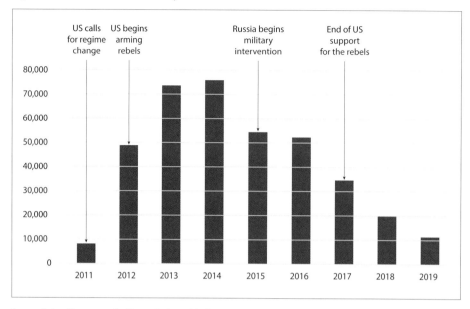

Source: Syrian Observatory for Human Rights. Table does not include the approximately 200,000 undocumented deaths across that time period.

The death toll in 2012 increased by more than six times to 49,361. In each of the two years after that, the number killed was more than nine times what it was in 2011, reaching a peak of more than 76,000 in 2014.

During this period, other governments also provided weapons to Syrian rebels through their own channels, so it is analytically difficult to disentangle the effects of those efforts from that of the US-coordinated one.[47] But the larger point is that when the US was most intensely engaged in arming rebels to overthrow the Assad regime, total deaths peaked. The Russian intervention, beginning in September 2015, coincided with a decline in the death rate. By 2017, it had dropped by 55% from its peak, to 34,700. As the government continued to establish control over the country, the total number of Syrians killed fell a further 42% in 2018, finally reaching 11,244 in 2019, the lowest of any year since the civil war began. The death toll in Syria has been highest when the US has been most involved, lowest when it has stepped back and done less.

This pattern is the opposite of what the madman theory of mass killing would predict. If Assad kills simply because he is evil or irrational, then he would kill more Syrians as he gains control over the country and is logistically more capable of slaughtering his enemies. Instead, the data suggests that the involvement of outside powers, including the US, on the side of the rebels probably exacerbated the violence and may have led to a death count orders of magnitude above what it otherwise would have been. Neither social scientists nor anyone else, of course, can say with certainty what would have happened if the US had not pursued regime change in Syria, however half-heartedly. But we can draw a strong inference that the US policy of economic warfare and pressuring the regime in Syria accelerated the deterioration of the humanitarian situation. The fact that the death toll increased precipitously in the aftermath of US intervention provides further confidence in this assessment.

Dealing with future uprisings

The US continues to have adversarial relationships with many dictatorships, some of which may face domestic uprisings in the future. When they do, decisions made in Washington will have major consequences for civilians in those nations, for nearby countries and for some Americans. According to Jay Solomon, the CIA 'has contingency plans for supporting democratic uprisings anywhere in the world. This includes providing dissidents with communications, money, and in extreme cases even arms.'[48] Although a large-scale invasion like that of Iraq in 2003, involving tens or hundreds of thousands of American troops, is unlikely in the near future, the US may be tempted to apply the same tools it used in Syria to try to overthrow the Assad government – that is, economic strangulation and arming rebels. This would become more likely if US leaders continued to believe, wrongly, that Syria was lost to Assad's depredations because the US did nothing. Even today, although it has ceased arming rebels who seek to overthrow the regime, the US is continuing its economic blockade and maintaining a troop presence that occupies a large portion of Syria, including oilfields, in an apparent effort to prevent the Assad regime from regaining territory and increasing state revenue.[49] Moreover, the United States' 'maximum pressure' campaign against Iran mirrors the efforts against Syria in practically every way other than the arming of rebels.

A proper understanding of what happened in Syria counsels against the interpretation of events favoured by interventionists. To avoid making bad situations worse, the US should absorb four lessons from its ineffective Syria policy. Firstly, foreign leaders, even those who commit atrocities, should be presumed rational actors unless there is strong evidence to the contrary. The academic literature on mass killings makes it clear that governments commit evil acts for self-interested reasons. Acknowledging the rationality of foreign leaders does not mean morally justifying their actions. Rather, it allows clearer thinking about how to incentivise them to adopt policies that cause the least harm possible to their civilian populations.

Foreign leaders should be presumed rational

Secondly, the US should understand that regime change is not the antidote to government atrocities. Rather, it is more likely to exacerbate mass violence. While dictatorship is common, mass killing is rare and tends to occur when leaders face political or personal threats. US policy currently works to amplify both by demanding that regimes leave power and that their leaders face personal consequences for their actions. The US was unable to protect religious minorities during its occupation of Iraq despite, at one point, having more than 150,000 troops in-country. Clearly Washington could not have made any credible guarantees to Assad and his supporters among the non-Sunni population of Syria that they would be protected in the event that its policy of regime change succeeded.

Acknowledging that Assad was unlikely to leave power or lose his base of support would have produced clearer thinking about what to do in Syria. Attempts to impose democratic change from abroad have rarely been successful, especially when, as in the case of Syria, states are poor and lack a history of democratic institutions.[50] The debate over whether the Obama administration should have done more in Iran during the Green Revolution of 2009 was similar to the discussion about Syria. In both cases, advocates of regime change offered no plausible explanation of how efforts to topple the state would lead to effective and humane governance instead of simply turning up the pressure on the regime and making it more brutal.[51]

Thirdly, Washington should cease trying to economically debilitate regimes facing domestic uprisings. The idea that a government that prioritises staying in power above all else, once deprived of resources, will be unable to sustain its armed forces or maintain their loyalty has only a tenuous basis in historical experience. Sanctions can have the opposite of their intended effect, causing the targeted regime to rely on cruder methods of repression that fail to distinguish between peaceful civilians and those that genuinely threaten the regime. Regardless of the geopolitical consequences, such policies tend to hurt the people of the targeted country. In Syria, the economic embargo aimed at the Assad regime has immiserated the population and hindered the delivery of food and medical aid, as Western banks and other businesses seek to avoid having anything to do with the country. According to *The Intercept*, a leaked internal UN email indicated that sanctions have been a 'principal factor' in the decline of the Syrian healthcare system, while contributing to increases in the price of fuel and basic foodstuffs.[52]

Finally, a policy of engagement is better than one of isolation. When Obama declared that Assad must go and began the American embargo, there had only been an estimated 2,000 civilian deaths in Syria. As the death toll has climbed into the hundreds of thousands, the US has been left with few realistic options for ratcheting up the pressure against Damascus, or even for discussing the issues involved with the regime. Although Washington did make genuine and serious diplomatic efforts to engage the regime alongside the external Syrian opposition, US terms always implicitly included Assad's eventual departure, which doomed its efforts in both Damascus and at the UN Security Council.[53] Every other power in the region – even those once seeking regime change – has found it useful to negotiate directly with the Assad government. But the US still effectively treats regime change as a precondition for talks.[54]

Engagement would not only help advance an ultimate settlement to the Syrian civil war, but also protect human rights. Even in the midst of conflicts, the US has historically pressured its allies towards positions that are more in accord with human-rights standards, as it did when it pushed the Netherlands to halt offensives against Indonesian rebels and eventually grant its colony independence after the Second World War.[55] While Syria is not the Netherlands, the US is often able to pressure even dictators with whom it has relationships, as it has done with Sunni Gulf leaders in facilitating the release of political prisoners.[56] In other words, the US can leverage its power to promote better human-rights practices. Working with Russia and Iran could generate greater pressure on the Assad regime to that end. Instead of demanding that the current government step down, which would likely require killing or imprisoning Assad and others, US power could be used to achieve more realistic and productive goals, such as winding down the civil war and preventing the most serious human-rights abuses.

*   *   *

For too long, Washington has pursued policies in the Middle East that are based on wishful thinking and divorced from a thorough and assimilated understanding of what social science says about mass killing and civil war. While ultimate moral responsibility lies with those who commit atrocities, US policy can help shape the conditions that make such acts more or less likely. In imposing economic sanctions and pursuing regime change, American leaders have inadvertently incentivised mass killing and other forms of civilian victimisation. The enduring myth that the United States stood back and did nothing in Syria should be soundly rejected, and precluded from serving as a justification for similar mistakes in the future.

Notes

1   John McCain, 'We Have a Stake in Syria, Yet We Have Done Nothing', *Washington Post*, 22 December 2016, https://www.washingtonpost.com/opinions/john-mccain-we-have-a-stake-in-syria-yet-we-have-done-nothing/2016/12/22/229678da-c7b7-11e6-8bee-54e800ef2a63_story.html.

2   Jane Eisner, 'Our Great Moral Failure in Syria', *Forward*, 27 December 2016, https://forward.com/opinion/357875/our-great-moral-failure-in-syria/. See also Richard Cohen, 'We Cannot Underestimate the Effects of Obama's Inaction in Syria', *Business Insider* (reprinted from the *Washington Post*), 6 October 2015, https://www.businessinsider.com/we-cannot-underestimate-the-effects-of-obamas-inaction-in-syria-2015-10;

and Bob Fredericks, 'Obama Says Not Bombing Syria Took Political Courage', *New York Post*, 15 May 2017, https://nypost.com/2017/05/15/obama-says-not-bombing-syria-took-political-courage/.

3 In criticising the Obama administration, the author writes that 'even as Syria's conflict escalated and the costs of inaction have mounted, the administration's risk calculus has remained static'. Steven Heydemann, 'Why the United States Hasn't Intervened in Syria', Brookings Institution, 17 March 2016, https://www.brookings.edu/blog/markaz/2016/03/17/why-the-united-states-hasnt-intervened-in-syria/.

4 Shadi Hamid, 'Why Doesn't Obama Seem to Listen to Syria Experts?', Brookings Institution, 10 February 2016, https://www.brookings.edu/blog/markaz/2016/02/10/why-doesnt-obama-seem-to-listen-to-syria-experts/.

5 Paul Wolfowitz, 'Undoing Trump's Syria Blunder', *New York Times*, 21 November 2019, https://www.nytimes.com/2019/11/21/opinion/trump-syria-blunder.html. The statement is contradicted by the reporting of the *New York Times* itself. See Mark Mazzetti and Ali Younes, 'C.I.A. Arms for Syrian Rebels Supplied Black Market, Officials Say', *New York Times*, 26 June 2016, https://www.nytimes.com/2016/06/27/world/middleeast/cia-arms-for-syrian-rebels-supplied-black-market-officials-say.html.

6 See, for example, Jeffrey Goldberg, 'The Obama Doctrine', *Atlantic*, April 2016, https://www.theatlantic.com/magazine/archive/2016/04/

the-obama-doctrine/471525/.

7 See Syrian Observatory for Human Rights, 'Nearly 585,000 People Have Been Killed Since the Beginning of the Syrian Revolution', 4 January 2020, https://www.syriahr.com/en/152189/.

8 See, for example, Rich Barlow, 'Here's What We Should Do About Syria', WBUR, 22 October 2019, https://www.wbur.org/cognoscenti/2019/10/22/kurds-syria-turkey-donald-trump-rich-barlow; Editorial Board, 'The Price Assad Should Pay for Gassing His People', *Chicago Tribune*, 9 April 2018, https://www.chicago-tribune.com/opinion/editorials/ct-edit-syria-assad-trump-chemical-weapons-20180409-story.html; and 'Bashar al-Assad's "Pathetic" Barbara Walters Interview: 4 Takeaways', *Week*, 8 December 2011, https://theweek.com/articles/479642/bashar-alassads-pathetic-barbara-walters-interview-4-takeaways.

9 David Schenker and Andrew J. Tabler, 'In Search of Leverage with Syria', Washington Institute for Near East Policy, 14 June 2011, https://www.washingtoninstitute.org/policy-analysis/view/in-search-of-leverage-with-syria.

10 Jamie Weinstein, 'American Ambassador to Syria: Bashar al-Assad Is Evil', *Daily Caller*, 21 September 2011, https://dailycaller.com/2011/09/21/american-ambassador-to-syria-bashar-al-assad-is-evil/. Over several years, Ambassador Ford has shifted from arguing that Obama should do more to support the Syrian opposition in 2014 to defending one of Donald Trump's announced

pull-outs in 2018. See Robert S. Ford, 'Arm Syria's Opposition', *New York Times*, 10 June 2014, https://www.nytimes.com/2014/06/11/opinion/ford-arm-syrias-opposition.html; and Robert S. Ford, 'Trump's Syria Decision Was Essentially Correct. Here's How He Can Make the Most of It', *Washington Post*, 27 December 2018, https://www.washingtonpost.com/opinions/even-without-troops-the-us-can-still-have-influence-in-syria/2018/12/27/757582b8-0a08-11e9-85b6-41cofeoc5b8f_story.html.

11 Sam Ser, 'Assad Is "Evil, Beyond Brutal, Not Rational", US State Department Says', *Times of Israel*, 8 January 2013, https://www.timesofisrael.com/assad-is-evil-beyond-brutal-not-rational-us-spokeswoman-says/. Economics and international-relations theories derived from it usually define 'rational' not in terms of a subject's goals, but in terms of the relationship between goals and actions. Richard Posner presents a simplified version of this idea when he says that rationality is 'defined as achieving one's ends … at least cost'. Richard A. Posner, 'Rational Choice, Behavioral Economics, and the Law', *Stanford Law Review*, vol. 50, 1997, p. 1,551. This is the sense in which the term 'rational' is used in this article.

12 Benjamin Valentino, Paul Huth and Dylan Balch-Lindsay, '"Draining the Sea": Mass Killing and Guerrilla Warfare', *International Organization*, vol. 58, no. 2, Spring 2004, pp. 375–407. See also Benjamin Valentino, *Final Solutions: Mass Killing and Genocide in the 20th Century* (Ithaca, NY: Cornell University Press, 2004). Mass killings occurring outside of wartime have also been found to be generally explicable through a focus on the political goals of leaders, particularly those at the top of communist regimes seeking to fundamentally remake society.

13 Frank W. Wayman and Atsushi Tago, 'Explaining the Onset of Mass Killing, 1949–87', *Journal of Peace Research*, vol. 47, no. 1, January 2010, pp. 3–13.

14 Gary Uzonyi and Richard Hanania, 'Government-sponsored Mass Killing and Civil War Reoccurrence', *International Studies Quarterly*, vol. 61, no. 3, September 2017, pp. 677–89.

15 Evan Perkoski and Erica Chenoweth, 'Non-violent Resistance and Prevention of Mass Killing during Popular Uprisings', International Center on Nonviolent Conflict, April 2018, https://www.nonviolent-conflict.org/wp-content/uploads/2017/07/nonviolent-resistance-and-prevention-of-mass-killings-perkoski-chenoweth-2018-icnc.pdf.

16 See Ore Koren, 'Means to an End: Pro-government Militias as a Predictive Indicator of Strategic Mass Killing', *Conflict Management and Peace Science*, vol. 34, no. 5, September 2017, pp. 461–84.

17 See Michael Freeman, 'The Theory and Prevention of Genocide', *Holocaust and Genocide Studies*, vol. 6, no. 2, February 1991, pp. 185–99; Uzonyi and Hanania, 'Government-sponsored Mass Killing', p. 682.

18 A story in the *Washington Post* published shortly after the Iraqi invasion of Kuwait begins with the sentence: 'Madman, crazy, insane and

maniac are the adjectives of choice to describe Iraq President Saddam Hussein.' Jack Anderson and Dale Van Atta, 'Saddam Hussein's House of Horrors', *Washington Post*, 13 August 1990, https://www.washingtonpost.com/archive/lifestyle/1990/08/13/saddam-husseins-house-of-horrors/afbf8df9-74be-4050-962d-7e21f01cc658/. According to Paul Wolfowitz, 'Saddam Hussein was much more than just another bad guy', and in terms of brutality was on a different level than other tyrants. 'Remarks Delivered to the Philadelphia World Affairs Council', Coalition Provisional Authority, 5 May 2004, http://govinfo.library.unt.edu/cpa-iraq/transcripts/20040508_wolf_enormous.html. Some of his behaviour, such as the alleged 1993 plot against the life of George H.W. Bush, seems to have indicated an unstable and self-destructive personality. Yet the point is that even in the case of Saddam, the patterns of atrocities across time are consistent with a rational-actor model. The Justice Department has investigated the supposed Bush-assassination plot and found the evidence uncovered by the Kuwaitis to be credible. Office of the Inspector General, US Department of Justice, 'The FBI Laboratory: An Investigation into Laboratory Practices and Alleged Misconduct in Explosives-Related and Other Cases', April 1997, Section D: 'The Bush Assassination Attempt', https://fas.org/irp/agency/doj/oig/fbilab1/05bush2.htm.

19   See Lisa Blaydes, *State of Repression: Iraq under Saddam Hussein* (Princeton, NJ: Princeton University Press, 2018);

and Samuel Helfont, *Compulsion in Religion: Saddam Hussein, Islam, and the Roots of Insurgencies in Iraq* (New York: Oxford University Press, 2018).

20   See, for example, Christopher Hitchens, *A Long Short War: The Postponed Liberation of Iraq* (New York: Plume, 2003).

21   Uzonyi and Hanania, 'Government-sponsored Mass Killing', p. 681.

22   Graeme Wood, 'What ISIS Really Wants', *Atlantic*, March 2015, https://www.theatlantic.com/magazine/archive/2015/03/what-isis-really-wants/384980/.

23   Scott Wilson and Joby Warrick, 'Assad Must Go, Obama Says', *Washington Post*, 18 August 2011, https://www.washingtonpost.com/politics/assad-must-go-obama-says/2011/08/18/gIQAelheOJ_story.html.

24   Jay Solomon, 'US Pushes to Try Syrian Regime', *Wall Street Journal*, 18 June 2011, https://www.wsj.com/articles/SB10001424052702303635604576391901761410060; 'UN Bid to Refer Syria to ICC Vetoed', Al-Jazeera, 23 May 2014, https://www.aljazeera.com/news/middleeast/2014/05/un-bid-refer-syria-icc-vetoed-2014522142710574665.html.

25   Scott Shane and Jo Becker, 'A New Libya, "With Very Little Time Left"', *New York Times*, 27 February 2016, https://www.nytimes.com/2016/02/28/us/politics/libya-isis-hillary-clinton.html.

26   Jeff Stein, 'Inside the CIA's Syrian Rebels Vetting Machine', *Newsweek*, 10 November 2014, https://www.newsweek.com/2014/11/21/moderate-rebels-please-raise-your-hands-283449.html.

27   See Mazzetti and Younes, 'C.I.A.

Arms'; and Steven Lee Myers and Thom Shanker, 'State Department and Pentagon Plan for Post-Assad Syria', *New York Times*, 4 August 2012, https://www.nytimes.com/2012/08/05/world/middleeast/state-dept-and-pentagon-planning-for-post-assad-syria.html.

28 Tom O'Connor, 'How ISIS Got Weapons from the US and Used Them to Take Iraq and Syria', *Newsweek*, 14 December 2017, https://www.newsweek.com/how-isis-got-weapons-us-used-them-take-iraq-syria-748468.

29 Conflict Armament Research, 'Weapons of the Islamic State', December 2017, pp. 5–8.

30 Mazzetti and Younes, 'C.I.A. Arms'.

31 *Ibid.*

32 Kenneth Pollack, 'An Army to Defeat Assad: How to Turn Syria's Opposition into a Real Fighting Force', Brookings Institution, 7 September 2014, https://www.brookings.edu/opinions/an-army-to-defeat-assad-how-to-turn-syrias-opposition-into-a-real-fighting-force/.

33 Ben Rhodes, *The World As It Is: A Memoir of the Obama White House* (New York: Random House, 2018), chapter 16.

34 Wilson and Warrick, 'Assad Must Go'.

35 Nada Bakri and Steven Erlanger, 'E.U. Bans Syrian Oil as Protests Continue', *New York Times*, 2 September 2011, https://www.nytimes.com/2011/09/03/world/middleeast/03syria.html.

36 See Jeanne Gobat and Kristina Kostial, 'Syria's Conflict Economy', IMF Working Paper, June 2016, https://www.imf.org/external/pubs/ft/wp/2016/wp16123.pdf; and Matt Phillips, 'The Collapse of the Syrian Economy Is Worse than Germany

after World War II', *Quartz*, 26 July 2016, https://qz.com/741432/the-collapse-of-the-syrian-economy-is-worse-than-germany-after-world-war-ii/.

37 Wilson and Warrick, 'Assad Must Go'.

38 Kongdan Oh and Ralph C. Hassig, *North Korea Through the Looking Glass* (Washington DC: Brookings Institution Press, 2004), pp. 32–3.

39 The embargo on Iraq may have caused more than 500,000 deaths, and although this figure has been disputed, Iraq certainly suffered more economic deprivation and a higher infant-mortality rate than its neighbours during the time it was sanctioned. See Tim Dyson and Valeria Cetorelli, 'Changing Views on Child Mortality and Economic Sanctions in Iraq: A History of Lies, Damned Lies and Statistics', *BMJ Global Health*, no. 2, 2017, https://gh.bmj.com/content/bmjgh/2/2/e000311.full.pdf.

40 Christoph V. Steinert, Janina I. Steinert and Sabine C. Carey, 'Spoilers of Peace: Pro-government Militias as Risk Factors for Conflict Recurrence', *Journal of Peace Research*, vol. 56, no. 2, October 2018, pp. 249–63.

41 Salwa Amor and Ruth Sherlock, 'How Bashar al-Assad Created the Feared Shabiha Militia: An Insider Speaks', *Daily Telegraph*, 23 March 2014, https://www.telegraph.co.uk/news/worldnews/middleeast/syria/10716289/How-Bashar-al-Assad-created-the-feared-shabiha-militia-an-insider-speaks.html.

42 In 2017, the Iranian government announced that it had lost 2,100 personnel in Iraq and Syria over the

previous five years, including recruits from Pakistan and Afghanistan, with the losses being about evenly distributed between the two theatres of war. See 'Iranian Official Says 2,100 Fighters Killed in Syria, Iraq', Radio Free Europe, 7 March 2017, https://www.rferl.org/a/iran-1-100-fighters-killed-syria/28355761.html. As of 2019, Russia had confirmed the deaths of 116 personnel in Syria, not including at least 73–101 military contractors, according to one conservative estimate. Scott Lucas, 'Syria Daily: Russia Acknowledges Deaths of 3 Troops', EA Worldview, 26 March 2019, https://eaworldview.com/2019/03/syria-daily-russia-acknowledges-deaths-of-3-troops/.

43   Amnesty International, '"It Breaks the Human": Torture, Disease and Death in Syria's Prisons', 2016, https://reliefweb.int/sites/reliefweb.int/files/resources/MDE2445082016ENGLISH.PDF.

44   Syrian Observatory for Human Rights, 'Nearly 585,000 People Have Been Killed Since the Beginning of the Syrian Revolution'.

45   The numbers used here are from the Syrian Observatory for Human Rights, see http://www.syriahr.com/?p=353886. While sources differ about the total number of people killed, all agree with the general outline put forth in Figure 1, in which the violence was relatively low in 2011, before peaking over the next few years and then declining again. Focusing on civilian deaths alone reveals a similar pattern.

46   See, for example, C.J. Chivers and Eric Schmitt, 'Arms Airlift to Syria Rebels Expands, With Aid From C.I.A.', *New York Times*, 24 March 2013, https://www.nytimes.com/2013/03/25/world/middleeast/arms-airlift-to-syrian-rebels-expands-with-cia-aid.html; and Mark Mazzetti, Adam Goldman and Michael S. Schmidt, 'Behind the Sudden Death of a $1 Billion Secret C.I.A. War in Syria', *New York Times*, 2 August 2017, https://www.nytimes.com/2017/08/02/world/middleeast/cia-syria-rebel-arm-train-trump.html.

47   See, for example, Meredith Buel, 'Saudi Arabia Offers Sophisticated Weapons to Syrian Rebels', Voice of America, 2 March 2014, https://www.voanews.com/world-news/middle-east-dont-use/saudi-arabia-offers-sophisticated-weapons-syrian-rebels; Frank Gardner, 'Gulf Arabs "Stepping Up" Arms Supplies to Syrian Rebels', BBC, 8 October 2015, https://www.bbc.co.uk/news/world-middle-east-34479929; Aron Lund, 'How Assad's Enemies Gave Up on the Syrian Opposition', Century Foundation, 17 October 2017, https://tcf.org/content/report/assads-enemies-gave-syrian-opposition/; and Frederic Wehry, 'Gulf Calculations in the Syrian Conflict', Carnegie Endowment for International Peace, 9 June 2014, https://carnegieendowment.org/2014/06/09/gulf-calculations-in-syrian-conflict-pub-55865.

48   John Solomon, *The Iran Wars: Spy Games, Bank Battles, and the Secret Deals that Reshaped the Middle East* (New York: Random House, 2016), p. 181.

49   Lucas Tomlinson, 'US Military Returns to Syria to Protect Oil Fields; Kurdish Leader Accuses Turkey of "Continuing Its War"', Fox News, 31 October 2019,

https://www.foxnews.com/world/us-military-returns-syria-oil-fields.

50 Alexander B. Downes and Jonathan Monten, 'Forced to Be Free? Why Foreign-imposed Regime Change Rarely Leads to Democratization', *International Security*, vol. 37, no. 4, Spring 2013, pp. 90–131.

51 According to Eli Lake, 'there is no guarantee that an Obama intervention would have been able to topple Khamenei back in 2009, when his people flooded the streets to protest an election the American president wouldn't say was stolen. But it was worth a try. Imagine if that uprising had succeeded.' Eli Lake, 'Why Obama Let Iran's Green Revolution Fail', Bloomberg, 24 August 2016, https://www.bloomberg.com/opinion/articles/2016-08-24/why-obama-let-iran-s-green-revolution-fail.

52 Rania Khalek, 'US and EU Sanctions Are Punishing Ordinary Syrians and Crippling Aid Work, UN Report Reveals', *Intercept*, 28 September 2016, https://theintercept.com/2016/09/28/u-s-sanctions-are-punishing-ordinary-syrians-and-crippling-aid-work-u-n-report-reveals/. See also Justine Walker, 'Humanitarian Impact of Syria-Related Unilateral Restrictive Measures', report prepared for the UN Economic and Social Commission for Western Asia's National Agenda for the Future of Syria, Swiss Agency for Development and Cooperation, May 2016, https://www.documentcloud.org/documents/3114567-Study-on-Humanitarian-Impact-of-Syria-Related.html.

53 See, for instance, Jonathan Stevenson, 'The Syrian Tragedy and Precedent', *Survival*, vol. 56, no. 3, June–July 2014, pp. 121–40.

54 Hannah Allam, '"Assad Must Go" Demand Should Go, Ex-White House Official Says', *McClatchy*, 12 May 2016, https://www.mcclatchydc.com/news/nation-world/national/national-security/article77313747.html.

55 Cees Wiebes and Bert Zeeman, 'United States' "Big Stick" Diplomacy: The Netherlands Between Decolonization and Alignment, 1945–1949', *International History Review*, vol. 14, no. 1, February 1992, pp. 45–70.

56 See Colleen McCain Nelson, Margherita Stancati and Ahmed Al Omran, 'Obama Says US and Gulf Arab Allies Share "Broad Common Vision"', *Wall Street Journal*, 21 April 2016, https://www.wsj.com/articles/obama-to-reassure-gulf-partners-1461225258; Elizabeth Llorente, 'Saudis Release Three Women's Rights Activists from Jail Temporarily Amid International Pressure', Fox News, 29 March 2019, https://www.foxnews.com/world/saudis-release-three-womens-rights-activist-from-jail-temporarily-amid-international-pressure; and Josh Rogin, 'Congress Presses Trump on Human Rights in the Gulf', *Washington Post*, 17 September 2019, https://www.washingtonpost.com/opinions/2019/09/17/congress-presses-trump-human-rights-gulf/.

Review Essay

Proper Spying

Rodric Braithwaite

How Spies Think: Ten Lessons in Intelligence
David Omand. London: Viking, 2020. £20.00. 352 pp.

Principled Spying: The Ethics of Secret Intelligence
David Omand and Mark Phythian. Oxford: Oxford University
Press, 2018. £20.00. 304 pp.

In his new book *How Spies Think*, David Omand recalls bringing an intelligence report to Margaret Thatcher on the afternoon of 31 March 1982. She read it, looked up and said 'This is very serious, isn't it?' 'Yes, Prime Minister', he replied. 'This intelligence can only be read in one way: the Argentine junta are in the final stages of preparing to invade the Falkland Islands, very likely this coming Sunday' (p. 1). It was a brilliant coup by Government Communications Headquarters (GCHQ), the United Kingdom's signals-intelligence agency. But it did not save the Falklands from invasion, which the British government had tried for months to persuade itself was improbable. The incident neatly encapsulates the weaknesses, as well as the strengths, of the intelligence process.

Omand spent his career in the rarefied upper reaches of the British defence and intelligence establishment: at GCHQ, which he directed in 1996–97; in the British delegation to NATO; in the Ministry of Defence;

Rodric Braithwaite was the British ambassador in Moscow (1988–92) and chairman of the Joint Intelligence Committee (1992–93). He is author of *Armageddon and Paranoia: The Nuclear Confrontation* (Profile Books, 2017).

Survival | vol. 62 no. 5 | October–November 2020 | pp. 193–202   DOI 10.1080/00396338.2020.1819655

in the Joint Intelligence Committee; as permanent secretary of the Home Office; and finally as security and intelligence coordinator in the Cabinet Office, where he was largely responsible for formulating Britain's present counter-terrorism policy. Since retiring in 2005 he has devoted himself to writing and teaching about the uses and abuses of secret intelligence, having also co-authored, with Mark Phythian, *Principled Spying: The Ethics of Secret Intelligence*. Omand brings to the subject mature experience, deep thought and high seriousness. It is difficult to imagine anyone better qualified.

A vexing game

Spying is about stealing other people's secrets in order to frustrate their designs against you and to promote your own designs against them. You

persuade foreigners to betray their countries, by appealing to a higher cause if possible, but if necessary by blackmail, bribery, sexual entrapment and threats. Or you filch their correspondence and documents to discover what they are up to. In the old days you read their secret writing and deciphered their coded messages by hand. Nowadays you can sift through millions of online messages by computer.

The secret world has a special allure all its own. The press takes a sensational, almost a prurient, interest in its doings. Politicians are flattered to think it tells them things that no one else knows. Ordinary people are happy for their government to spy on foreigners, though they are less enthusiastic when their government spies on them. We are all entranced by stories of derring-do in the shadows.

The secret agencies themselves, not surprisingly, enjoy the adulation. In countries such as Russia, they see themselves rather than their ostensible masters – the tsars, the commissars, the presidents – as the ultimate guardians of the state. The thought lingers even in democracies. In the 1970s, a maverick group in the British Security Service (also known as MI5) managed to convince themselves that the prime minister, Harold Wilson, and even their own director general were Soviet agents. Robert Gates, a distinguished

US director of central intelligence, told his new recruits that 'this nation is at peace because we in intelligence are constantly at war' (quoted in *Principled Spying*, p. 93). John le Carré, whose novels chart the moral complexity of spying, still feels 'shifty' about the extent to which he, too, has contributed to its glamorisation.[1]

The moral complexity is unavoidable. If you think that the noble end of protecting your state and your fellow citizens justifies whatever means deliver the goods, then the opportunities and temptations to push the limits of acceptable behaviour will multiply. In extreme circumstances, in wartime or faced by an imminent terrorist threat, even respectable governments may be tempted to use repugnant techniques, including assassination and torture. Democracies, at least, try to keep the thing under control. That is not easy, since spying has to remain secret if it is to be effective.

Principled Spying is a work of moral philosophy. Omand calls it a 'Socratic dialogue' between himself and Phythian, a professor of politics and international relations. It tackles this central problem: can moral limits be defined for the business of spying and how, in a liberal society, can you ensure they are observed? The language borders on the technical. 'Aretaic', for example, is not a word in common use. At first I thought that 'deontological' was something to do with trees. So you do have to pay attention. But the writing is lively and accessible, despite the subtlety and complexity of  the subject. And it is well worth the effort. Though it reaches well back into the past, the book is bang up to date, and deals at length with the transformation brought about by the burgeoning digital revolution.

The authors divide the history of espionage into three periods. The first is the prerogative-agent model: intelligence agents operate secretly under their sovereigns' authority, to protect them and the public from harm, as when Francis Walsingham saved Queen Elizabeth I from assassination and the country from invasion. The model conveniently combines a maximum of freedom for intelligence agencies with a minimum of public oversight. It is therefore popular with many governments, including Russia's.

Democratic countries came to adopt the hidden-guardian model. Their legislatures decided – by implication, mostly – that their countries needed effective intelligence agencies operating in secret on the outer margins of the law. But they preferred to leave the details and the responsibility to the executive arm. This was the model for Britain until well beyond the middle of the twentieth century. British governments routinely refused to discuss the work of the intelligence agencies, or even denied their existence, and the British Parliament and people accepted that.

But as people began to lose their belief that the government always knew best, a series of intelligence scandals blew up in the UK and the United States. Press, Parliament and Congress demanded explanations. Liberals insisted on knowing if governments were spying on their own people. By the turn of the century, in both countries, the social-contract model had emerged – a complex system of laws and practices designed to hold the agencies to account while allowing them to go on working in secret. It was mirrored in other democracies.

In wartime the conflict between necessity and morality becomes dramatically stark. Omand recognises that governments will feel justified in taking extreme measures when the very existence of the state is in danger. But even in times of great danger we should never contemplate operating beyond the boundary of our obligation to preserve human rights.[2] A major responsibility falls on the spymasters themselves, who must 'have a clear sense of what the democratic society they exist to protect expects of them' and be able 'confidently to refuse instructions that fall outside their remit' (*Principled Spying*, p. 95).

It is a high test. It has to survive the counter-arguments of those who believe that we are entitled to use the same weapons as our enemies. And it can fray under stress, when the agencies are under pressure to deliver the goods. The major powers have all used their agencies to deploy what the Russians call 'active measures', overthrowing foreign governments, manipulating their elections, bribing and subverting their officials and politicians, spreading black propaganda. The CIA has a long history of mounting elaborate covert actions, some barely distinguishable from wars, to make the world safe for democracy.[3] The handling of spies and informants raises particularly stark problems. It involves very personal kinds of deception.

Agents can cheat you for financial gain or because the other side has turned them. They can slip into crime and even murder to preserve their cover. Covert operations against Irish terrorists by the British army and against environmental activists by the Metropolitan Police, and British intelligence agencies' collusion in the American practice (known as 'rendition') of kidnapping suspected terrorists and delivering them to torture or detention without trial, crossed the line. They were condemned after public inquiry.

The ability governments now have to intercept and exploit huge masses of information raises different but equally stark ethical questions. Our governments – as we now all know, not least thanks to Edward Snowden – can hack into our communications and our computers. They press private companies to hand over our digital records. They keep our personal data in bulk. They insist that they have to do this to counter the disruptive and sometimes murderous plans of others. People in most democratic countries are inclined to believe them: better to give up some personal privacy than to get blown up by a terrorist. But the debate has encouraged – or forced – the British and other governments to pass increasingly stringent legislation to ensure that their digital operations do not unduly damage the innocent public.

Omand and Phythian believe the public debate Snowden triggered was useful, even necessary. Such revelations help to keep democratic governments honest. Whistle-blowers are often people of courage and moral principle. But their actions, too, are fraught with moral ambiguity: they are blowing the whistle on employers who trust them, and to whom they owe their loyalty.

Omand and Phythian rely on the centuries-old tradition of just-war theory to support their arguments. War, they believe, should only be entered into 'with extreme reluctance and a sense of moral tragedy and foreboding' (p. 90). But war – and spying – can nevertheless be waged properly, provided that the cause is just and the methods proportionate and necessary, and that there is a firm determination not to harm innocent people.

This may be the only coherent theory within which to think about the ethics of war and espionage. But its tests are subjective. Who decides whether our cause is just? At what point do we conclude that our use of force has become disproportionate, and call off our operations? At the beginning of the Second World War, Britain and America condemned the indiscriminate bombing of civilians. They ended the war with Hiroshima and the area bombing of German cities. The authors themselves conclude sadly that just-war theory provides an intellectual framework for inquiry, but cannot provide answers (p. 193).

The law, too, helps only up to a point. As the authors say, what is lawful is not at all necessarily ethical. Some of us may believe it is wrong to use drones to assassinate our opponents at a distance. We like to think that torture is ineffective as well as immoral because under extreme pressure your prisoner will tell you what he thinks you want to hear, rather than what you need to know. But, after the attack on the Twin Towers in New York, a bunch of then-president George W. Bush's lawyers persuaded themselves and him that practices internationally condemned as torture could be justified under American law. It's the 'ticking bomb' argument. You've captured a terrorist who knows where a bomb has been placed that will kill many people if it goes off. You are justified in using every physical pressure on him to avert catastrophe.

The 1966 Algerian–Italian film *The Battle of Algiers* is a brilliant exploration of the complexities. A French paratroop colonel, sent to pacify Algiers, successfully tortures a prisoner into revealing the whereabouts of a guerrilla leader. The leader is eliminated, the guerrilla movement is crushed and peace returns to the city. But at the end of the film, the people of Algiers rise against their colonial oppressors and the French lose the war. The film was reportedly shown to American commanders and troops serving in Iraq.[4] It's not clear what conclusion they drew from it. Torture may have generated actionable intelligence during the wars in Iraq and Afghanistan, as it seems to have done in Algeria. It did not, and could not, stop all three wars from tottering to an ignominious close far short of anything resembling victory.

Information and truth

In his latest book, *How Spies Think*, Omand deals with another central problem. How do you ensure that the information spies collect is accurate, timely and actionable? Spies and their masters are as human as the rest of us. They make mistakes through organisational confusion, managerial incompetence and muddled thinking. Their failures can have catastrophic consequences: Pearl Harbor, Adolf Hitler's surprise attack on Russia, the shambles in Iraq and Afghanistan. Joseph Stalin used to shoot his spies when they got things wrong. In democracies the penalties are less severe. The spies lose their jobs; they are publicly investigated; and the press covers them with abuse, often unfair and ignorant.

If the earlier book is intended to supply a moral compass for spies and their customers, *How Spies Think* deals with the space between, where the analysts apply their brains to puzzle out the messy, contradictory, sometimes dubious information they get from their spies, in order to produce conclusions that can usefully guide the decision-makers. Unlike Tony Blair, who as prime minister believed that the intelligence showed 'beyond doubt' that Saddam Hussein had weapons of mass destruction, Omand knows that there are strict limits to what intelligence can do.[5] Intelligence officers are not soothsayers, though they are often blamed for not foreseeing the unforeseeable when some row breaks out over a so-called intelligence failure.

Omand aims 'to empower ordinary people to take better decisions by learning how intelligence analysts think' (p. 2). That is an ambitious objective, perhaps too ambitious. In the course of his book, Omand demonstrates not that the analysts have an easily communicated skill, but that their thinking is prone to the same kinds of pitfalls as that of the rest of us.

His method is to illustrate the traps, and to show how the analysts try to scramble out of them by deliberately cross-examining their own intellectual habits and prejudices. He believes in the power of meticulous logic, dispassionately applied. Even if we cannot foretell the future, we can at least analyse the various ways it might unfold and so reduce the risk of surprise. But he also cautions us that our knowledge and understanding of the world is always fragmentary and sometimes wrong. Facts are never simple: they need explaining. We should guard against the manipulation and deception of others. We can be misled at least as much by our own preconceptions, our obsessions, our conspiracy theories, our paranoia, our preference for the familiar. Beware, he warns us above all, of the 'consensual hallucination': our instinct to stick with our group and – alas – to tell our bosses what they want to hear.[6] He conveys his central message with sceptical and sometimes quirky clarity: you must be aware of your own weaknesses if you are to analyse those of others correctly; that is a skill that can indeed be applied to our everyday lives.

It is still not enough. Omand emphasises that you must also seek to under-stand what is going on in your opponent's mind – to empathise with him – if you want to deal with him effectively. Raymond Garthoff, a wise CIA analyst, believed that 'the inability to empathize with the other side and visualize its interests in other than adversarial terms' was one reason why American ana-lysts often got the USSR wrong. But too much empathy raises eyebrows. An American official who departed from 'the implicit stereotypical cold war con-sensus', Garthoff warned, risked damage to his career and influence.[7] That kind of stereotype – an ideological view of the world that was mirrored on both sides of the divide – led intelligence analysts in Moscow astray at least as often as it confused those in London and Washington.

Grumpy sceptics say that you delude yourself if you think that it is possible to penetrate the minds of others, especially if they are foreigners from a totally different background. That is an oversimplification, a counsel of despair. In the first half of the 1980s, the Cold War was heating up as the aggressive poli-cies of Ronald Reagan's new administration provoked an answering paranoia among the Russians. The Soviet Union staggered as three of its elderly leaders died in rapid succession. The burning question was: who would take over? No one knew, of course. But in KGB officer Oleg Gordievsky the British had a well-placed agent who, though he was not close to the leadership and its manoeuvrings, was a highly intelligent observer of the Moscow scene and the emotions that drove it. He tipped off the British that Mikhail Gorbachev – young, energetic, effective – was a plausible candidate. When Gorbachev became the Soviet leader in March 1985, Thatcher, and later Reagan, rightly judged that they could do business with him. The intelligence prepared the ground. But it was the instinct of the politicians that made the choice. Indeed, some intelligence chiefs in London and Washington thought it was the wrong one, and that the politicians had been hoodwinked. It is an excellent example of how the worlds of the spies, the analysts and the politicians intersect.

There is an implied question of much broader implication here. How does a government – or a business organisation, or an individual – profit from the work of experts? One cannot simply dismiss expertise outright, as Michael Gove did in 2016, when he announced that 'people in this country have had enough of experts'.[8] There can be no excuse for decision-makers to ignore the available evidence, whether it comes from experts on coronavirus or experts on intelligence. But it is their job to take the final – and if necessary sceptical – judgement on the plausibility of the advice, and on its applicability to the problem in hand. Heads of government, chief executives and individuals all have to make the best judgement they can and act in good faith. It is they, and not their advisers, who must accept responsibility for success or failure.

*   *   *

At the end of the day another question stands out. If we use the same methods of secret war – seduction, subversion, surveillance, assassination, even torture – how are we better than our opponents? The Crusaders favoured a simple answer: 'Pagans are wrong and the Christians are right.'[9] Some still hope that an unexacting division of the world into black and white will enable them to evade the moral complexities.

The historian Max Hastings has said about the performance of the Western allies in the Second World War that 'all belligerents in all conflicts are morally compromised, but this does not render all causes equally worthless'.[10] Omand and Phythian try to come up with something better: what distinguishes us from our opponents is our determination to subject our actions to the disciplines of morality and the law. That is not a very good answer – even in democratic societies raw human nature has a habit of breaking through. But it is the best we have. British laws and parliamentary oversight have been successively strengthened to prevent abuse, to punish perpetrators and to compensate victims. But the intrinsically difficult problem of overseeing a necessarily secret activity remains what Peter Spiegel has called 'that most unsquareable of democratic challenges'.[11] We are lucky in Britain to have spymasters like Omand and his successors, who are well aware of their daunting and sometimes conflicting responsibilities.

Notes

[1]   John le Carré, 'The Influence of Spies Has Become Too Much. It's Time Politicians Said No', *Guardian*, 14

June 2013.

[2]   Reversing a saying of Cicero – 'in time of war the law is silent' – Lord Justice

Atkin famously dissented in 1941 from his House of Lords colleagues' judgement that the government had the right to suspend habeas corpus in wartime. 'In England, amidst the clash of arms, the laws are not silent. They may be changed, but they speak the same language in war as in peace. It has always been one of the pillars of freedom, one of the principles of liberty for which on recent authority we are now fighting, that the judges are no respecters of persons, and stand between the subject and any attempted encroachments on his liberty by the executive, alert to see that any coercive action is justified in law.' *Liversidge v Anderson*, AC 206 (HL), 1942. Atkin's view has not gone away. It was cited in American litigation over actions by the US government post-9/11.

3 Two lively accounts on this subject are Steve Coll, *Ghost Wars: The Secret History of the CIA, Afghanistan and Bin Laden, from the Soviet Invasion to September 10, 2001* (New York: Penguin, 2004); and John Prados, *Safe for Democracy: The Secret Wars of the CIA* (Chicago, IL: Ivan R. Dee, 2006).

4 See, for example, Jonathan Kim, 'ReThinking The Battle of Algiers: A Movie the Pentagon, the Black Panthers and the IRA Can Agree On', *Huffington Post*, 10 November 2009.

5 See 'Full Text of Tony Blair's Foreword to the Dossier on Iraq', *Guardian*, 24 September 2002.

6 Because events are always confusing, because nothing ever quite works as it should, people everywhere are prone to believe that their lives are governed, not by their ostensible rulers, but by hidden forces – the gods, the worldwide Judaeo-Masonic conspiracy, the CIA or the KGB, or the 'deep state' that President Donald Trump is determined to drain. The BBC's 1988 TV drama *A Very British Coup* vividly showed a Labour government that wanted to pull out of NATO and get rid of the bomb being overthrown by a conspiratorial group of officials led by the chairman of the Joint Intelligence Committee.

7 Raymond L. Garthoff, *Assessing the Adversary: Estimates by the Eisenhower Administration of Soviet Intentions and Capabilities* (Washington DC: Brookings Institution Press, 1991), p. 51.

8 See Henry Mance, 'Britain Has Had Enough of Experts, Says Gove', *Financial Times*, 3 June 2016.

9 The origin of this phrase is unclear. Some firmly attribute it to the 'Chanson de Roland', a line of which reads 'Paien unt tort e chrestiens unt dreit'. Others attribute it to Marco Polo. G.K. Chesterton, who also saw the world in black and white, calls the phrase an 'unanswerable and terrible truism' in his novel *The Man Who Was Thursday*.

10 Max Hastings, 'Human Smoke by Nicholson Baker', *Sunday Times*, 4 May 2008.

11 More fully, he cited 'that most unsquareable of democratic challenges: how to run clandestine intelligence and security agencies in a system that is ostensibly accountable to the people'. Peter Spiegel, 'The FBI, the CIA and the Truth About America's Deep State', *Financial Times*, 6 May 2020.

Book Reviews

Middle East
Ray Takeyh

To Start a War: How the Bush Administration Took America into Iraq
Robert Draper. New York: Penguin Press, 2020. $30.00. 496 pp.

Books on the Iraq War all ask the same question: how did this disaster come about? The road to Baghdad is judiciously chronicled by Robert Draper in his important new book, *To Start a War*. Draper is a natural storyteller, and his narrative encompasses a president certain of his beliefs; foreign-policy mandarins who called for war; a compliant press; and a secretary of state who too often withheld his reservations from the president. Most importantly, secretary of defense Donald Rumsfeld's eagerness for war was matched only by his indifference to its aftermath.

The war in Iraq cannot be understood without appreciating the inconclusive nature of the First Gulf War. The army of Saddam Hussein was defeated, but he remained in power. Nearly everyone believed that he possessed weapons of mass destruction and would use them again if given a chance. Throughout the 1990s, both Democrats and Republicans insisted on regime change, but sanctions, covert actions and no-fly zones were not enough to nudge Saddam from the seat of power. In 1998, Bill Clinton went even further, signing a congressional resolution that was passed unanimously by the Senate declaring regime change to be the United States' objective. Secretary of state Madeleine Albright and national security advisor Samuel Berger's rhetoric scarcely differed from that of the most hawkish of Republicans. And then came the tragedies of 9/11.

George Bush did not begin his presidency seeking war with Iraq. His preoccupations were domestic, and his foreign policy would most likely have featured

Survival | vol. 62 no. 5 | October–November 2020 | pp. 203–209   DOI 10.1080/00396338.2020.1819656

summits with allies and arms-control negotiations with adversaries. But after 9/11 all threats were magnified, and the public wanted revenge. Afghanistan would not suffice, and Saddam seemed menacing. There are no inevitabilities in history, but the force of events was pushing America toward another war in the Middle East.

In some ways, Draper's book represents the revenge of the mid-level intelligence analyst. Those who spoke to Draper insist that they disputed the notion that Saddam had ties with Islamist terrorists or possessed a cache of biological and chemical weapons. They claimed to be shocked by the notion that Iraq had a nuclear apparatus, however embryonic. One of the villains of this book (and there are many) is George Tenet, director of the CIA, who is portrayed as so eager for a seat at the table that he often ignored the warnings of his own staff in order to placate his top customer, the president. Of course, basing a book on interviews presents certain challenges. The Iraq War has produced its share of officials claiming they opposed the war all along, or that their memos somehow did not reach key policymakers at the right time. These assertions are impossible to verify without access to the documentary evidence. Draper is a cautious and careful journalist, and he tries to present a balanced picture, but he still lacks the most essential tool of historical research: primary sources. An important contribution to this debate would be for the White House to declassify the full Iraq record of the Bush administration. This may not change the verdict, but it would allow a more complete assessment of one of the most contentious conflicts in modern American history.

Fraternal Enemies: Israel and the Gulf Monarchies
Clive Jones and Yoel Guzansky. London: C. Hurst & Co., 2019.
£45.00. 297 pp.

Fraternal Enemies was written before the announcement of Israel's normalisation of diplomatic relations with the United Arab Emirates (UAE). As such, it is replete with the assertion that a full-scale rapprochement between Israel and the Arab states cannot come about so long as the Palestinian issue remains unresolved. Still, this misjudgement should not deter readers from what is a compact and well-written book that thoughtfully sets out the history of Israel's relations with the Gulf regimes.

The recent convulsions of the Middle East – the Iraq War, the Arab Spring and finally the Syrian civil war – have focused the Gulf rulers' attention on new threats, such as Iran, and new opportunities, such as ties with Israel. The current generation of Gulf leaders, as well as the public, seem less preoccupied with a Palestinian struggle that for seven decades has generated costly wars and inconclusive diplomacy. It seems that many Middle Easterners are finally ready to move on.

The surprising aspect of all this is not that a small sheikhdom decided to forge formal ties with Israel, but that it was not Oman that led the way. As the authors demonstrate, the relationship between Jerusalem and Muscat has deep roots. In the early 1970s, Israel helped the sultan of Oman with his war against leftist guerrillas. The relationship steadily expanded to encompass both commercial and security interests. After Jordan signed a peace agreement with Israel in 1994, it was expected that Oman would follow suit. Prime minister Yitzhak Rabin even made a brief visit to Oman. But the anticipated normalisation did not come about because of the Palestinian obstacle. This did not stop Israel and the Gulf rulers from developing discreet ties, particularly as the security situation in the region deteriorated and strange new alignments came to the surface.

The subtext of all this is the perennial complaint of the Gulf states that the US is not doing enough to protect them. Today, the charge is that Washington, beginning with the Obama presidency, is becoming less interested in the region, and that both Democrats and Republicans are talking about ending the 'forever wars' there. To the Gulf states, Iran seems menacing and its nuclear programme well on track. In their telling, America's hostility to Iran has been tentative, with the Obama administration inking a nuclear agreement with Tehran that Joseph Biden has pledged to revive should he become president. Not even Donald Trump makes the grade in their eyes, as he seems obsessed with securing his own deal with Iran. Israel, on the other hand, seems steady in its animus toward the Islamic Republic, and has even taken its fight with Tehran to Syria.

Accusations of American indifference to the Middle East ring hollow given the number of US bases that litter the region. Moreover, at a time when a pandemic is ravaging the US and China is growing ever stronger, it is hard to explain why the White House should be preoccupied with the region's intractable conflicts. As the US withdraws, what remains may not be chaos and disorder, but rather a region that is sorting itself out and moving beyond its convenient enmities. The UAE has taken a big step in that direction. The question is whether other Arab states will follow its path toward maturity.

China's Western Horizon: Beijing and the New Geopolitics of Eurasia
Daniel S. Markey. New York and Oxford: Oxford University Press, 2020. $19.99/$29.95. 344 pp.

China is much in the news these days. It is a nation that has generated a rare bipartisan agreement in the US, namely that its ascendance will come at

America's expense. The assumption that a prosperous China integrated into the world economy would become a responsible stakeholder is today a much-contested notion. The hawks, and there are very few doves anymore, argue that Beijing has somehow discovered the key to geopolitical mastery that long eluded the US. The argument seems to be not how to avoid a new cold war, but how best to manage it.

Daniel Markey's sober and engaging book tracks China's policies in Central and South Asia, as well as in the Middle East. The author traces China's much-vaunted Belt and Road Initiative, detailing both its achievements and its limitations. Chinese diplomacy can be ham-fisted, and the country's billion-dollar infrastructure projects seem often to become entangled in the same political intrigues that bedevil the US. At times, Beijing appears just as confused and bewildered as Washington. Countries such as Pakistan and Kazakhstan are not always easy places to do business, after all.

Nevertheless, China has certain advantages in its approach to the Middle East. Beijing recently made news by signing a comprehensive agreement with the Islamic Republic that, if executed, would leave its imprint on nearly every major industrial sector in Iran. Telecommunications, clean energy, the banking system and infrastructural projects are all on the agenda. A humbled clerical regime even conceded that it would take China's concerns into account when negotiating oil prices. As Markey demonstrates, however, China has a history of inking accords that are more aspirational than real, and of promising Iran much but delivering little. Still, the agreement as presented constituted a dramatic reversal for an Islamist regime that once made self-reliance a core aspect of its mission. The mullahs have given away more to China than the Persian monarchs ever did to Britain and America.

Even more impressive is the fact that China has done all this without jeopardising its relations with Iran's principal Arab nemesis, Saudi Arabia. The Kingdom has done its own share of courting China, with a succession of princes journeying to Beijing and signing commercial agreements. Hundreds of Chinese firms are already operating in Saudi Arabia, and lately there has been talk of nuclear cooperation. In some ways, Beijing's relations with Riyadh are more substantial than its ties with Tehran. In the end, American sanctions are still deterring China from breaching certain parameters, belying the notion of its recklessness.

Markey's impressive and well-researched book is a must-read for anyone trying to decipher China's uneasy path as it moves beyond its region into the contested waters of the Middle East and South Asia. If China is to be the West's new adversary, then both its power and its vulnerabilities should be better understood. As such, this book is a welcome addition to the emerging literature on China's foreign policy under Xi Jinping.

MBS: The Rise to Power of Mohammed bin Salman
Ben Hubbard. New York: Tim Duggan Books, 2020. $28.00.
384 pp.

Muhammad bin Salman is a prince in a hurry, and after his gradual assumption of total power in Saudi Arabia something unusual took place. MBS, as he became known, spoke vaguely of reform while delegations of American foreign-policy luminaries journeyed to the Kingdom and came away wide-eyed, proclaiming that they had seen the future and it was Jeddah. Ben Hubbard's account of MBS is not so much a biography as a study of his path to absolute power. It is rich in detail, perceptive in its observations and thoughtful in its dissection of a society that is often shrouded in mystery. Despite all the efforts of the Kingdom to deny access to a resourceful reporter, Hubbard has managed to penetrate the country's many layers and come up with his share of gems. His conclusions are as stark as they are convincing.

The Saudi national compact as contrived in the early twentieth century rested on a simple bargain. The monarchy would provide its citizens with financial benefits, and they would reciprocate with political loyalty. What held the system together was massive oil wealth, religious orthodoxy and considerable corruption. To his credit, MBS recognises that this bargain is unsustainable in the twenty-first century. He wants to trim the power of the Kingdom's clerical enablers, create free-trade zones, attract tourists and diversify a workforce that currently relies on expatriates for nearly all tasks. His plan, concocted by Western management-consulting firms, is audaciously called Vision 2030. MBS appears to be a true believer, seemingly convinced that he can rearrange the social order that has sustained the monarchy. It is a big bet, and if it fails, he could end up being the Kingdom's last ruler from the House of Saud.

It did not take long for MBS to reveal his cruel streak. In 2017 he locked up Saudi Arabia's most prominent billionaires in the Ritz-Carlton Hotel and extorted money from them before letting them out. He callously disposed of his elders when they got in his way. He has waged a merciless and ultimately inconclusive war in Yemen. And then came the gruesome murder of Jamal Khashoggi, a Saudi journalist who paid for his criticisms of MBS with his life. Khashoggi's killing in a Saudi consulate in Turkey was both pitiless and stupid. Everyone knows that consulates are typically surveilled closely by the host country, and Turkey made the most of the awkward position that Riyadh found itself in. Yet Khashoggi's murder had remarkably little impact on the monarchy's standing in the West. After a spasm of condemnations, it was back to business as usual. Trade delegations resumed their visits and foreign-policy mandarins renewed their praise of Vision 2030. MBS is still seen in many Western quarters as a modernising monarch.

Saudi Arabia today feels like the Iran of the 1970s, with an enterprising autocrat promoting reforms that he poorly understands; Western consulting firms rushing in to sell their programmes of change at the highest possible price; rampant corruption that is selectively prosecuted, thus generating popular cynicism; lavish spending on weapons systems that the country's military cannot use and its treasury can ill afford; and a looming economic crisis as the complexion of the world's energy markets changes and Saudi oil becomes less relevant. The House of Saud may not go the way of the Pahlavi dynasty, but if history does not always repeat itself, it has been known to rhyme.

Rise and Kill First: The Secret History of Israel's Targeted Assassinations
Ronen Bergman. New York: Random House, 2018. $35.00.
784 pp.

Ronen Bergman's massive account of Israel's practice of targeted killing has been much praised for its thoroughness. It is a lucid account that at times reads more like a novel than a work of history – one could easily believe that a movie version was in the works. Numerous veterans of the Israeli intelligence services chose to confide in Bergman, seeming never to tire of recalling their triumphs. To be fair, the author also chronicles the disasters and asks probing questions, the most important of which is whether the practice of targeted killing has actually made Israel safer.

Upon its creation, Israel faced a wall of Arab hostility. Terrorism was often wielded against the Jewish state by Palestinians seeking revenge. Bergman's account jumps from one episode to another with such speed that a casual reader could easily get lost amid all the operational details. At times, the context of events is missing as the narrative focuses more on who died and who survived than on the reason operations were launched in the first place. A more sustained historical framework would have allowed the reader to better appreciate why Israel did what it did at various times in its history. Israel has gone from a struggling nation to a regional superpower. Through it all, it has made a point of tracking its enemies before they discharge their plans. At times, such pre-emption can go terribly wrong. Yet one has to marvel at the ability of Israel's agents to so easily penetrate various Arab states and movements.

In the end, the targeted killing that would have had the greatest impact on Israel's security was the one it did not carry out. Bergman asserts that the Iranian shah's last prime minister, Shapour Bakhtiar, approached Mossad about killing Ayatollah Ruhollah Khomeini in Paris. The story is entirely believable, as Bakhtiar was a liberal with guts who was desperately trying to wrestle the revolution from Khomeini. Had the Israelis killed Khomeini, it is entirely possible that the course of the revolution would have been different. The shah's monarchy may have been doomed, but it need not have been replaced by a regime whose ideological character is animated by anti-Semitism.

Bergman has done the public a grand service by producing a comprehensive and readable account of one of the most contentious practices of the Israeli state. Israel's fortunes have been changing as the region realigns and Arab states come to see Jerusalem more as an ally than a convenient foe. How all this will affect Israel's fixation with targeted killings remains to be seen.

Economy
Erik Jones

Narrative Economics: How Stories Go Viral and Drive Major Economic Events
Robert J. Shiller. Princeton, NJ: Princeton University Press, 2019. £20.00/$27.95. 400 pp.

Stories influence behaviour. Indeed, that is why people tell stories in the first place. If a story is not going to generate some kind of reaction, what would be the point in telling it? It is therefore worth noting that most economists exclude stories from the list of important influences in their models for economic performance. The usual excuse is that such models need to be parsimonious to be tractable. More important, perhaps, is that simpler models allow for more sophisticated forms of statistical analysis. If parsimony and sophistication come at the cost of 'completeness' in capturing the world around us, the advantages they offer to economics as a scientific discipline are more than worth it. At least, that is the conventional wisdom.

Robert Shiller disagrees. He believes that stories, or 'narratives', are an essential part of economics as a social construct. Narratives capture how people perceive the world around them and, in turn, shape how they respond to it. Since their responses make up economic activity in the aggregate, it makes no sense to exclude either narratives or the responses they generate from economic analysis. On the contrary, given the huge advances in the digitisation of books and articles, and in the elaboration of models for harvesting and analysing narrative components (or word combinations) as data, there is no excuse for economists to sideline such powerful influences on economic performance.

Shiller throws down the gauntlet, arguing not only that economists should learn from other disciplines, but also that 'collaborative research between economists and experts in other disciplines holds the promise of revolutionizing economics' (p. 17). He highlights the insights from epidemiology as particularly important and uses them to frame much of the rest of his argument.

This analogy is not as strong as others that Shiller might have chosen. Although 'contagion' works as a metaphor, ideas are not like diseases in two crucial respects: they do not need physical proximity to spread, and human beings control their mutation (in other words, ideas do not mutate without human involvement). These differences do not rule out a comparison with disease transmission, but they do mean that the underlying causal mechanism is different, no matter how similar the statistical graphs for phrase repetition (idea spread) and case infections (disease spread) may appear.

Survival | vol. 62 no. 5 | October–November 2020 | pp. 210–216   DOI 10.1080/00396338.2020.1819657

There are better models that Shiller cites in his list of references and that he might have used more effectively. One comes from the study of how ideas influence economic policymakers (Mark Blyth's book *Austerity*) and the other from the study of viral marketing (Jonah Berger's *Contagious*). These references do not appear in the main body of Shiller's text or notes, but they should. Shiller might also have cited the wider schools of thought that inspired these works, as exemplified by Charles Kindleberger's classic *Manias, Panics, and Crashes*, among others.

If economists really want to revolutionise their discipline, they need to read Blyth's book in the context of Peter Hall's work on the spread of Keynesianism and Kathleen McNamara's work on the creation of the euro. Berger's book should be read in the context of the Heath brothers' *Made to Stick* and Malcolm Gladwell's *The Tipping Point*. Shiller is absolutely right to insist that economists look outside their own discipline to bring in this narrative dimension; they should not have to look far to find the inspiration they have been missing.

The Great Reversal: How America Gave up on Free Markets
Thomas Philippon. Cambridge, MA: The Belknap Press of
Harvard University Press, 2019. £23.95/$29.95. 368 pp.

Europeans have cheaper broadband access, better healthcare, stronger protection of data privacy and more efficient banks than Americans do. This is because European markets are more competitive, having built their competition policies based on lessons learned from the United States. The US used to have the most competitive markets on the planet, but somehow, during the past 20 years or so, American politicians and policymakers threw it all away.

Thomas Philippon offers a remarkable narrative – to borrow from Robert Shiller – with wide-ranging implications for economic performance. He builds his case with a compelling mixture of patience and data. Each chapter adds a new layer to the argument, starting with the impact of market power at the firm level on economic performance in the aggregate, passing through the complex political economy of regulation, and winding up with a thorough analysis of finance, healthcare and the major players in the gig economy. At the outset, Philippon says that *The Great Reversal* could be a textbook as well as a commentary, and he is not kidding. The book is suitable for coffee table and classroom alike.

Like any narrative, however, Philippon's tale is wrapped in other stories – what Shiller calls 'narrative constellations'. These need to be disentangled to avoid confusion. For example, the author relies heavily on the notion of 'free' markets, which he describes as free from arbitrary interference and artificial protection. None of these modifiers are helpful, because each has narrative implications that Philippon rejects time and again in his own argument. Nothing in the marketplace is free, and everyone who participates in it is either producer, consumer or product. Politics is always motivated, not arbitrary – just follow the money. And economics is a social arrangement, which makes it organic, not artificial. There is no 'right' policy, because policymakers are only human and therefore prone to mistakes.

The most troubling narrative in Philippon's book is about regulation. Sometimes, on the surface at least, he seems to accept the conventional idea that regulation is like an on–off switch that alternates between regulation and deregulation. Regulation stifles competition; deregulation unleashes it. This impression is strongest when he sketches the history of telecommunications and airlines. But dig a little deeper and it becomes apparent that the choice is not between regulation and deregulation, yes or no, more or less. The real choice is between regulation that allows for, or even reinforces, the concentration of market power, and regulation that promotes the diffusion of market power. It is also about ensuring that no single player or group of players can take over the regulatory process.

The distinction here is vital to the extent that Philippon's argument is that European markets work better than American markets because they are better regulated, and because the regulatory process is better insulated from monied politics. This is a liberal argument insofar as it implies that only rules can create freedom. The US did not give up on free markets; Americans embraced a narrative within which freedom means there are no rules, or that any rules are kept to a minimum. This story of American freedom is what exposed the country and its citizens to the accumulation of market power in the hands of an ever-smaller group of individuals who have, in turn, hijacked the legislative process to serve their own goals. We should not pretend their actions are arbitrary or artificial. As Philippon shows, brilliantly, the effects of this group on the US economy are intentional. That argument is too important to ignore.

A Great Deal of Ruin: Financial Crises Since 1929
James Gerber. Cambridge: Cambridge University Press, 2019.
£26.99. 348 pp.

Financial crises are not all the same. They may share common features in terms of the risk factors that bring them about, the dynamics they unleash or the scars they leave behind, and they tend to create similar feelings of uncertainty and panic. Moreover, every crisis yields its own 'lessons' for future policymakers. But to examine the engine that drove each crisis – or its recovery – is to reveal a lot of variety.

This diversity is an important theme running through James Gerber's excellent introduction to the major financial crises of the past 100 years. Gerber uses the highly contingent nature of financial crises to explain why they are so hard to predict, so easy to underestimate once they get started and so challenging to address; he also uses that contingency to explain why economists disagree on the strengths and weaknesses of the policy responses. His point is not that we cannot learn from past crises; on the contrary, his book shows how they have shaped the intellectual history of macroeconomics and finance in many ways. Nevertheless, the overriding message is that we should combine data and humility in equal measure when drawing conclusions or offering policy recommendations.

Although published in 2019, Gerber's book is ideal for anyone confused about how governments are responding to the economic consequences of the COVID-19 pandemic. As with the crises of the past, the economic consequences of government efforts to stop the spread of the novel coronavirus are unique. Nevertheless, Gerber identifies certain risk factors that can help explain why some countries seem to be more vulnerable than others. These same risk factors can help readers to anticipate how economic consequences will evolve as the shockwave extends from the real economy into the financial sector, and from one country to the next.

Most important, perhaps, *A Great Deal of Ruin* explains why some themes are emerging so strongly in the policy debates both within and among national governments: the importance of global leadership, the threat of economic contagion, the limits of monetary accommodation, the scope for fiscal stimulus and the perils of moral hazard. Each of these is but an echo of the lessons 'learned' through the experience of the Great Depression, the Latin American debt crisis, the Asian financial crisis, the subprime crisis and the European sovereign-debt crisis.

A sub-theme in Gerber's book is the power of ideas. This only stands to reason. If crises are as contingent and diverse as the author paints them to be, they necessarily create uncertainty. This is precisely when people reach for models in search of instructions on how best to protect their interests or to foster some sort of recovery. These models provide the 'narratives' that Robert Shiller says are so central to economics – and it is clear from repeated citation that Gerber draws on Shiller's work.

The striking point is how much of Gerber's analysis is also caught up in narrative structures. The story he tells of the eurozone crisis is a good illustration. His argument mirrors the conventional wisdom among American economists; it skews somewhat from the conventional wisdom in Europe. Gerber places more emphasis on fiscal integration and less on the role of the European Central Bank, for example. He also puts greater stress on the theory of optimum currency areas and almost none on the problem of sudden stops in Europe's integrated financial markets. These 'shortcomings' are not serious in such an ambitious survey. It is a terrific book. But as Gerber shows time and again, even subtle shades of emphasis are important in policy deliberations. Here, too, narrative is critical to economic success.

The UK and Multi-level Financial Regulation: From Post-crisis Reform to Brexit
Scott James and Lucia Quaglia. Oxford: Oxford University Press, 2020. £60.00. 240 pp.

Financial crisis is a recurrent problem, even for those countries with the longest experience in banking or the greatest focus on financial services. Indeed, as James Gerber points out in his historical survey, countries usually experience a crisis soon after they convince themselves they have found the secret to stability. The puzzle is why this should be the case. Given some governments' long experience of financial regulation, it should be possible to devise a formula for keeping the economy safe. The problem is that finance is not 'one thing', nor is regulation and nor are financial markets. Neither, for that matter, are states.

Scott James and Lucia Quaglia do an outstanding job illustrating what this combination of differences entails for the challenge of stabilising the financial economy. They start with a simple question: why, after the financial crisis of 2007–08, did the British government have such a mixed response – tough in some areas, weaker in others? The answer is anything but simple. Once James and Quaglia start to map the different actors who played a role, the objects of their attention, the arenas for setting rules and the interests at play in any given context, it becomes almost impossible to keep track of the overall picture. We can follow the negotiations over a single regulation, such as capital-adequacy requirements, as they evolve domestically within Europe and at the global level. We can see when the different actors come into play, what strategies they pursue, where they exert influence and what compromises they have to swallow.

Yet it is almost impossible to generalise from any one case study, or to see how the results across many different agreements add up to a coherent regulatory framework. In such a context, it is unsurprising that the banking sector gets treated very differently from the hedge-fund sector. This variation can be explained: James and Quaglia note that banking regulation was a higher priority for the public after the crisis, while hedge-fund managers were more influential with politicians. Understanding the pattern, however, does little to reassure that the regulatory outcome will be resilient when faced with the next crisis. Indeed, one of Gerber's lessons from the financial crisis is that shadow banks are really just banks in terms of their potential influence on financial stability – and hedge funds are active in shadow banking.

The authors use this kind of argument to unlock another puzzle, which is why the British financial industry did not mount a more effective opposition to Brexit. It turns out that finance is not monolithic in politics either. While this does not explain why the United Kingdom voted to leave the European Union, it does explain why the negotiations to do so have poorly reflected what we might imagine to be the vested interests of the City of London. This finding leaves us with considerable scope to speculate about what Britain's financial future will be outside the EU. James and Quaglia try to sketch the possibilities, but contend that we will not know what the new UK–EU relationship will look like until we see it.

This uncertainty adds another source of concern about the prospects for financial stability. Even before the onset of the COVID-19 pandemic, the possibility that separating the UK from the EU would create new sources of instability was manifest. The authors' chapter on derivatives clearing is worth the price of the volume on its own – offering an analysis that seems very technical on the surface, but that turns out to be dramatically important. Finance not only comprises many things, but each of them could lead to crisis. No wonder financial stability is so hard to engineer through regulation.

The Perils of International Capital
Faisal Z. Ahmed. Cambridge: Cambridge University Press, 2019. £22.99. 198 pp.

A good book does not close the conversation, but opens it. Faisal Ahmed has written a really good book, opening a conversation about the influence of foreign capital on non-democratic governments. His claim is that autocratic regimes can take advantage of foreign aid, remittance income and foreign direct investment to extend their hold on power. This claim is controversial in different ways depending upon which source of funds is involved. The international-development community is already debating the effectiveness of foreign aid; Ahmed suggests it may be counterproductive for democratisation. As for foreign direct investment, the author pours cold water on the idea that democratic freedom follows naturally from economic development. His book is sure to capture the attention of scholars who work on both sets of issues.

Ahmed's most striking argument is arguably about remittances. By establishing how foreign remittances strengthen autocratic governments, he challenges the deeply held conventional wisdom that remittances are the lifeblood of democratising development. Flowing within families and therefore largely outside the reach of governments, no matter how corrupt or autocratic, remittances allow for individual-level investment in both human and physical capital. They also carry ideas about opportunity and liberty that can channel directly into the promotion of civil society and democratic opposition. By arguing that these flows are actually supporting autocracy, the author darkens the last ray of hope in the wider debate about globalisation. People are sure to take note.

The method Ahmed uses is clever. His biggest challenge is to separate cause and effect, aiming to show that remittances cause a substitution of government expenditure on welfare goods (which will decrease) with patronage in the form of spending on public-sector employment. The problem is that the causal arrow could go both ways, and lower government spending on welfare could raise the need for remittances rather than the other way around. So the author looks for a pattern in remittance flows that he can explain using factors outside this conversation. He notes that the price of oil fluctuates, and that remittance flows from the Gulf region fluctuate along with it. Therefore, if he can show that oil-price fluctuation mirrors the pattern in government spending on welfare, this would be good evidence that remittances are driving the show rather than vice versa. And this is what he discovers: autocratic governments spend less on welfare and more on patronage when remittances increase along with oil prices.

This is an important argument. The question is whether it is convincing. We must remember that Ahmed is opening a conversation; he is careful to qualify his interpretation of the data and to encourage others to express competing views. The big issue he leaves out is the fact that remittances are earned by migrants. To borrow from the brilliant work of Jonathon Moses, migrants travel to the Gulf states when oil prices rise, leaving their children behind with their grandparents. When they leave, migrants no longer work (or pay taxes) in their home countries, nor do they consume welfare goods provided by the state. Moreover, the remittances they send back may be enough to free their parents (the children's grandparents) from relying on state subsidies (which is Ahmed's measure of welfare). Unfortunately, since remittance-earners are in the prime of their lives, this also drains civil society of potential recruits for the political opposition to the government. Of course, when oil prices fall, these former remittance-earners return home, relying on subsidies and protesting against the government. In other words, maybe we should focus less on the money and more on the people – their exit and their voice.

South Asia
Teresita C. Schaffer

Pakistan: A Kaleidoscope of Islam
Mariam Abou Zahab. London: C. Hurst & Co., 2020. £20.00.
256 pp.

Mariam Abou Zahab was born in France and became fascinated by Islam as a young woman travelling in South Asia, eventually converting to Shi'ism. She plunged into life in the conflict zones of the Middle East and South Asia, working as an activist and writing extensively. She studied Urdu in France, and eventually added Persian and Pashtu to her repertoire. The obituary released upon her death in 2017 appears as the preface to this book. It paints a picture of a witty, engaging and sometimes enigmatic woman who was passionate about the causes to which she devoted her life and driven to understand deeply the cultures that animated them.

Abou Zahab examines the Islamist scene in Pakistan through several lenses: religious belief and traditions; sociology; local and regional politics; and relations with the army. The big theme running through the book is her observation that among all these perspectives, local factors were far more important than international ones, both in explaining the dynamics of individual movements and especially in driving the relations among them. She identifies the various ideological strands familiar to students of Pakistani and Indian Islam – Deobandis (including the major Sunni groups), Barelvis (the face of popular Islam), the more politically engaged Jamaat-e-Islami, Ahl-e-Hadith – but she convincingly shows that the real fault lines within the Islamist 'family' come from social class and local rivalries.

I found the chapter on Jhang most fascinating. Jhang is a region of southern Punjab, close to the Indian border, with a distinctive local language. It has produced a number of prominent national politicians. The major landholders are Shia, but those who work the land are often Sunni. Abou Zahab superimposes on this familiar landscape a few more fault lines, including commercial rivalries between urban and rural areas, 'feudal' Shi'ites versus those who migrated to the area, and different microgroups within both the Shia and Sunni communities. This area saw the birth of the Sipah-e-Sahaba Pakistan (SSP), an anti-Shia militant group, which also had a violent rivalry with other Sunni groups. All these local rivalries carry more weight than the ideological differences that too often dominate discussions of Islam in Pakistan.

Another riveting chapter discusses the Pashtun and Punjabi Taliban. It explores the complicated relationships between these groups and Pakistan's

Survival | vol. 62 no. 5 | October–November 2020 | pp. 217–222   DOI 10.1080/00396338.2020.1819658

government and army. The author argues that former president Pervez Musharraf legitimised the SSP, allowing its leader to run for parliament. At the same time, two competing organisations, Lashkar-e-Taiba and Jaish-e-Muhammad, had the closest ties with the army. This is not the first time Pakistani authorities have been accused of backing both sides in an internecine quarrel, but it is an interesting setting.

Most of this book appeared in other publications between 2004 and 2013. Abou Zahab's perspective is unusual, but it is an important one, and having these chapters between the same covers gives those seeking a deeper under-standing of Pakistan a valuable resource.

Backstage: The Story Behind India's High Growth Years
Montek Singh Ahluwalia. New Delhi: Rupa, 2020. ₹595.00.
464 pp.

Montek Singh Ahluwalia, universally known as Montek, is a name to be reck-oned with on the Indian economic scene. Many people reflexively think of him as a pillar of the elite Indian Administrative Service (IAS). In fact, he started his career in the World Bank, which technically makes him an outsider who came 'inside'. As the title of the book suggests, he is best known for the three decades he spent as one of India's most senior and most powerful economic officials. This period dominates his memoir.

The beginning of his long stint in Indian government service involved not just a return home from Washington DC, but also a culture change. He arrived just as the government that followed Indira Gandhi's experiment with autocracy was falling apart, a time I remember as one of great uncertainty. Manmohan Singh, who later became finance minister and then prime minister, was then chief economic adviser to the government. He had lured Montek away from the World Bank, installed him in the economic adviser's office, and became his most important backer in the government. For Montek, the challenge was to fit into a ministry staffed overwhelmingly by IAS officers, with that service's fixed etiquette and well-established networks.

A few months later, an election brought Indira Gandhi back to power. After her assassination, her son Rajiv became prime minister. Montek credits Rajiv with seeing India's possibilities in ways that many policymakers were unable to. He started the process – the book cites in particular the telecommunications sector and the empowerment of local governments – but these were relatively small and cautious steps.

The book conveys well the drama that ensued when the reform effort began in earnest. Montek writes that he had been convinced that making bold reforms was important. But the caution in the DNA of the Indian government was readily apparent. He depicts the struggle to change the government's rule reserving certain sectors of the economy for small industry. So many of the changes that were undertaken seemed frightening to long-time officials. The government implemented a currency devaluation in stages; liberalised foreign-investment policy amid considerable controversy; wrestled with a broadside from the politicians of the left, arguing that the government should use controls rather than market mechanisms; and put in place a complex system for gradually reducing quantitative controls on trade.

The results were dramatic. India's economic growth surged and millions were lifted out of poverty. India is now recognised as an important economic power. Montek and Manmohan Singh had good reason to be pleased with what they accomplished. But the caution that characterised each of these decisions is still an important feature of the Indian government. The success of the programme did not make successor governments confident about continuing to open the market. After the trade reforms were announced, the minister of state for commerce, P. Chidambaram, was quoted in a newspaper as having said 'we have always had wings but suffered a fear of flying' (p. 137). Reform fatigue is especially apparent now, following the dislocation caused by the pandemic. Prime Minister Narendra Modi, who ran as a reformer, is now stressing the more traditional approach – 'Make in India'.

This is an engaging memoir. Even those who lived the story will find nuggets of history they probably did not know about. Montek shares his personal views on the people he worked with. Manmohan Singh and Rajiv come out as heroes. He also shares, in some detail, his economic reasoning. This part is a bit more taxing, but is certainly a critical part of the story. *Backstage* supplies not just the 'backstory', but also the human story behind the decisions that changed the face of the Indian economy.

Fateful Triangle: How China Shaped U.S.–India Relations During the Cold War

Tanvi Madan. Washington DC: Brookings Institution Press, 2020. $35.99. 380 pp.

Tanvi Madan is a star in the rising generation of US-based scholars of Indian foreign relations. She set out to complicate the oversimplified picture of the US–China–India triangle that constitutes the conventional wisdom. In the process, she has produced an excellent account of the drivers of Indian foreign policy, showing both its ebbs and flows through the period she covers (1949–79) and its major enduring themes.

Madan argues that China shaped the context in which India operated throughout this period, and that India's ties with China and the United States pulled the centre of gravity of India's policy back and forth. She identifies four phases. The first was characterised by divergence (1949–56): the US looked on China with clear hostility; India had hopes for harmony between the two Asian giants; and India's commitment to non-alignment ensured that Delhi would not get particularly close to Washington. This was followed by a period of US–India policy convergence (1956–62), culminating in China's successful attack on India in October 1962 and the opening of a military pipeline from the US to India. This represented the zenith of Cold War-era India–US ties. In the third phase, marked by dependence and disillusionment between the US and India (1963–68), the warmth of 1962 cooled – but India began to worry that distancing itself from the US would create an uncomfortable degree of Indian dependence on Russia. Finally, the disengagement phase (1969–79) was characterised by a general decline in the priority that India and the US gave to their mutual relationship. These years included Henry Kissinger's and Richard Nixon's opening to China, India's intervention in Bangladesh's freedom war and the Indo-Soviet treaty of 1971.

A few recurring themes took on particular importance during these phases. The most striking was the argument, made by foreign-policy professionals in every US administration from Harry Truman to Nixon, that the US had a major interest in seeing India succeed as an economically successful democracy, lest China look like a better model for economic development. This is an argument that I associate particularly with Chester Bowles, who was US ambassador for two years in the 1950s and again from 1964–68, but Madan quotes a long string of others to the same effect.

A second theme was the shifting meaning of non-alignment. Jawaharlal Nehru's signature contribution to foreign policy, 'non-alignment' remains a hallowed term, and its intellectual impact on Indian foreign-policy thinking remains strong. In recent years, however, foreign-policy commentators have begun to look at the term in a different light. The phrase often used today is 'strategic autonomy'. Madan traces the concept of non-alignment through the policy debates chronicled in her book. In concluding, she argues that the real core of India's foreign policy is 'diversification'. This is the goal that the country's policymakers have pursued during the 73 years of independence.

Putting these two themes together, the Indian government's internal debates, as Madan depicts them from her archival research, are fascinating. India's foreign-policy leaders are painfully aware that they need the United States – and that once the US had normalised relations with China, Washington did not need Delhi as much as in the past. Unfortunately, the ethos of non-alignment discouraged candid discussion between the two governments on this apparent asymmetry. The two sides might have had an easier time improving relations if they allowed more candour into the room!

My one regret is that the story stops, at least in this book, in 1979. The remarkable transformation of US–India relations did not really start until 2000. China is still important in setting the context. But the role India seeks to play, and especially its capacity to shape the international environment, have both expanded dramatically. India's economic success is one important reason – but China's economic success has been even more spectacular than India's. I hope we can look forward to the next instalment.

Closing Argument

Living and Dying Nations and the Age of COVID-19

Benjamin Rhode

I

On 4 May 1898, the British prime minister and statesman Lord Salisbury delivered a speech at the Royal Albert Hall in which he divided the nations of the world into two categories: the 'living' and the 'dying'. The 'living' were 'great countries of enormous power growing in power every year, growing in wealth, growing in dominion, growing in the perfection of their organisation'. Salisbury claimed that the living nations would inevitably 'encroach' upon the territory of the dying nations, and that disputes about 'curing or cutting up these unfortunate patients' might provoke war among the great powers.[1]

Salisbury and his audience would have primarily associated 'living' states with the great and rising powers such as the British Empire, the United States, Russia and Japan, and the 'dying' states with precarious non-Christian polities such as the Chinese or Ottoman empires, the latter described for decades as the 'sick man' of the European continent. Yet there were plenty of other candidates for the 'dying' category, including some Christian and European states.[2] Four hundred years earlier, Spain had seized the world's greatest maritime empire in the Americas. But three days before Salisbury's speech, the US Navy had blown Spain's Pacific fleet out of the water without suffering a single casualty. The Spanish–American War would deprive Spain of the last of its significant colonies.

Benjamin Rhode is IISS Senior Fellow for Transatlantic Affairs and Editor of the *Adelphi* book series.

Survival | vol. 62 no. 5 | October–November 2020 | pp. 223–234   DOI 10.1080/00396338.2020.1819659

Once hostilities ended, the US purchased the Philippines and annexed Puerto Rico, and Cuba became a de facto US protectorate.

For most observers, military defeat tended to be a key indicator of whether a nation should be categorised among the dying, but any state or empire that appeared to be on the downslope of decline – whether Portugal, Persia, Morocco, Austria-Hungry or even France – might fear that it too was on the verge of disintegration and dismemberment, its lands to be divided up among the strong or its autonomy removed in all but name. Mounting national debts could allow foreign creditors to exert powerful political control, often through embedded 'advisers', and demand territorial concessions. The great powers jealously scrutinised each other's efforts to lend to weaker, insolvent states, fearing that their rivals might acquire exclusive access to fresh markets, land or other resources.

Salisbury's speech has frequently been discussed in the same breath as 'social Darwinism' – an oversimplified and overused term that signifies, essentially, a belief that the principles of biology apply to human affairs and international relations; that struggle is a natural and beneficial process; and that the destruction of the weak is an inevitable aspect of survival of the 'fittest', those best adapted to their environment.[3] Conflations of Salisbury's speech with social Darwinism ignore important realities, including the fact that Salisbury did not subscribe to the theory of natural selection even in the biological realm, and that he did not glorify war as an agent of progress.[4] Moreover, even some self-identified social Darwinists did not espouse territorial expansion or policies allowing or encouraging the 'weak' to perish.[5] Salisbury did, however, subscribe to a fatalistic view of international affairs with a long pedigree: that the law of the jungle prevailed.[6] And his speech captured something of the spirit of the time, which often carried a deep emphasis on ruthless struggle.[7]

There was no consensus, however, on precisely which attributes determined success in the struggle among nations. While judgements often clustered around certain traits that might seem obvious in 2020 – population, landmass, industrial output, the size of the armed forces and social organisation – contemporary preoccupations and assumptions meant that many observers understood national superiority to encompass other key dimensions beyond numbers of battleships or blast furnaces. Sometimes they focused on factors that today we might consider essentialist, puzzling or repellent, including 'energy', religion, racial 'willpower' or even the supposedly gendered character of a race or nation.[8]

Categorising polities as 'living' or 'dying' was not always entirely figurative. The biological metaphor in which the state resembled a living organism could sometimes become an organicist model that informed policy prescriptions. The year before Salisbury's speech, the political geographer Friedrich Ratzel made perhaps the most famous exposition of the idea that states, like organisms, must expand or die. Ratzel coined the term *Lebensraum*.[9]

The health of the body politic might have a bidirectional causal relationship with the bodily health of its citizens. Levels of disease and mental illness could serve as both indicators and determinants of national or racial health and efficiency.[10] Many Americans took pride in the fact that, after removing Cuba from Spain's yoke, they not only closed Spanish 'reconcentration camps' where thousands of Cuban civilians had died in squalor, but also brought under control the yellow fever that had taken the lives of many American soldiers, and which had in earlier years spread to the US, prompting one newspaper to suggest that 'the extirpation of Spanish rule in Cuba is a sanitary measure essential to the safety of the United States'.[11]

Many deemed it quite natural for those states considered incapable of 'self-government' to be governed instead by those who were, or to have their ineffectively or inhumanely governed colonies appropriated by others who could do the job properly. This apparent reality was often justified using Darwinian rhetoric. For example, Henry Cabot Lodge, later chairman of the US Senate Committee on Foreign Relations, argued that Spain was 'unfit to govern' and that, 'for the unfit among nations, there is no pity in the relentless world-forces which shape the destinies of mankind'.[12]

A good number of contemporary British observers (and more than a few Americans, including Lodge) believed that the 'Anglo-Saxons' were the paragons of self-government. In the words of George Steevens, one of the best-known British journalists of the time, the logic of imperialism was that 'we rule better than other nations, and therefore we ought to rule more than other nations'.[13] In May 1899, almost exactly a year after Salisbury's Royal

Albert Hall speech, the *Daily Mail* claimed in an article on 'dying nations' that if the British Empire continued to expand 'along the lines of least resistance' and at a steady pace, then it would take 450 years to absorb the rest of the world's landmass. Recognising that those lands included Germany, Russia and the US, it acknowledged magnanimously that 'even if we could, we have no wish to swallow these or any other decently governed countries'. This left only half as much territory ripe for British control, meaning that 'all the world will be properly governed by the year 2012'. Of course, even the proudest imperialist needed to avoid hubris: no empire could indefinitely postpone its decline and fall. The *Mail* predicted that, in the case of the British Empire, this would take another 1,500 years.[14]

II

The brutal reality of counter-insurgency in the Philippines moderated American reveries of further protectorates or annexations in Asia and Latin America. Britain's self-confidence also soon took a knock, following its disastrous early performance in the Boer War. Nevertheless, Britain did eventually and at great cost win that war, with its inadequacies inspiring the 'national efficiency' movement. One of imperialism's loudest cheerleaders, the poet Rudyard Kipling, advised his compatriots: 'Let us admit it fairly, as a business people should / We have had no end of a lesson: it will do us no end of good … So the more we work and the less we talk the better results we shall get – / We have had an Imperial lesson; it may make us an Empire yet!'[15]

While the coming half-century or so would witness the demise of most European territorial empires, Britain emerged victorious from both world wars, albeit battered and bankrupt. Unlike many European countries, it did not endure a defeat or occupation that served as an indictment of national performance or forced it to reassess its political or social model. Whereas, for example, the events of 1940 represent France's darkest hour in the twentieth century, Britain's 'finest hour' that same year fed into national myths and self-images of heroism, pluck and independence. For many years after the Second World War, many Britons could convince themselves that they would continue to punch above their weight through their supposedly 'special' relationship with the United States, sometimes consciously described as an imperial successor to the British Empire. The British would, it was assumed, prove themselves indispensable partners through their wisdom, wit and experienced statecraft, and exert influence from behind the throne. In 1943, the future prime minister Harold Macmillan remarked that 'these Americans represent the new Roman Empire and we Britons, like the Greeks of old, must teach them how to make it go'.[16] For some Britons, this pleasant self-deception has never lost its appeal.

Many Anglo-American advantages were not illusory. Not only did London and Washington enjoy military victory in the world wars but, by the end of the century, victory in the Cold War seemed to confirm the supremacy of their generally shared creed of liberal-democratic free-market capitalism. Anglo-American triumphs now tended to be explained in terms of superior institutions and political culture, rather than superior racial attributes. It did become apparent, to some observers at least, that other states could adopt successful elements of the Anglo-American political and economic models and combine them with more effective public administration and more equitable societies. Despite this awareness, a belief in an exceptional Anglo-American or 'Anglo-Saxon' trait of particularly effective self-government seemed to endure.

III

The performance of populist and often inept governments in Washington and London in recent years has severely dented this belief – or, at least, it should have done. Moreover, in the time of coronavirus, the self-satisfied self-images of the two main English-speaking states – supposedly blessed not only with pragmatic and practical political cultures but also with a fair degree of efficiency in the material matters of government – appear painfully outdated.

COVID-19 has provided a worldwide test of a vital measure of national capability: how effectively can a state protect the health and lives of its people? Direct comparisons between national pandemic performances are fraught with difficulty: the methodologies of recording deaths vary among countries and are applied with uneven accuracy; the pandemic is still in its early stages and it may be some time before a final picture of relative death rates emerges; and some of the differences in death rates may be accounted for more by factors such as the relative age of populations than by national responses.

Disclaimers aside, it would be difficult to argue with a straight face that either the United Kingdom or the United States has performed well. At the time of writing, the US had suffered the largest number of confirmed infections and deaths of any country worldwide. The UK had one of the highest death rates in Europe (if not the highest, depending on when the measurement was made), and had Europe's highest overall death toll during COVID-19's first wave. While in earlier periods of economic gloom Britain had been described, rather hyperbolically, as 'the sick man of Europe', this was now true in a very literal sense. In July 2020, the UK's chief scientific adviser, Sir Patrick Vallance, admitted with some understatement that it was 'clear that the outcome has not been good in the UK'.[17] This poor performance came despite the fact that both Washington and London had strategic warning that other developed nations, where the sickness had taken hold earlier, did not. Their suffering should have alerted the US and the UK to the perils of delaying decisive preventative action. This warning was not adequately heeded.

Nor were positive examples from abroad. The British government rarely seemed to acknowledge or explain, in public at least, why it had been unable to emulate South Korea's rapid implementation of a mass-testing system and containment of the disease without a single day of national lockdown, even though South Korea was a democratic state with a roughly equivalent population, a smaller economy and a higher population density than the United Kingdom.[18] Sometimes, popular explanations for the disparity between the success of East Asian states and the failures of the Anglo-Americans fell back on vague cultural factors, such as 'Confucian values'. The reality was probably more prosaic, and more damning. Having already encountered dangerous, novel coronaviruses more than once during the twenty-first century, states in East and Southeast Asia were less susceptible to complacent assumptions that COVID-19 would resemble modelled influenza pandemics.[19]

London had prided itself on its pandemic preparedness but, in addition to its misplaced early extrapolations from influenza outbreaks, for a vital period in March much of the government's official scientific advice seemed to be informed by an unsupported belief that the British populace would only tolerate a few weeks of lockdown.[20] It seems likely that these complacent and unexamined beliefs contributed to Britain's unnecessarily large death toll. In geopolitical terms, the poor performance of the UK and the US will probably not soon be forgotten, and will shape international narratives of relative prestige and power. These narratives might perhaps only be mitigated by the speedy production of safe and effective vaccines, in which Anglo-American scientific capabilities could at least partially compensate for failures of national leadership.

The pandemic seemed to produce some surprising national success stories. Over the previous decade, Greece had often been described in terms reminiscent of those reserved for 'dying' nations – disorganised, dishonest and incapable of self-government. At times, it was murmured that foreigners might be required to administer Greek affairs; some German politicians even suggested that Greece sell the Parthenon and some of its islands to pay down its debt.[21] In 2020, however, Greece was able to implement one of the most effective and prompt containment measures against COVID-19 seen in Europe. As of late May, despite cash-starved public services, an elderly population and a crowded capital city, its death rate was one-sixth of Germany's and one thirty-fifth of Britain's.[22] This raises the question of which nations were truly 'dying': those indebted financially, or those unable to protect the lives of their own citizens due to a lack of timely and decisive leadership.

It would be easy to overstate the significance of this observation. Greece's excellent pandemic performance certainly does not translate into global leadership in any broader sense. The past few months, though, are a useful reminder of the brute fact – which historically tended to be delivered in wartime – that when the chips are down, a nation's response to crisis can surprise most observers. Public-health performance will not supplant war as the ultimate test of national capability but may well supplement it, with some nations which, in earlier decades or centuries, prided themselves on superior public health perhaps acknowledging and responding to painful realities about their own capacities. Defeat, even in a non-military context, can be a salutary experience.

Since history began, people have tried to divine the determinants of the rise and fall of tribes, kingdoms and empires. At the turn of the twentieth century, our recent ancestors were preoccupied with the supposed life force of nations, and conjured any number of medical–biological metaphors and models to explain and predict international affairs. In hindsight, many of their assumptions and crude attempts to map contemporary scientific or cultural preoccupations onto their interpretation of the international realm appear deluded at best and dangerous at worst. Yet recent decades have featured their own delusions about the inevitable trajectory of global trends. Confidence recently placed in the capacity of certain states to govern effectively may appear to be based on outdated or misplaced assumptions. And some recent notions about what really counts in national performance and international competition are likely to appear just as bizarre to our descendants as those of our ancestors do to us.

The next few years, marked by COVID-19's disruption of our comfortable postmodern lives, may perhaps witness a reversion to earlier tendencies to assess relative national success by categorising states as 'living' or 'dying'. We must hope, however, that such depictions remain metaphorical: not following earlier misguided models of the state as an organism composed of its subjects, or of public health as a proxy for inherent national or racial attributes, but confining themselves to more straightforward extrapolations, with public health serving as an indication of the effective government, institutions and leadership a state requires to prevent a pitiless virus from extinguishing the lives and livelihoods of its people.

Notes

1 For a transcript of Salisbury's speech, see 'The Primrose League', *The Times*, 5 May 1898.

2 Margaret MacMillan, *The War That Ended Peace: How Europe Abandoned*

Peace for the First World War (London: Profile Books, 2013), pp. 39–40.

3 On the outlines of social Darwinism, see Stuart Anderson, *Race and Rapprochement: Anglo-Saxonism and*

Anglo-American Relations, 1895–1904
(London: Associated University
Presses, 1981), pp. 28–9; MacMillan,
The War That Ended Peace, pp. 246–7;
and Bradford Perkins, *The Great
Rapprochement: England and the
United States, 1895–1914* (New York:
Atheneum, 1968), pp. 74–6. For an
overview of the oversimplified use
and complexities of this term, and
its lack of precision in describing
intellectual trends in the nineteenth
century, including imperialism, see
Peter J. Bowler, *Darwinism* (New
York: Twayne Publishers, 1993),
pp. 57–62; Gregory Claeys, 'The
"Survival of the Fittest" and the
Origins of Social Darwinism', *Journal
of the History of Ideas*, vol. 61, no. 2,
April 2000, pp. 223–40; Paul Crook,
'Historical Monkey Business: The
Myth of a Darwinized British Imperial
Discourse', *History*, vol. 84, no. 276,
October 1999, pp. 633–57; and James
Allen Rogers, 'Darwinism and Social
Darwinism', *Journal of the History of
Ideas*, vol. 33, no. 2, April–June 1972,
pp. 265–80. Examples of Salisbury's
speech being mentioned in the context
of social Darwinism can be found
in J.A.S. Grenville, *Lord Salisbury
and Foreign Policy: The Close of the
Nineteenth Century* (London: Athlone
Press, 1964), p. 165; William Langer,
*The Diplomacy of Imperialism, 1890–
1902* (New York: Alfred A. Knopf,
1951), pp. 504–5; MacMillan, *The War
That Ended Peace*, pp. 246–7; and T.G.
Otte, *The China Question: Great Power
Rivalry and British Isolation, 1894–1905*
(Oxford: Oxford University Press,
2007), p. 17.

4   See Anderson, *Race and Rapprochement*,

p. 87; Otte, *The China Question*, pp.
17–18; and Andrew Roberts, *Salisbury:
Victorian Titan* (London: Weidenfeld &
Nicolson, 1999), pp. 593–6.

5   See Claeys, 'The "Survival of the
Fittest" and the Origins of Social
Darwinism', pp. 228–9; Crook,
'Historical Monkey Business', p. 633;
and William G. Sumner, *The Conquest
of the United States by Spain* (Boston,
MA: D. Estes & Company, 1899).

6   Roberts, *Salisbury*, pp. 691–2.

7   Claeys, 'The "Survival of the Fittest"
and the Origins of Social Darwinism',
p. 226; and MacMillan, *The War That
Ended Peace*, pp. 246–7.

8   For a longer discussion of many
of the ideas presented in this
article, including these themes, see
Benjamin Rhode, *'The Living and the
Dying': The Rise of the United States
and Anglo-French Perceptions of Power,
1898–1899*, PhD thesis, University of
Oxford, 2017, pp. 1–45.

9   Michael Heffernan, 'Fin de Siècle,
Fin du Monde? On the Origins of
European Geopolitics, 1890–1920',
in Klaus Dodds and David Atkinson
(eds), *Geopolitical Traditions: A Century
of Geopolitical Thought* (London:
Routledge, 2000), pp. 45–7; Charles S.
Maier, *Once Within Borders: Territories of
Power, Wealth, and Belonging Since 1500*
(Cambridge, MA: Harvard University
Press, 2016), pp. 238–9; and Geoffrey
Parker, *Western Geopolitical Thought in
the Twentieth Century* (London: Croom
Helm, 1985), pp. 11–12.

10 See R.B. Kershner, Jr, 'Degeneration:
The Explanatory Nightmare', *Georgia
Review*, vol. 40, no. 2, Summer 1986,
p. 423; Robert A. Nye, *Crime, Madness,
and Politics in Modern France: The*

Medical Concept of National Decline (Princeton, NJ: Princeton University Press, 1984), pp. 119, 143–4; and Daniel Pick, *Faces of Degeneration: A European Disorder, c.1848–c.1918* (Cambridge: Cambridge University Press, 1989), pp. 21, 189–203.

11 Mariola Espinosa, 'The Threat from Havana: Southern Public Health, Yellow Fever, and the U.S. Intervention in the Cuban Struggle for Independence, 1878–1898', *Journal of Southern History*, vol. 72, no. 3, August 2006, pp. 541–68.

12 Anderson, *Race and Rapprochement*, p. 119; Edward Caudill, *Darwinian Myths: The Legends and Misuses of a Theory* (Knoxville, TN: University of Tennessee Press, 1997), p. 92; and Henry Cabot Lodge, *The War with Spain* (New York: Harper and Brothers, 1899), p. 2.

13 G.W. Steevens, *Naval Policy: With Some Account of the Warships of the Principal Powers* (London: Methuen, 1896), p. 182.

14 'Dying Nations', *Daily Mail*, 3 May 1899.

15 See Paul M. Kennedy, *The Rise of the Anglo-German Antagonism, 1860–1914* (London: Allen & Unwin, 1980), p. 265; David Reynolds, *Britannia Overruled: British Policy and World Power in the Twentieth Century* (London: Longman, 1991), pp. 68–78; and G.R. Searle, *The Quest for National Efficiency* (Oxford: Blackwell, 1971).

16 Graham Allison, *Destined for War* (New York: Houghton Mifflin, 2017), p. 200.

17 Alistair Smout and Paul Sandle, 'UK's COVID-19 Outcome Has Not Been Good, Mistakes Were Likely Made –

Chief Scientist', Reuters, 16 July 2020, https://www.reuters.com/article/us-health-coronavirus-britain-vallance/uks-covid-19-outcome-has-not-been-good-mistakes-were-likely-made-chief-scientist-idUSKCN24H28D.

18 In 2018, the United Kingdom had a population density of 274.8 people per square kilometre, compared to South Korea's 529.7 people/km². 'World Development Indicators', World Bank, https://databank.worldbank.org/. The UK government was, however, willing to make misleading statements comparing absolute numbers of tests conducted each day: see Georgina Lee, 'Government's South Korea Testing Claim Needs Context', Channel 4 News, 30 April 2020, https://www.channel4.com/news/factcheck/factcheck-governments-south-korea-testing-claim-needs-context.

19 Andrew Leonard, 'Taiwan Is Beating the Coronavirus. Can the US Do the Same?', *Wired*, 18 March 2020, https://www.wired.com/story/taiwan-is-beating-the-coronavirus-can-the-us-do-the-same/; and S. Nathan Park, 'Confucianism Isn't Helping Beat the Coronavirus', *Foreign Policy*, 2 April 2020, https://foreignpolicy.com/2020/04/02/confucianism-south-korea-coronavirus-testing-cultural-trope-orientalism/.

20 For a discussion of assumptions relating to influenza and 'behavioural fatigue', see George Parker et al., 'Inside Westminster's Coronavirus Blame Game', *Financial Times*, 16 July 2020. In fact, the Scientific Pandemic Influenza Group on Behaviours had not actually argued the case for

'behavioural fatigue'. See Lawrence Freedman, 'Strategy for a Pandemic: The UK and COVID-19', *Survival*, vol. 62, no. 3, June–July 2020, pp. 61–2; and Elisabeth Mahase, 'Covid-19: Was the Decision to Delay the UK's Lockdown Over Fears of "Behavioural Fatigue" Based on Evidence?', *British Medical Journal*, 7 August 2020, https://www.bmj.com/content/370/bmj.m3166.

21 Phillip Inman and Helena Smith, 'Greece Should Sell Islands to Keep Bankruptcy at Bay, Say German MPs', *Guardian*, 4 March 2010, https://www.theguardian.com/business/2010/mar/04/greece-sell-islands-german-mps.

22 William J. Antholis and Filippos Letsas, 'How Greece Can Reopen Without Ruining Its Coronavirus Containment Success', *Fortune*, 27 May 2020, https://fortune.com/2020/05/26/greece-coronavirus-lockdown-reopening-tourism/.

Correction

Article title: Notes from a Pandemic: Bologna, Rome, Nanjing, Vienna and San Jose
Authors: Emma Mika Riley, Christopher Olivares, Laura Rong, Niklas Hintermayer and Zoe Mize
Journal: *Survival*
Bibliometrics: Volume 62, Number 4, pages 245–260
DOI: http://dx.doi.org/10.1080/00396338.2020.1792145

When this article was first published online, the third sentence on the first page read as follows:

In the second week of March, 20 fellow students who didn't evacuate to their home countries were arrested during a birthday party because groups of more than six people had been made illegal.

This has now been corrected to read:

In the second week of March, 20 fellow students who didn't evacuate to their home countries were reported by the police during a birthday party because groups of more than six people had been made illegal.

This has been corrected in the online article.